Midst Africa's Southern Wilds

The British Settlers to South Africa of 1820

Edited by: Johan Hefer

TheirStory
Volume 1

Copyright © 2020 Johannis Antonius Publishers (Pty) Ltd

All rights reserved.

ISBN: 9798681025801

Editor & Development Editor: Johan Hefer

Content Editor: Yvonne Labuschagne

Over the waters wide and deep.
Where the storm-waves roll, and the storm-winds sweep.
Over the waters see them come!
Breasting the billows' curling foam;
Fathers for children seeking a home
   In Africa's Southern wilds.

Forthcoming from Johannis Antonius Publishers

TheirStory

Volume 1: Midst Africa's Southern Wilds

Volume 2: Rough Outlines

Volume 3: Rediscovered: British South Africa

Volume 4: Ladies in White

Visit our website on www.japublishers.online for more information

Foreword

I love first person accounts. That is why the philosophy behind *TheirStory* is to publish first hand accounts that illustrate history. The benefit of first hand accounts is that the events had not been filtered through various historian's world views. These people have views that are influenced by their own world view, but they tend to be honest.

The impact of the 1820 Settlers on South Africa has been immence. Their likes included great statesmen, fighters for civil rights and other people who made South Africa what it is today (for good and bad).

Why was these settlers so important? Firstly they were a very large homogenous group that came from a far more liberal population than what had been in South Africa.

The Dutch/German immigrants from the VOC (Dutch East Indies) period were literally employees. They then asked permission to stay in the country and many tried to get as far away from the "Company" as they could. The educational opportunities were almost non-existent, especially in frontier areas. Very few were people were literate. The VOC were trying to make profits not educate their people. In the colony before British rule the population had very few civil rights and almost no representation in government.

These British Settlers were generally well educated (As can be seen in some of the parts of this book). They believed in free press and representative government. They came to South Africa to act as a buffer in the border areas but ended up changing the colony in fundamental ways.

In this year, which is the 200 year anniversary of the British Settlers of 1820 coming to South Africa, a book of this nature is apt. We hope that you will enjoy the selection of texts we have put together.

Johan Hefer – September 2020.

Table of Contents

Foreword..5
Introduction to the Volume..10
Background and the first five years of settlement...11
The Reminiscences of An Albany Settler..20
A Long and Tedious Voyage..63
The Cobblers Tale — A Disembarking Yarn..68
Very much vexed that no one could go on shore..72
Travel to Our Wild Domain..78
By Flood and Field – The Life of a Post-Holder..89
Satisfied with their Situation and Prospects..98
The memories of James Samuel Reed..107
Norton I, Emperor of the United States and Protector of Mexico.........................119
Fetcani command (1827-8)...131
The Loss of a good Wife...135
Early Years of the Baptist Church..144
Biographies of the Leaders..155
    Bailie's Party...155
    Willson's Party..159
    Parker's Party...163
Biographies of British Settlers...169
    Atherstone, John...169
    Atherstone, William Guybon..170
    Attwell..170
    Ayliff, Reverend John..171
    Biggar, Alexander...174
    Bisset, Lieutenant Alexander..174
    Boardman, Reverend William...175
    Booth, Benjamin...176
    Bowker, Miles...176
    Bradfield, John..178
    Butler, Captain Thomas..178
    Caldecott, Dr Charles...179
    Campbell, Dr Ambrose George..180
    Campbell, Captain Duncan...181
    Campbell, Major-General Charles..183
    Campbell, Dr. Peter...184
    Damant, Edward...185
    Carlisle, John..185
    Carlisle, Frederick...185
    Cawood, David..186
    Cawood, Samuel...187
    Chase, John Centlivres...188

Collett, James...189
Cock, William...189
Currie, Sir Walter..191
Dyason...193
Forbes, Alexander...194
Garcia, Maurice..194
Glass, Thomas..195
Godlonton, Robert..195
Gray, William..198
Greathead, James..199
Griffith, Charles..200
Hartley...201
Haw, Simon..204
Hobson, David..204
Holditch, Dr. Robert..205
Hoole, James...205
Hudson, Hougham...205
Huntley, Charles Hugh...207
Jarvis, George...208
Keeton, Benjamin...209
Lucas, Philip...209
Mahoney, Thomas..210
Mandy, John...211
Mandy, Joseph...211
Maynard...212
McCleland, Rev Francis...212
Mills, Daniel..213
Moodie...214
Moorcroft, James...214
Oates, John..214
Painter, Samuel...215
Palmer, George..215
Phillipps, Thomas...216
Pigot, George...217
Pote, Robert...217
Pringle, Thomas...219
Pullen, Thomas..219
Roberts, Dr Edward..220
Surmon, William Henry..220
Scanlen, William...221
Shaw, Rev William...223
Shepstone, John..224
Southey, George..225
Southey, Richard..226
Slater, Charles..227
Slater, Thomas...227
Smith..227

Stanton, William 228
Stringfellow, Thomas 229
Stubbs, John 229
Temlett, James 229
Trollip 230
Wedderburn, Christopher 230
White, Thomas Charles 232
Wood, George 233
Wright, William 235
Bibliography 237

Table of Figures

Figure 1: Sleeping on Deck - Thomas Baines..22
Figure 2: Crossing the Zak River 04/09/1811 - William John Burchell..............24
Figure 3: Artificers Square, Grahamstown - Janek Szymanowski....................34
Figure 4: Front view of house in Beaufort St, 1834 - Frederick Timpson I'ons...37
Figure 5: Plan of Fort Wilshire - Henry Foley..39
Figure 6: Probably Edward Turvey - Frederick Timpson I'Ons........................45
Figure 7: Grahamstown (South Side), 1823 - Henry Foley..............................51
Figure 8: Rolling to Windward - Thomas Baines...63
Figure 9: Going ashore in Table Bay - Thomas Baines...................................70
Figure 10: Dick at the Wheel - Thomas Baines...72
Figure 11: Thomas Pringle - Unknown Artist..78
Figure 12: Andries, A Khoi. Celebrated wagon Driver in Grahamstown - Henry Foley.......79
Figure 13: Train of Wagons at Karreebergen Poort - William John Burchell.....85
Figure 14: Boer Huntsman, c1802 - Samuel Daniell.......................................89
Figure 15: Grahamstown (North Side), 1823 - Henry Foley.............................97
Figure 16: A black man leading two oxen - Henry Clifford De Meillon.............98
Figure 17: Thornhill near Port Frances - H Coburn (1827)............................101
Figure 18: Zak River 04/09/1811 (2) - Willliam John Burchell.......................106
Figure 19: James Samuel Reed..107
Figure 20: Elizabeth Elliot..112
Figure 21: James Samuel Reed..112
Figure 22: Reed family gravestone..112
Figure 23: Ceclily Emily Mabel Reed...118
Figure 24: Elizabeth Elliot..118
Figure 25: George Thomas and Fanny Reed...118
Figure 26: Joshua A. Norton...119
Figure 27: Joshua A. Norton...120
Figure 28: Emperor Norton, Lazarus and Bummer - Edward Jump.................126
Figure 29: The funeral of Lazarus...127
Figure 30: Emperor Norton..130
Figure 31: Thomas Stubbs...131
Figure 32: Grahamstown, 1827 - H. Coburn..134
Figure 33: Two men drinking at a table - Frederick Timpson I'Ons................135
Figure 34: Back view of house in Beaufort St, 1835 - Frederick Timpson I'Ons...143
Figure 35: William Miller, 1854 - Frederick Timpson I'Ons...........................144
Figure 36: The converted carpenter's shop...146
Figure 37: Bathurst Street Church, 1843...154
Figure 38: William Kidson, 1849 - Frederick Timpson I'Ons..........................155
Figure 39: High Street, Grahamstown, 1856 - Charles Jay............................171
Figure 40: A camp of 1820 Settlers - Frederick Timpson I'Ons......................179
Figure 41: Mr. Quinn - Unknown A*rtist*...208
Figure 42: Mrs. Quinn - Unknown Artist...208

Introduction to the Volume

By Johan Hefer

My personal interests lie in my ancestors, which were not 1820 Settlers. They are generally of Dutch or German descent and came to South Africa before the British Annexation of the Cape. First person accounts of this period is few and far between.

This is not true, for the British Settlers of 1820 were not only literate but seems to have enjoyed writing down their thoughts. It was therefore not too difficult to put together this book as there were many options to choose from.

This book contains accounts from various settlers as well as other stories written by their descendants based on their stories. This is not a history book, we are not trying to make any comment on the accuracy of their views or understand their world view. We are trying to provide you, the reader with insights into the day-to-day lives of these settlers in their own words wherever possible.

Editorial Approach

Many of the parts of this book had been previously published and as such we as a rule published them as is. Here and there were changed paragraph breaks to make the text easier to read. In some cases the source transcriptions had corrections in them, as a rule we simply included these corrections as text. The aim is not to be totally accurate but to make the text easy to read.

It is important to note that the word Caffer and Hotentot was used widely in the originals throughout the book. We have simply changed these to Xhosa and Khoi/Khoisan. The words did not have the racial connotations they have today but was simply used to refer to the people. No inference can therefore be made through the use of these words by the authors in this book.

Various geographical names have changed over the years. As a rule we have left the name as given or where appropriate indicated the new name. We have not noted the more recent change from Grahamstown to Makhanda in the text.

Background and the first five years of settlement.[1]

By John Centilivres Chase[2]

During the height of political upheavals in England that on the 12th July 1819, being the last day of the session, Mr. Vansittart, Chancellor of the Exchequer, made that far-famed speech which was the leading cause of the embarkation for the Cape of Good Hope of more than four thousand Settlers of various descriptions. Lord Sidmouth, in the House of Lords, harangued to the same purport, and fanned the deluding flame which had been lighted up in the Commons. Mr. Vansittart is reported to have said, "The Cape is suited to most of the productions both of temperate and warm climates, to the olive, the mulberry, and the vine, as tell as to most sorts of culmiferous and leguminous plants, and the persons emigrating to this Settlement would soon find themselves comfortable." The considerate and grave character of two Ministers so at war heretofore with everything like fancy or fable caused their Statements to be received with full credit and confidence, and they were regarded as a warrant of success. It is strange to relate such to have been the infatuation, that those who disagreed on all other subjects agreed in this. On the representation of the Minister, the 'faithful Commons' at once and unreluctantly voted to carry the emigration into effect. The promulgation of the governmental scheme was received with avidity by the public, and the applications for permission to avail themselves of the facilities offered were numerous beyond expectation. The number to be accepted was restricted to 4,000 souls, and the disappointment of the unsuccessful candidates, amounting to above 90,000, was bitter beyond conception. The utmost care was employed in the selection of the emigrants. The regulations issued from Downing street required certificates of to character from the ministers of parishes, or some persons in whom the Government could repose confidence; offered passages to those persons who, possessing the means, would engage to carry out at the least ten able-bodied individuals above eighteen years of age with or without families; that a deposit should be made of £10 for every family of one man, one woman, and two children; others beyond this number to pay £5 each, etc. that, notwithstanding an ungenerous sneer of the 'Civil Servant' "that it wag the wish of the Ministry to get rid of the dangerously disaffected," Government had reserved to itself the right, and exerted it

---
1. Extract taken from Wilmot & Chase (1869)
2. See page 188

successfully, to prevent the migration of such useless and ill-assorted characters for its new Settlement.

The two first vessels with the adventurers (the *Chapman* and *Nautilus*, transports) left Gravesend on the 3rd of December 1819, lost sight of the white cliffs of Albion on the 9th, and arrived in Table Bay on the 17th March following, on the 9th April anchored in Algoa Bay, and safely debarked on the following morning at its little fishing village with anxious, beating hearts, made still more uneasy by the forbidding and wild aspect of the shore. This, however, was quickly relieved by the hearty welcome of the few officers of the little garrison, and others, whose kindness and solicitude was beyond all praise.

Alas! As this is penned, hardly one of these now survive to receive the acknowledgements of gratitude, and but few of the pioneers by these vessels live to make those acknowledgements.

Upon landing, the Settlers were disappointed to find their locations distant full one hundred miles from the port, although one party had solicited to be set down near the mouth of the Great Fish River, where some of the most sanguine had already planted—in imagination—sufferance wharves, and dreamed of innumerable vessels to be anchored in that estuary. Wagons were, however, provided by Government in sufficient number, at the cost of the immigrants, a debt which was afterwards most considerately remitted, as was the charge also of rations issued for several months; in fact, the British Government of that day behaved with the greatest liberality to the young Plantation. On the 18th of April, the first or Chapman party commenced their inland progress in ninety-six wagons from Algoa Bay, afterwards named Port Elizabeth, which at that time numbered thirty-five souls (including its small garrison) inhabiting two houses stone built, and a few huts, a more desolate and unpromising place indeed can hardly be conceived.

The journey was propitious; splendid rains had fallen a few months before, the rivers were running, the ponds (vleys) overflowing, the pasturage luxuriantly rich, astonishing the travellers, who had pictured Africa as arid, water less, and sterile. Game, too, was abundant—the hartebeest, springbok, quagga, ostrich—but the country devoid of inhabitants and cattle, while the blackened gables of the farmhouses recently burnt by the Xhosa savages furnished proof how terrible the invasion of 1819 had been. On the 26th, the party with great ease crossed in their wagons the Kowie River mouth, where now vessels of more than 800 tons lie at anchor, and on the evening of the 28th arrived at a deserted farm called "Korn Place" (a promising, but delusive, augury) under the mud walls of a house not long consumed by the enemy. Here the immigrants decided to sit down permanently, and called the embryo village "Cuylerville," in compliment to Colonel Cuyler, whose attentions and kindly manners during the time he accompanied them on their long and fatiguing journey were unremitting. On the following day a few of the party, with some military officers and Colonel Cuyler, proceeded to inspect the mouth of the Great Fish River, which raised high expectations of its future navigability; and on the 3rd of May Colonel Cuyler took his leave with this ominous caution, "Gentlemen, when you go out to plough never leave your guns at home."

The remainder of this, to them, eventful year was occupied in hutting or housing, for which a small detachment of the Cape Corps, skilled in these matters, and for defence, had been most considerately left; and very soon a large breadth of soil was sown with wheat, Indian corn, and seeds of vegetables. The immigrants were now left to themselves in a vast wilderness, the nearest occupied spot being the small military post of Kafirs Drift, seven miles, and the head-quarters, Graham's Town, forty miles away; and the wolf[3], the jackal, and the tiger[4] nightly serenaded them; at first frightening the new-comers out of their propriety, until custom-made them familiar with what was somewhat alarming, but never proved dangerous.

By the end of the year 1820 most of the emigrant ships had touched at the Cape and proceeded to Algoa Bay, and by its close there had been landed there 4,659 persons, which number was soon supplemented by the relations and friends of the first arrivals, so that in the total 5,000 souls settled in the new Colony in the Zuurvelden or Sourfields, a belt of land extending eastwardly from the Sundays River to the Great Fish River, and southwardly from Graham's Town to the sea, an area of some 3,000 square miles.

The Governor of the Colony, Lord Charles Somerset, having gone to England on leave, the administration devolved on that talented, amiable, but subsequently ill-fated officer, Sir Rufane Shaw Donkin, who after dispatching some of the earlier Settlers' ships as they arrived in Table Bay, himself soon followed. Landing in Algoa Bay he called the village he there founded "Port Elizabeth" after his late wife, who had recently died in India, marking the event by erecting a pyramid on the Hill, dedicated to her memory, little creditable it must be said to the taste of the architect, but still of some use as a beacon for shipping. He then visited the several locations, encouraging the newcomers by cheering words of kind encouragement,

---

3. Hyena
4. Leopard

founded a town and magistracy at Bathurst on a branch of the Kowie River, the Mansfield, as the nucleus of the Settlement, at which place he had providently collected Commissariat stores of food, implements and other necessaries.

Up to nearly the close of the year everything portended success; the season was genial, the crops luxuriant and promising, the cattle which the Settlers had purchased from the Dutch farmers from the interior were fat and healthy, and joyous expectancy filled the bosoms of all, alas! How soon to be extinguished, for in November the wheat crops began to exhibit the symptoms of that fatal disease, the rust, which became general throughout the Settlement before the time of harvest. The blow was severe—disheartening, and much distress and despondency followed, for all the bread-stuff remaining to them was very limited, and they were chiefly obliged to have recourse to maize (Indian corn), food to which none had been accustomed.

1821—The ensuing year, thus commenced gloomily enough; but hopes were still indulged that better times were in store. The majority of the immigrants were young, healthy, and naturally sanguine; the fact too, known to them, that the Colony had the credit of producing the finest wheat in the world, sustained their confidence; and their firm reliance upon Providence inspired them to renewed exertion. In June Sir Rufane Donkin again visited the Locations, sympathized with the disappointed, and animated the trusting. Provisions, in consequence of the failure, continued to be issued from the Government stores at a reasonable rate, on credit; an increase to the miserably insufficient grants of land (originally only 100 acres for each adult) was promised; a Military Settlement founded in the ceded or neutral territory between the Great Fish and Keiskamma Rivers, with a Fort at Fredericksburg on the Gualana River, calculated to keep the lately expelled barbarians in check; popular Chief Magistrate, a Colonel Jones, was appointed for the District of Albany, and with him were associated two of the leading Settlers as Heemraaden (i.e., assessors) to his Court, viz., Captain Duncan Campbell and Mr. Miles Bowker, both gentlemen possessing the good opinion of the immigrants.

Confidence was thus restored, and the Settlers began again to till the land which had proved so ungrateful for past attentions, when adverse circumstances arose to scatter their fondest hopes.

Unfortunately for the peace and progress of the Settlement, differences having arisen, out of some infraction of military routine, between Sir Rufane and the son of the absent Governor (an officer on the Frontier), occasioned such a breach, that it began to be rumoured that Lord Charles Somerset, whose return was daily expected, being moved by his son, had expressed entire displeasure at all the acts of Sir Rufane, and was disposed vindictively to reverse them—a rumour too quickly realized; to add to the alarm occasioned by these reports, symptoms of that cruel scourge, the rust, reappeared, and the wheat crops for the second time entirely failed. Lord Charles arrived on the 30th November, harbouring feelings of resentment against the immigrants, who naturally held strong sentiments of gratitude to their benefactor, the Acting-Governor, and were disposed to espouse his cause, the fatal results of which were at once exhibited, and he treated that officer with humiliating disrespect.

The annals of the Western portion of the Colony at this period afford little of value to warrant notice. Affairs there went on in their usual routine, the supplies required for the age of the Settlers gave good and profitable employment for a portion of its capital *pour les miserable* in the East, and the only events of real value were the commencement of a Light-house, the first on its coast, on Green Point, at the entrance of Table Bay, and the foundation of the Cape Town Library.

One of the first acts of 'the Restoration' was the removal from the Magistracy of the British Settlement of Albany of Colonel Jones, "a gentleman of noble descent, and a brave, open, and kind-hearted man." This ungracious procedure was adopted too within six days of His Excellency's arrival, and in the most offensive manner. The successor appointed was a person known to be a staunch supporter and protégé of Lord Charles, and consequently, although a man of ability, not very acceptable to the Settlers, soured by misfortune, and now become distrustful of the Government. Such early indications of temper at head-quarters, added to the gloom occasioned by the adverse dispensations of Providence, and the prospect of political persecution to which the adventurers on the Frontier had in no way made themselves obnoxious, heightened the dismay.

The animosity the returned Governor displayed in those instances just recorded was soon made farther apparent by the treatment of Sir Rufane's favourite and judicious settlement of Fredericksburg. Immediately on His Excellency's arrival it was industriously circulated that he intended to suppress it, and the privates of the Royal African Corps, who had been disbanded, but placed under contract with the officers, grantees, and others for a limited period of service, began to desert without the slightest check. To aid the dissolution, an order was also issued for the of the small military post quartered for the protection of the village, as well as for the discontinuance of the road to it, then constructing at Kafir's Drift, across the Great Fish River. The effect of these and other hostile measures tended to embolden the Xhosa, who, taking advantage of this unstable policy and manifest indication of weakness, threatened the new little Colony, commenced robbing the

Settlers on both sides of the Fish River, and committed several barbarous murders; so that before the end of March 1822, the whole of the Fredericksburg party were forced to retire, leaving houses and standing crops to the mercy of the delighted barbarians, who soon burnt the village. Beyond this the safety of the Albany Settlement also compromised by the permission given to that and worst foe, the Chief Macomo, to occupy on sufferance a portion of these lands so vacated, and by ill-planned military movements, ending in disgraceful failures, afforded the ever-ready enemy a colourable pretext for his recommencement of encroachments.

Another token of His Excellency's utter disapproval of Donkin system was the removal of the Albany seat of magistracy from Bathurst to Graham's Town, which, although in itself probably a necessary change, was felt at time as a vexatious proof of hostility. Dispirited by past, and suspicious of the future, many of the Settlers began seriously to contemplate removal to some more favoured home: New South Wales (the present great Australian Colonies then 'were not'), Canada, the United States, and even the little isolated Island of Tristan da Cunha, were speculated upon. The mechanics too, as well as others, began to disperse into the other districts of the Colony, a movement which it was vainly attempted to arrest, and there wag every symptom of general disruption of the Settlement. At length a Select Committee of twelve gentlemen was appointed to draw up a statement of the aspect of affairs, to be laid before the Cape Town Government, and in May (11th) a requisition was addressed to the leading Settlers to meet on the following 24th at Graham's Town, "to consider the best means to be adopted at the present crisis," but this British and constitutional method of seeking redress was met by a furious Government proclamation, bearing the same date, declaring the proposed meeting unlawful, and threatening "arrest and the bringing to justice all and every individual who shall infringe the ancient laws of the colony." Foiled in their legitimate course the Settlers prudently abstained from any public demonstration, but undaunted by their harsh repulse at once prepared (at private meetings, held at their respective homes) and transmitted to the Imperial Government memorials containing full representations of their present condition and future prospects, repelling the insinuations of disaffection, and indignantly denying, as they were designated in the Governor's proclamation, they were "either ignorant, malevolent, or designing persons."

To increase the general dejection, disease in the wheat crops began once more to appear, and by the end of September a general failure—the third—was announced, the malady even spreading among the hitherto secure Bengal variety. During the year also, an unpopular and impotent attempt was made to incorporate the impoverished and harassed Settlers into a Yeomanry Corps, and to impose upon them an Oath of Allegiance, which, under the circumstances, was resented as a slur upon their conscious loyalty. The two Special Heemraaden, Captain Campbell and Mr. Bowker, now felt themselves bound to resign their commissions; and the Kafirs, after robbing the Settlers and committing some murders, and assembling in masses within their own country on the Border, seemed to menace attack. The only ray of hope now left to the unfortunate immigrants was furnished by rumours, fondly accepted, that the Home Govemment were preparing to inquire into the fate of their South African experiment in the remote pastures of the Zuurvelden.

1823—Weary of waiting for the expected inquiry into their grievances, the Settlers, on the 16th March 1823 again addressed Earl Bathurst, Secretary of State for the Colonies, with full explanations of their position, and as the principal difficulty therein enumerated still remains unredressed, although urged year after year, it is given here in as condensed a form as possible : — "We do not complain," say they, "of the natural disadvantages of the country to which we have been sent. We are actuated by one undivided feeling of respect and gratitude to the British Government, which future reverses will never efface; but it is a peculiar hardship being placed in a remote corner of the British dominions, with our interests and prospects committed to the control of one individual, and that our situation is neither thoroughly understood nor properly represented; that we have been debarred all means of |expressing our collective sentiments upon matters of the | utmost importance to our common interests. It has long — and from the most distressing proofs — become evident to the Settlers that the Colonial Government, situated at the opposite extremity of the Colony, where every particular, whether of soil and climate, or the constitution, pursuits, and interests of society, is totally different, possesses no adequate means of ascertaining their actual wants. That under this conviction it was contemplated by a small number of the principal Settlers to consult together upon the most advisable mode of making His Excellency the Governor acquainted with their situation, but this intention was not only met by positive prevention but by public imputations against the views and motives of the Settlers in general," &c. This document was signed by 374 individuals of the most respectable classes.

After transmitting this appeal they awaited patiently the progress of events, when to their delight the expected 'Royal Commissioners of Inquiry'[5] arrived on the 12th of July at Cape Town, where they were duly sworn in at Government-

---

5. The names of the Commissioners were J. T. Bigge, Colonel, W. M. G. Colebrooke, and W. Blair.

house. To fill up, as it were, their cup of calamity, violent tempests of wind and rain now visited the Eastern Districts in the month of October — still remembered as 'The Flood' — causing the destruction of much life and property, and leaving the apparently doomed Settlement at its zero point of depression.

1824. — Buoyed up by the hope of relief from the Royal Commissioners, the new year (1824) was hailed with pleasure, not unmixed with anxiety, by the almost ruined and nearly despairing immigrants. On the 5th February these gentlemen arrived in Graham's Town, where they were received by the authorities with sullen courtesy — by the people with open arms; the then little town was illuminated, and great rejoicings exhibited under the belief that the "Reign of Gubernatorial' Terror!" was at an end.

They were, however, for a time mistaken. In the evening of that day a few of the most respectable of the people who had assembled in the streets to witness the rejoicings were charged by the mounted men of the Cape Corps, and were hauled off to the common prison, with the threat of incarceration; and a most cruel and mendacious semi-official statement was published in the Government Gazette of the 21st of February, designating the affair as 'Riots in Graham's Town,' accusing the people—who it called a rabble—with insulting the Government and 'firing upon' the soldiery. This distortion of a natural and harmless demonstration was intended to abuse the minds of the Commissioners, in which it signally failed, and for the purpose of hoodwinking the Imperial Government by representing the body of immigrants as belonging to that violent class of political reformers of 1820 opprobriously designated as 'Radicals.'

The Commissioners on the spot were not so easily to be duped, and in their report to the Honourable the Secretary of State, dated the 26th September 1826, they thus nobly vindicated the character of the maligned immigrants:—"The introduction, however, of the English Settlers, and the right of free discussion which they have claimed and exercised, together with the bold defiance they have given to the suspicions entertained of their disloyalty and disaffection to the Government, have had the effect of exciting in the Dutch and native population a spirit of vigilance and attention that never existed before, and which may render all future exertion of authority objectionable that is not founded upon the law."

No doubt encouraged by the visit of the Commissioners of Inquiry, an attempt to establish free press in the Colony, a thing hitherto unknown, was now made; and early in the year (January 7) Mr. John Fairbairn and a British Settler, Mr. Thomas Pringle (the sweet lyrist of Glen Lynden, whose muse has immortalized the scenery of the Frontier and Kaffraria), published the first number of a newspaper called

The South African Commercial Advertiser, printed in Cape Town by Mr. George Greig.

A South African journal was also begun by the same party, and the Rev. Mr. Faure, the pastor of the Dutch Reformed Church, commenced a similar work, entitled *De Zuid-Afrikaanshe Tydschrift.* This dawn of a press was hailed with universal pleasure, but unfortunately destined in such Tory times to be of short duration.

A German philosopher, Böme, somewhere in his terse writings remarks that "Luther well knew what he was about when he threw his ink-bottle at the Devils head; there is nothing the Devil hates more than ink," and so, true to the saying, the hatred of the Colonial Government to free journalizing was soon exhibited. On the 17th May, Lord Charles Somerset assumed the censorship of the press; The Advertiser was suspended, the types and presses seized by the Fiscal (Anglice, Attorney-General), and an order for the banishment of the proprietor, Mr. Greig, issued; but very soon, through fright, this was recalled.

The natural result of these violences was pasquinading[6] and the promulgation of manuscript libels against the actors in the stupid crusade. At length the temper of the Colonists was roused, and memorials from both Cape Town and the Eastern town were transmitted to the British Government, and the inestimable privilege of a free press was granted (April 30, 1829) after a long and weary struggle, mainly through the exertions of Mr. Fairbairn, to whom the public presented a silver vase, as a testimony of gratitude for his consistency and public spirit, which he richly deserved.

1825.—The effects of the Royal Commission began now gradually to develop themselves. In March, the huge monopoly of the Government Farm under the "Boschberg" at Somerset East, established ostensibly for the advantage of the Cavalry Force on the Frontier, but in fact for the Governor's benefit whose name it bore, was abolished, and the present village thereon and district founded, while on the 2nd of May instructions issued by His Majesty George IV. were received, for the erection of a Council of seven members, including the Governor, to advise and assist him, placing the Imperial representative under some slight but wholesome restraint.

---

6. a composition that imitates or misrepresents somebody's style, usually in a humorous way.

The Reminiscences of An Albany Settler

Rev. H.H. Dugmore[7]

This piece is a lecture delivered in Graham's Town at the British Settlers Jubilee, May 1870. It provides an overview of the settler experience and world view. It would appear that this speech was delivered both in Grahamstown and Queenstown.

Part 1

"Tis fifty years since!"

Descendants of the Pioneers of 1820, we are looking back over the lapse of half a century! Few and feeble are the genuine Fathers and Mothers of the Settlement that still linger among us; yet even of these there are some with us in this Jubilee gathering.

Men and women who headed their families from the home beyond the waters; and who have lived in this sunny clime to see their children's children, even down to the fourth generation.

These are they who really "bore the burden and heat of the day" in the work of colonizing South-Eastern Africa, for their anxieties on behalf of their offspring doubled their care and toil. And now those Children stand, themselves grey-headed and almost patriarchal, the link between the old country and the land of their adoption: — born in the one, naturalized in the other. It is for the information of their children that I would on this occasion call up some reminiscences of the past, and hold up to their view a few of memory's pictures of what their fathers' fathers, and their mothers' mothers did and bore in the olden time.

But little more than fifty years ago, when the few surviving hoary-headed Fathers of the Albany Settlement were yet dwellers in "The dear Old Land," the word "Africa" was suggestive of little but waterless wilds, burning suns, the death-wind of the desert, and the slave trade. In many minds the distinctions of South, East, and West coasts were little recognised, and their differences — physical, climatic, or social — hardly known. But despite the appalling, which is so often associated with the unknown, and despite the gloomy pictures drawn by those who would fain have detained them, there was courage enough in the breasts of these pioneers, and of their life-companions, to brave the dangers, real or imaginary, of a

---

7. Dugmore, H.H. (1871). Reminiscences of an Albany Settler. Richards, Clanville and Co, Grahamstown.

voyage to, and a settlement on, the shores of South Africa, although that was the point remotest of all from the land of their birth. Some four thousand British Settlers sailed from the Island Home of their fathers, in the year 1820, to found the Anglo-African Community which now exists in the Eastern Province of the Cape Colony.

It is hardly to be supposed that a child of nine years old could enter into full sympathy with the feelings of those who were rending the ties of home and kindred, and launching the boat of life upon an unknown sea. But the picture of the last parting which I myself beheld has never faded from my memory.

It has rather become more vivid with the lapse of years, as growing faculties enabled me the better to appreciate what I remembered — the last wish and blessing of neighbours and friends, mingling hopes and fears for us — the last clasp of brothers' hands — the last falling upon sisters' necks by those who were never to look into each other's eyes again. I see them still! The faint hope of one day returning to visit once more the old home was never realised by those who then ventured to give utterance to it. Every one of them lies in an African grave.

I affect no Statesman's view of the expediency of settling our Eastern frontier with an English colony, though the subject is one that invites some political reflections. Nor will I, just now, attempt any estimate, or hazard any prophecy as to its results — present or future. My task is the humbler one of "reminiscence." I am trying to gather up some of the fragments that memory has saved from, oblivion.

Long delays interfered with the departure of the *Sir George Osborn*, the ship in — which our party were to sail. We chafed under them, but they, perhaps, saved our lives, for a few days before our expected time of starting, one of those January gales, for which the coast of England is so fearfully noted, burst upon us as we lay moored in the Thames. Whole tiers of vessels were driven from their moorings, and drifted in the darkness down the river. Lads sleep soundly, and so the first effects of the storm did not disturb me ; but I remember being awakened by a crashing noise soon after daybreak, and looking up through the hatchway just in time to see the rigging of our ship torn away like cobwebs by the yards of another that had come foul of us.

This first and involuntary stage of our voyage ended in our running aground just opposite Greenwich Hospital, and having all the women and children landed, lest the ship should heel over and capsize with the ebb tide. Had the gale (which was said to be the severest that had been known for forty years) caught us while going down the channel, we should, perhaps, have foundered, as many others did.

I would apologise for adverting to these *personal* matters, did I not know that such references are among the best means of calling up kindred reminiscences in the minds of those who passed through experiences more or less similar. I have no doubt that what I have just said has recalled to the recollection of some present the circumstances of their own embarkation.

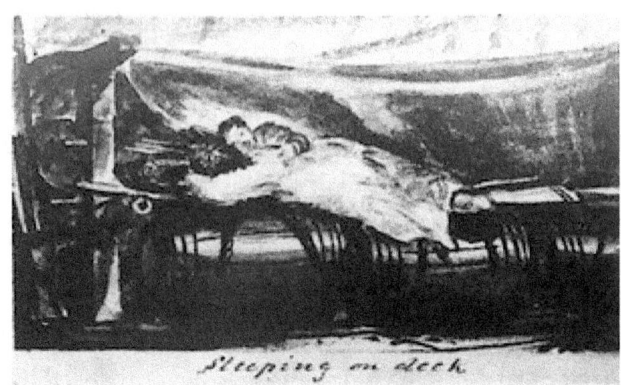

Figure 1: Sleeping on Deck - Thomas Baines

The sailing day did arrive at last, and "the last glimpse," not "of Erin," but of "Old England," was obtained through many an eye dimmed with tears, as the Land's End faded finally from view, and then the wide shore-less ocean spread around us.

I know nothing about the regular emigrant ships of the present day; that is, so far as respects the quality of the food, or the accommodation they supply; but I remember the close packing "between decks," the "banyan days," and the hard salt junk and harder biscuit of 1820. I have not forgotten how salt the outside of the puddings used to taste which the old weather-beaten coot had boiled with seawater in the general "copper;" nor how the passengers sometimes quarrelled with the steward for cheating them out of the supplies. I remember, too, how the little fellows, who were too young to see danger, having got over the sea-sickness in the channel, would climb into the long boat amidships, or cling to the 'main shrouds,' singing in chorus to the rocking of the vessel —

"There she lay.
All that day.
In the Bay of Biscay, O!"

as the rough seas were rolling around us. And I remember the steep vine-clad lulls, and the grapes and oranges of Madeira; where the boats with their tempting freight, and their dark-looking rowers, swarmed around the ships. Then came the tantalizing "variables," — the calms of the "line," — the rough shaving operations of old Father Neptune, the lather of whose brush, and the edge of whose razor stuck, the one to the chin and the other to the memory, for some time afterwards. Nor have I forgotten the one or two fearful storms we encountered, when the hatches were battened down, the heavy seas were shipped, and while the torrents poured down among us in the midnight darkness, the mothers clasped their children to their bosoms, exclaiming, "We'll all go together!"

But, thanks to Him who "holds the waters in the hollow of His hand," the storms were weathered, the perils passed; and after many a weary day, the welcome cry of "Land!" rang through the ship, gladdened every heart, and made young and old start to their feet, and strain every eye to catch a first glimpse of what they had long been pining to see. And the scene was repeated as ship after ship made the coast. The *Chapman* and the *Nautilus*, the *Northampton*, the *Garland*, the *Kennersly Castle*, the *Ocean*, the *Amphitrite*, the *John*, the *Stenton*, the *Weymouth*, the *Canada, Brilliant, Aurora, Zowaster, Belle Alliance*, and all the rest, as they ranged along the coast, with its high blue mountains full in view, had their decks thronged with anxious gazers on the new strange land in which their future lot was to be cast. At length Cape Recife was rounded, Algoa Bay spread its broad bosom, and ship after ship bore its living freight to the last anchorage.

> Over the waters wide and deep.
> Where the storm-waves roll, and the storm-winds sweep.
> Over the waters see them come !
> Breasting the billows' curling foam;
> Fathers for children seeking a home
> In Africa's Southern wilds.

The desolate sand-hills and salt-marshes of their then solitary landing place were not calculated to raise the spirits of the newcomers, or realise the visions which had probably flitted before the eyes of the sanguine when the Mountains of George first loomed into view. The "Liverpool of the Cape" was not yet in existence, and a dreary barren looming waste met many a disappointed eye. A few, indeed, landed only to die; and, as in the case of Dr. Cotton, the "Head" of the Nottingham party. Dr. Caldecott[8], and some others, ended their emigrant's career before it had well begun. I can well believe that many a doubt and fear were exchanged by the anxious elders of the new colony, as they first made each other's acquaintance among the tents of "Settler's Town" behind the sand hills. But the adventurers had bidden a long "Farewell" to the land of their fathers, and for weal or for woe they had come to dwell in the wilds of Africa.

---

8. See page 180

They must e'en make the best of it. There was little prospect of seeing waving corn-fields where they first pitched their tents, and some of the agriculturists might look back despondingly on the golden harvests of old England. But this was not to be their resting place. A journey of a hundred miles "up the country" might give brighter prospects to their eyes; and so they braced themselves for action. And then began to arrive the strange-looking conveyances that were to carry them inland, — the light loosely-made wagons, — the long "spans" of long-horned oxen, — the drivers with their monster whips and strange speech, — the little impish-looking leaders with dark skins and scanty clothing, and with stranger speech than their masters. We have long since become used to all these things; but they were wonders then. Next came the visit to the stores provided by the government; and the picks and spades, the axes and hammers; the ploughs and harrows, that were to "subdue the earth" for its new occupants, were added to their miscellaneous luggage.

And so the trains of pilgrims began to wend their way towards a centre of attraction, where the hope of bettering their condition was the only shrine — for there were, as yet, no temples in the wilderness.

Figure 2: Crossing the Zak River 04/09/1811 - William John Burchell

We "little ones" of those days felt none of the care that weighed on the hearts of our fathers and mothers. The gipsy—looking camp-fires of the first night's outspanning[9] at the Zwartkops — the ringing echo of the whips among the hills, as

---

9. Camp.

driver assisted driver up the steep bush-paths — the scarlet blossoms and the honey-dew of the aloes, that stood like soldiers on the mountain sides — the wild flowers of the wilderness, so new and strange — the bounding of the springboks over the plains — these were excitements for us that banished both care and fear, and made the journey a happy and beguiling one.

And now the Sunday's River is crossed, and the terrible old Ado Hill is climbed, and Quaggas Flat is passed, and the Bushman's River heights are scaled. The points of divergence are reached, and the long column breaks into divisions. Baillie's party made their way to the mouth of the Fish River, where, it was said, the "Head" had been allowed to choose a territory, and where he hoped to realize imaginations of commercial wealth by founding a seaport town. And the Duke of Newcastle's proteges from Nottingham took possession of the beautiful vale of Clumber, naming it in honour of their noble patron. And Wilson's party settled between the plains of Waay-plaats and the Kowie bush, right across the path of the elephants, some of which they tried to shoot with fowling-pieces. And Sephton's party, after an unceremonious ousting from their first location at Reed Fountain, founded the village of Salem, the religious importance of which to the early progress of the Settlement is not to be estimated by its present size and population. These four were the large parties.

The smaller ones filled up the intervening spaces between them. Behind the thicket-clad sand hills of the Kowie and Green Fountain, and extending over the low plains beyond Bathurst, were the locations of Cock's, Thornhill's, Osler's, Smith's, and Richardson's parties. Skirting the wooded kloofs from Bathurst towards the banks of the Kleinemonden, were ranged the parties of James and Hyman. It was the latter who gravely announced to Captain Trapps, the Bathurst Magistrate, the discovery of "precious stones" on his location; and which the irascible gentleman, jealous of the reserved rights of Government, found on farther enquiry were only "precious big ones."

The rich valley of Lushington afforded a resting place to Dyason's party. Holder's people called their location New Bristol; which never, however, acquired any resemblance to old Bristol. Passing on towards the front, there were Mouncey's party, Hayhurst's party, Bradshaw's party, Southey's party, stretching along the edge of the wide plains of the Round Hill, and drinking their Western waters. The post of honour and danger was the line of the Kap River. This was occupied by the party of Scott below Kaffer Drift, and by the Irish party above it. The Forlorn Hope of the entire settlement was Mahoney's party at the Clay pits, who had to bear the first brunt of every Xhosa depredation in the Lower Albany direction. Names thicken as we proceed from Waay-plaats towards Graham's Town.

Passing Greathead's location, we come among the men of Dalgairns at Blauw Krantz. Then those of Liversage, about Manley's Flat. John Stanley, "Head of all Parties," as he styled himself, belonged to the same neighbourhood. Turvey's party were in Grobblaar's Kloof; William Smith's at Stony Vale; Dr. Clarke's at Collingham. Howard's, Morgan's, and Carlisle's bring us by successive steps to the neighbourhood of Graham's Town; the suburbs of which were indicated by the painted pigeon-house at Burnett's. To the South-westward, the valley of the Kareiga was occupied by Menzies-, Mills-, and Gardner's parties. The rear-guard of the Settlement may be said to have been formed by the men of Norman's and Captain Butler's parties, who occupied Seven Fountains, and the upper end of the Assegai Bush River.

Besides these "parties," there were other companies of a more select and exclusive kind. Elderly gentlemen of upper-class connections, and retired officers from various departments of the king's service, came with small numbers of men under special conditions, and engaged for a term of years. The names of Bowker, Campbell, Philips, Piggott, and others, will suggest themselves; and such designations as Piggott Park and Barville Park, given to their domains, indicate the social position assumed by their owners.

My "reminiscences" are those of an *Albany* settler; but I do not forget that there was another party, who, though locally separated from the main body, occupied a position, the importance of which developed itself in the after-history of the Settlement. I refer to the Scotch party, who were located on the Baviaan's River, among mountains and glens that have been rendered classic by the poetry of their leader, and historic by the gallant deeds and indomitable endurance of his compatriots, in the after-struggles of the frontier. I need to make no particular reference, however, to the early circumstances of that body of men, as in Pringle's "African Sketches" they have a most graphically written history of their own.[10]

Of the many "Heads of Parties" whose names I have mentioned, I know of but one who still survives. That one is a man who surely must, when first located near the mouth of the Kowie, have had some prophetic instinct that looked on into the future; and, true to that instinct, though half a century has elapsed, there he is now, white with the snows of age; but with energy unexhausted; destined, I trust, to reap the reward of long years of labour in the realization of his wish to give Albany a free and safe port of her own. If ever man *deserved* success for perseverance in the

---

10. See an extract from this book reprinted in the current volume.

face of multiplied discouragements, and for bearing up against that "deferring of hope" which "maketh the heart sick," William Cock deserves it. *Finis coronat opus*; and most heartily do I hope, that before the last of our old leaders passes from amongst us, he may see *his* "work crowned" with a result that shall carry its benefits down to future generations.

As to the rest of the "Heads," some of them soon found that—

"Twas distance lent enchantment to the view"

of manorial dignities and immunities to which they had looked forward across the broad waters. These soon left their parties to shift for themselves, and sought their own fortunes elsewhere. Others manfully stood by those whom they represented till their early struggles were over. All have passed away, and even the names of some of them are almost forgotten.

But now to return to the first arrival "on the location." It was a forlorn-looking plight in which we found ourselves, when the Dutch wagoners had emptied us and our luggage on to the green-sward, and left us sitting on our boxes and bundles "under the open firmament of heaven." Our roughly-kind carriers seemed, as they wished us good-bye, to wonder what would become of us. There we were in the wilderness; and when they were gone we had no means of following, had we wished to do so.

Towns, villages, inns, hostelries, there were none. We must take root and grow, or die where we stood. But we were standing on our own ground, and it was the first time many could say so. This thought roused to action, — the tents were pitched — the night-fires kindled around them to scare away the wild beasts, and the life of a settler was begun.

Thus was the land overspread by a new race of occupiers; sanguine in their hopes, and eager to develop its capabilities. Tribes of barbarians had dwelt in it — had hunted in the forests of Oliphant's Hoek and made their *Vee places*[11] along the banks of the Kareiga. But they had gone before the British Settlers came, and the new occupants had to dispute the possession of the soil with inhabitants of other kinds.

> Wilderness lands of brake and glen, —
> The wolf's and the leopard's gloomy den;
> Wilderness plains where the springbok bounds
> And the lion's voice from the hills resounds
> And the vulture circles in airy rounds —

---

11. Seasonal livestock farms.

Are Afric's southern wilds.

Elephants in hundreds roamed leisurely from the Kooms to the Kowie, and from thence to the Ado. The rhinoceros crushed at will the thickets of the Fish River ravines. The lion stalked in undisputed sovereignty on the slopes of the Winterberg, and his roar was occasionally heard in the lower districts. The howl and laugh of the hyena, and the shrill yell of the jackal; were the regular nightly serenade of the new settlers, to which the little ones listened and trembled. By day even, the tiger's[12] deep bass sounded for hours together among the *krantzes*[13], and the ominous responsive call of the wild dog to his fellow, too often sent its melancholy sound on the breeze, as the pack ranged ravenously over the pasture grounds; while from every high ridge whole armies of baboons shouted their defiance, and demanded what business we had on their domains. And then, over the plains of Mount Donkin, and the Salem flats, springboks in thousands bounded playfully, as their snowy backs shone in the sunlight, while the ostriches ruffled their plumes, the hartebeest raised their horned crests, and the quaggas galloped heavily among them. We must go far from Albany to see such sights now, but the long-range rifles of Ayton and Bowker had not then arrived.

A bird's-eye view of Albany, at the earliest stage of the Settlement, would have shown a widely-spread camp of many divisions. The tents supplied by the government studded the locations in all directions, and marked the first phase of life there. And then came the selection of sites, and the preparation of material for more permanent dwellings. The nervous looked out for defensible positions. The men of sentiment sought picturesque spots, where the beauties of nature might be seen to advantage, forgetting, however, sometimes to enquire whether they were within the reach of water or not. More practically, the sober father of a family of healthy lads from the rural districts examined the soils, and fixed on a homestead in the midst of his prospective corn-fields. As to the first dwellings themselves, they were of very various, and very original orders of architecture. A young brotherhood of bachelors built for themselves a booth of leafy branches, after the manner of the Israelites of old.

An economist of materials dug his house out of the bank of a river. The wattled framework of two or three square rooms looked, in the eyes of some, like the founding of a mansion.

Many a father and son, with axe on shoulder, ranged the wooded kloofs in search of door-posts and rafters; and many a mother and daughter cut wattles and

---

12. Leopard
13. Cliffs

thatch nearer home for walls and roof; aye, and many a back ached under successive loads, borne toilsomely from tangled thicket and rushy swamp. Stone and brick were among the visions of an advanced order of things belonging to the future. Even the Devonshire Cot was rarely ventured upon at first.

The "Great Flood" of 1823 made strange work with many of these primitive dwellings. The bachelors' booths did not keep out the rain like Roman cement. The underground residence in the river's bank presented a remarkable appearance when the flood had subsided. One man was heard asking his neighbour if he had seen anything of his house passing that way.

The Settlers were earnest and energetic in their first attempts to make Albany an agricultural district. When they took their first survey of their new possessions, the language of many a father was, in substance —

Hand to the labour! *Heart* and hand!
Our sons shall inherit an alter'd land.
Harvests shall wave o'er the virgin soil;
Cottages stand and gardens smiley
And the songs of our children the hours beguile
   'Midst Africa's Southern Wilds.

But there were days of trial and privation before them. The romance of first impressions had to give place to the stern realities that followed. Crops failed. The terrible "rust" blighted the hopes of season after season, and the hearts of many began to sink within them. Want stared them in the face, and the extension of the period of Government rationing became an absolute necessity. They were pinching times when one, though not a Spartan boy, had to fast in the morning till he could shoot a wild pigeon for his breakfast; and another, being somewhat less of a sportsman, waited anxiously for the noisy signal from his solitary barn-door fowl that there was a fresh egg ready for boiling — which, like a true husband, he divided equally with his wife; and another, leaving his family to a "dinner of herbs," with as much of "love" as there might be to give it a relish, trudged a twenty miles journey through the rain for a back-load of meal, which he managed to lose at midnight in the flooded river at his own door on his return. These are little specimens of the "hungry days," which I dare say could be easily multiplied from the memories of some of my hearers. They have served to laugh over many a time since, but they were hardly laughing matters then.

I may here introduce a little episode that belongs to the same period of our history, and presents one of the phases of early settler life. Three men went from Salem to Graham's Town to look for work. It so happened that their wives wanted a supply of meat while their husbands were away. One of the future members of parliament was then the shepherd of the ration flock, little dreaming of the distant honours in store for him. A sheep was procured. But the good women had no one with them who would undertake to slaughter it for them. What was to be done? They had no compunction about eating the sheep; but they all seemed to have qualms of conscience about reducing it to a state in which it *could* be eaten. They managed to tie its feet together, and then tried to "screw up" each other's "courage to the sticking point." While they were in animated discussion however, on a subject which threatened to require the drawing of lots, the sheep whose bonds were by no means as indissoluble as their own, suddenly started to its feet, and ran for its life, pursued of course by all three ladies.

The "situation" was by no means an ordinary one, and a view of the chase must have been very interesting. The result was, that the sheep was so hard-pressed as to be obliged to take to the water, and there was nothing left for the amateur lady butchers but to take to the water after it. I do not mean to say that they might have been seen *swimming* in chase of the fugitive mutton, but I believe that a step or two more would have set them floating, or sinking, as the case might be.

However, they gained possession of their prize once more; and this time they secured it. And then, with averted heads, the fatal stroke, or rather succession of strokes, was struck. Poor sheep! Had the good creatures been less tender-hearted it would have suffered less. But now the sheep was dead, they were still in the midst of their difficulties. They knew no more about skinning than slaughtering; and as little about cutting up as skinning.

But the indomitable "three" were not to be beaten. The skin came off at last — I rather think by piecemeal — the meat was carried home in most extraordinary joints, and the ladies ate their dinner in triumph, with appetites sharpened, no doubt, by the labour of procuring it. The skin became literally the "crowning" trophy of the exploit, for it was cut up into hats for the children.

To the material wants of the people the Government were as attentive and considerate as could have been expected; but the supplies they had provided were not always easy to be got at.

The little flocks of ration sheep used to play sad pranks with the inexperienced English drivers, and the wolves[14] and wild dogs used to play sad pranks with them. As one sample out of many, take the following: — One of our old Queenstown Field-cornets, in the days of his youth, took charge of the party's ration sheep from

---

14. Hyena

Bathurst to Green Fountain. The sheep numbered, probably, twelve or fifteen. Those who know that part of the country know what an excellent field it is for a sheep chase; and how a dozen of startled hamels, just separated from a large flock, would be likely to try a driver's legs, and lungs too, in crossing it. If the course of the journey could have been afterwards traced on a chart, it would have looked like the working out of some intricate geometrical problem. Such a succession of zigzags, angles, and arcs of circles, no ship, beating up against contrary winds, ever described. To mend matters, after miles of open plain had been traversed, there lay a tract of "enchanted ground" in the shape of a belt of thick mimosa woodland, right across the way home.

By dint of unconquerable perseverance the sheep were brought thus far; and then! One starting this way, two in that, three in the other; a rent in the coat in stopping these; face scratched and eyes endangered in turning those; a shout to his two companions to ascertain where the rest were; an impenetrable barrier of bush stopping all access to them. Before giving up all for lost, our friend declared he had run the sheep so hard that, though they had large tails at starting, they had melted away to half the size by the time he had done with them! Driven to desperation, he at length exclaimed, "Dead or alive I'll secure one of you at any rate!" as a discharge from his fowling-piece stretched it on the ground before him. But he was still miles away from home. Of his two companions one couldn't and the other wouldn't take his share in carrying the dead sheep. There was nothing left for it but to shoulder it himself; and sturdy John Staples shewed that if his own staple was not very long it was very good, for he carried his load home. It was the only sheep of the lot that reached its intended destination — the wild dogs, wolves[15], and jackals got all the rest.

A fate equally tragical, though different, overtook another little flock. The drivers, when five miles on the road, had to turn back for something they had forgotten. Rather than drive the sheep back with them, they left them in charge of a little boy of their company. They had taken certain precautions to prevent their running away; and so they left them at the edge of the Kowie bush, tying their legs together to keep them from straying. It was not long, however, before the spectacle of the disabled sheep attracted the notice of some keen-sighted ass-vogel[16] far up in the sky. The vulture telegraph was at once put in motion, and, appearing on all sides, as they are wont to do, like ghosts, from nobody can see where, a whole flight swooped down on their helpless victims, terrified the little shepherd from his

---

15. Hyena
16. Vulture

charge, and devoured them all alive before his eyes.

Such were some of the difficulties in the way of getting the government meat. Then, as to the bread. Twenty or thirty miles was a long way to carry a sack of flour on one's shoulders; especially in the early state of the roads through Howison's and Brookhuisen's poorts, and about Cadell's hill and Blauw Krantz.

The days of buck-wagons were still far off — even the block wheeled trucks without tiers or bushings, that wore out of the circular and jolted limpingly along, taking fire as they rolled, were to be seen only here and there. These were indeed a step or two in advance of the sledges made of forked branches, that used to stick fast in every mud-hole and sand-drift. As to the pack-oxen, they were stiff-necked in more senses than one, and managed now and then to leave both riders and loads behind them on their way home. I can testify, from the best of all knowledge, that a seat on the loose back of a fresh young pack-ox in full trot is neither easy nor safe, and it certainly puts a load of crockery in great peril, as I imagine old William Lee could have testified when his ox shook of its burden on the Salem flats.

Mrs. Lee had been assisting her husband either by leading or driving, I don't know which — wives can occasionally do both. He now left her to look after the load, while he set off to look after the ox that had left him. She in due time, feeling solitary, set off to look after the husband who had left her, and the load was left, — to look after itself.

The early struggles and privations of the settlers appealed to the heart of British humanity — never appealed to in vain. Contributions generous and hearty came from east and west. India joined the Mother country in subscriptions which amounted to several thousand pounds. "Boards of Relief" sat, and many cases of painful interest came before them, which it would be invidious to specify now, but which stand recorded in the "Reports" and "Official Correspondence" of those days. Of course, as is usual in such cases, there were heart-burnings caused by the distribution, and some were accused of receiving most who needed least. It is not, however, to be questioned, that to many the aid was most seasonable. In some instances, like the raising of the long-winged swallow to "The level of the daisy's head," it proved the starting point in life to those who received it.

The testing time enabled the settlers to ascertain how far they were fitted for the work of bringing the wilderness into cultivation ; and taught some of them that it was not their vocation to till from year to year ground which refused to yield them the bread they had been accustomed to eating in the old country.

The trades and professions of many had done little towards training them for agricultural life. I heard of some who sowed carrot seed at the bottom of trenches two spades deep, filling up the trenches with soil as soon as it was done. The remark of one who saw them was, "It will come up, most likely, in England about the time it does here." In another case, a man wishing to get some mealies for seed, applied to his neighbour who had obtained a supply just before, but found he had planted the whole without knocking it off the cobs! A third person planted out a lot of young onions, roots upwards.

The results of these blunders rather disgusted some of the "cockney gardeners," as the wags called them. And then they did not take kindly to mealie bread and pumpkin fritters, even when fried in sheeps-tail. The engraver and the copper-plate printer found little to do "on the location." Cutting initials on the bark of the wild fig-tree might look sentimental, but it yielded a poor return, and was hardly enough to keep the hand in. The coach-painter did not get much to do in the valley of the Kareiga, or on the borders of the Kowie bush. Armorial bearings on the panels of their carriages were not required by the settlers in those days. Some of them indeed had not yet found out the family crest.

Even the tailor was obliged to come down from the manufacture of broadcloth swallowtails to that of leather jackets with no tails at all. The young bucks had to dress in sheepskin. If, indeed, they could afford to sport cuffs and facings of jackal's or tiger's fur, so much the better, they might then calculate on making quite a sensation among the fair sex; especially if the *Zumin* had done its Saturday duty, and had given the proper bright yellow to the "crackers." Veldschoen[17] usurped the place of Wellingtons in many quarters, and the beaver gave way to the home-made palmiet, or coffee straw, and the tiger[18]-skin cap, flat-crowned generally, though not of the Oxford university cut. So were the hatter's and shoemaker's occupation either "gone" or greatly modified.

Take an illustrative incident on this point. A "ladies' shoemaker," who had worn out his own shoes, wished to take a walk from Wilson's party to Graham's Town. A neighbour suggested that it would be easy for him to supply himself by making a pair of the material which the hides and skins of the ration cattle provided. He did so, and remembering his own neat style of workmanship in the "ladies' line,"' he seems to have applied it in his own case. The shoes, put on damp and soft, fitted "Like a glove," and he started on his journey.

But the farther he walked the tighter the fit grew, and the harder the green hide, now becoming dry very fast from the heat of the dusty road. His plight soon

---

17. Literally field-shoe, the traditional shoe of the Dutch settlers in South Africa.
18. Leopard

became as bad as that of the poor fellow who was sent for penance to Loretto with peas in his shoes, and hadn't the wit to boil them before starting. In fact our settler's case was the worse of the two, for when he wished to relieve himself from torture by walking barefoot, he couldn't get his shoes off again. He had to endure his misery as far as Cadell's Hill, where a friend assisted him with his knife in the eel-skinning process of getting rid of his close-fitting appendages, and lent him a pair of his own for the rest of the journey. The ladies' shoemaker never forgot his walk, and perhaps never repeated it, for he took up his residence in Graham's Town.

Figure 3: Artificers Square, Grahamstown - Janek Szymanowski

Bricklayers and carpenters, and men of kindred trades, were very soon attracted in the same direction. The infant metropolis gave them more remunerative employment than the "location." Indeed, the tradesmen soon built a distinct "quarter" for themselves in the embryo city, and thus "Settlers' Hill" and "Artificers' Square" received their inhabitants and their names.

But there were adventurous spirits among the settlers — men with souls above shop-boards, carpenters' benches, or plough-tails. There was ivory in the kloofs of the Kooms and the Fish River, and a bold shot from a daring hunter might put him in possession of five hundred dollars worth at once, without any labour but such as would give zest to the achievement; — for what are toil, and exposure, and even half-starvation to the man who is bent on bringing home half a score of elephant's tusks as his trophy?

And there was a more adventurous career still for such as had courage to enter upon it. There was, among the Xhosa "over the border," ivory ready collected, as well as cattle ready reared. And for those who did not mind risking "the penalty of death," which governmental unwisdom had attached to a trade it had made contraband, there seemed to be the chance of getting rich rapidly.

Then began the romantic period of the Frontier Settlers' history, the formation of elephant-hunting parties, the wild life in the woods, the cautious tracking of the noble game; the daring venture among the monster herds, the sudden report waking the echoes of the hills, the fall of the victim, the terrific rush and ringing scream of the startled troop of giants, the crash of the trodden down forest in all directions, the hair breadth escapes of the hunters, sometimes within a trunk's length of their infuriated pursuers — the whole crowned by the triumphant contemplation of success as the party of hunters gathered around the prostrate game, and calculated the worth of the tusks which had been the perilous attraction. Nor must the other class of adventurers be forgotten — the stealthy crossing of the border, the appointed meeting place beyond it, the life-in-hand venture into the power of the Xhosa, the perilous return when dark nights and difficult ways had to be selected, and quick-sighted patrols of mounted riflemen dodged in the bushpaths.

    The Scotch party in the highland had their share of frontier adventure life. They had not only the elephants as occasional visitors, but also the lions as standing neighbours, and it was not long before they came into contact with them. Pringle, in his sketches, gives a graphic description of their first lion hunt, the spirit of which is well embodied in the poetic picture of it by the same hand.

THE LION HUNT.
Mount — mount for the hunting — with musket and spear !
Call our friends to the field — for the Lion is near!
Call Arend and Ekhard and Groepe to the spoor;
Call Muller and Coetzer and Lucas Van Vurr.

Side up Eildon-Cleugh, and blow loudly the bugle:
Call Slinger and Allie and Dikkop and Dugal;
And George with the Elephant-gun on his shoulder —
In a perilous pinch none is better or bolder.

In the gorge of the glen the bones of my steed.
And the hoofs of a heifer of fatherland's breed:
But mount, my brave boys! if our rifles prove true.
We'll soon make the spoiler his ravages rue.

Ho! the Hottentot lads have discovered the track —
To his den in the desert we'll follow him back;
But tighten your girths, and look well to your flints.
For heavy and fresh are the villain's foot-prints.

Through the rough rocky kloof into grey Huntly-Glen,
Past the wild-olive clump where the wolf has his den.

By the black-eagle's rock at the foot of the fell.
We have tracked him at length to the buffalo's well.

Now mark yonder brake where the blood-hounds are howling;
And hark that hoarse sound — like the deep thunder growling;
'Tis his lair — 'tis his voice! — from your saddles alight;
He's at bay in the brushwood preparing for fight.

Leave the horses behind — and be still every man:
Let the Mullers and Rennies advance in the van:
Keep fast in your ranks ; — by the yell of yon hound.
The savage, I guess, will be out — with a bound.

He comes! the tall jungle before him loud crashing.
His mane bristled fiercely, his fiery eyes flashing;
With a roar of disdain, he leaps forth in his wrath.
To challenge the foe that dare 'leaguer his path.

He couches — ay now we'll see mischief, I dread:
Quick — level your rifles — and aim at his head:
Thrust forward the spears, and unsheathe every knife —
St. George! he's upon us! now, fire, lads, for life!

He's wounded — but yet he'll draw blood ere he falls —
Ha! under his paw see Bezuidenhout sprawls —
Now Diederik! Christian! right in the brain
Plant each man his bullet — Hurrah! he is slain!

Bezuidenhout — up, man ! — 'tis only a scratch —
(You were always a scamp and have met with your match !)
What a glorious lion! — what sinews — what claws —
And seven-feet-ten from the rump to the jaws!

His hide, with the paws and the bones of his skull,
With the spoils of the leopard and buffalo bull,
We'll send to Sir Walter — Now, boys, let us dine.
And talk of our deeds over a flask of old wine.

What was begun from necessity was afterwards continued from choice. George Rennie seemed resolved to avenge on the whole race the insult his brother received when the lion put his paw upon him, looked round in contemptuous majesty, and then turned away as if he did not think him worth killing. Lion hunting parties crossed the Winterberg range, and the plains and valleys which the Queenstown grantees are now quietly cultivating became the theatre of many a scene of adventure which ought to have been chronicled for future generations.

Most of the leaders in these exploits of bygone days have passed away. Poor old Harry Stirraker, and the cool-headed and steady-handed William Gradwell and little John Thackwray, who engaged to write his own initials on the haunches of an elephant and shoot him afterwards, and who died the victim of his own daring.

George Rennie, too, the lion hunter, — I saw the white head and broad shoulders of the solitary old bachelor not many years since. These are gone, but others remain. The elder Cawood, William Hartley, and especially the old veteran Edward Driver, should be induced to write the story of their early adventures, or one of the most exciting chapters of Frontier history will be lost.

I had another name on my list of survivors, and I little expected to have to transfer it to the sadder one of those that are gone. Of the romance of early settler life there was one who could have told much ten days ago. The outspoken, open-handed, generous-hearted Carey Hobson had his full share of perilous adventure in the early days, and stirring to the younger spirits of the present would a recital of them from his own lips have been,

>He was a man, take him for all in all,
>I shall not look upon his like again.

Bold as a lion in spirit and bearing, he was full to overflowing of the milk of human kindness. With an energy and perseverance that never wearied, he created an oasis of civilization in what was at once a physical and a moral desert. His untimely death, while hastening to share in our festivities, has changed a time of gladness into one of mourning to every member of his family, and to all his friends has shorn the Jubilee joy of not a few of its rays.

Figure 4: Front view of house in Beaufort St, 1834 - Frederick Timpson I'ons

Part II

There was another class, less daring indeed, but of great importance to the formation of the future character of the province. The young men of mercantile tastes soon tired of "the location," and soon found that money was to be made by becoming commercial travellers on their own account; and so, rising from shoulder bundle to horse-pack, from horse-pack to cart-load, and from cart to wagon, did our incipient merchants carry their wares through the upper districts, and among the old established Dutch farmers, their devoted young wives being, in some instances, the companions and cheerers of their toilsome journeyings. Then was found the benefit of a London or Manchester training, when powers of persuasion had to be employed with oude Tanta[19] Nieuwkerk, as she sat by the ever simmering brass kettle, or with Oom[20] Dederik, as he puffed away his summer evenings on the stoep. The qualities of the *linebayi*[21] and the *wolkombersen*[22] were elaborately discussed — the recommendations of the material for *onderbaaige oordentlyk voor nachtmaal's tyd*[23] cautiously listened to. As for Nechi[24] Sanna, she needed no persuasion to admire the *mooi handschoen and halsdocken*[25]; while Neef[26] Gert, when the *nieuwe Engelsche zadel*[27] was exhibited, was prompt with his "*Ja! als vader maar ook ja zegt, dan neem ik dat zoomaar.*[28]"

So were the hamels[29] and kapaters[30] gradually gathered together for the return journey, sometimes (it has been waggishly asserted) under the idea that they would make excellent breeding stock(!) and occasionally a few of the hoarded rixdaalders[31] were added as *kontante geldt*[32], when the goods were specially attractive. And so were laid the foundations of an internal trade, which did very much towards breaking up the phlegmatic stagnation of rural life among the Dutch Afrikanders of the frontier, and introduced new currents of thought and feeling which have carried the present generation to a social condition greatly in advance

---

19. Directly translated old aunt, a colloquial term for an old lady.
20. Directly translated uncle, a colloquial term for a man.
21. Linen Jacket
22. Wool blankets
23. Waistcoats suitable for sacramental occasions.
24. Directly translated a female cousin, a colloquial term for a young lady.
25. Pretty gloves and neckerckiefs [or scarfs].
26. Directly translated male cousin, colloquial term for young man.
27. New English saddle.
28. Yes! if father will only say 'Yes' too, then I'll take it at once.
29. Castrated ram.
30. Castrated goat.
31. Local currency.
32. Cash.

of that of their fathers half a century ago.

There was another opportunity afforded for the exercise of the commercial talents of the new colonists. The Government, yielding at length to representations that were made to it on the subject, permitted, under certain restrictions, the opening of trade with the Xhosa. A periodical 'fair' was established at Fort Wilshire, where the colonial traders by scores, and the Xhosa by hundreds or thousands, met to exchange wares. The old post, long ago deserted, was a place of note in those days as the chief defence of the frontier. It has been silent and desolate enough since. Many years have elapsed since its stables were occupied by troop horses — since its officers' quarters were scenes of jollity, or the reveille and "tattoo" sounded in the square; but it was a place of some animation, and that of a strange and wild character when 'fair-day' arrived.

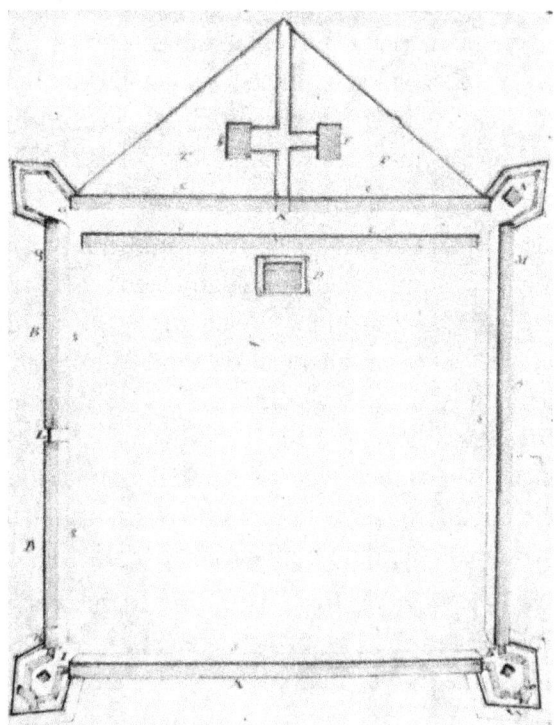

Figure 5: Plan of Fort Wilshire - Henry Foley

The traders were there with their beads, buttons, and brass wire; and the Xhosa were there from mountain range and sea coast lowland, from the Keiskamma to the Kei. Long files of women, headed by their lords and masters, and laden with ox-hides, horns, and gum, and here and there the more precious merchandise of an elephant's tusk among them, threaded the bush-paths in single file, or converged down the hill sides towards the centre of attraction under the guns of the Fort. The trees that fringed the banks of the Keiskamma below the post gave shelter to hundreds of swarthy groups of eager barbarians, wondering at the newly acquired value of articles they had formerly deemed worthless.

Xhosas have since gleefully told me what diligent search they used to make for the horns that had long been thrown away; and how the troops of children swarmed among the thorn-tree thickets, gathering gum for the new market.

There were no photographers in those days, nor had Mr. Ions begun his Xhosa sketches, or we might have had some amusing scenes from life fixed for us to contemplate. The grim old fort, with its wild scenery around it, would have formed the centre of a very characteristic picture. The motley throng of black, and white, and brown, varied by the red, green, and blue uniforms of "Line" Rifles and Artillery; the groups of women with their crushing loads gladly laid upon the ground before them; the men, seated on their heels, *kerrie*[33] in hand, jealously watching their property, or chaffering with the traders who were making them rival offers for the coveted merchandise; the greedy chiefs, headed by Gaika himself, laying seigniorial taxation on their own people, or pestering the white man for bribes and brandy.

Strange Xhosa was spoken on these occasions; and strange Dutch and English too. Interpreters were at a premium; and sadly perplexed were the traders now and then by the changes in the Xhosa fashions. Beads that were worth seventy dollars the pound, and buttons that were in universal demand one month, might be worth almost nothing the next. Speculators even in the Fort Wilshire market sometimes burnt their fingers. There was little to do in brocades or artificial flowers, and as little in thin steel; but the Xhosa men were as particular about their necklaces, and the women about their turban covers and karos back-stripes, as the leaders of the *mode* in London or Paris are about their bonnets and ball dresses.

The Fort Wilshire Fair gave a fresh impulse to the young commerce of Graham's Town, and it formed the commencement of an international trade with the Xhosa tribes that acquired great importance in a short time; and, but for the ruinous wars which followed, the result of barbarian cupidity, stimulated by civilized smugglers of guns and gunpowder, would have aided more than it has done in promoting their civilization.

I have said that the Government was considerate and kind in reference to the early material wants of the people. But there was a strong disposition to keep them

---

33. Walking / throwing stick.

under civil and political disabilities, against which the freeborn British spirit soon began to revolt. To have no "paper" to read but one, which a jealous and despotic Governor had first revised, did not suit the notions of men who had come from a land where every form and phase of opinion received public expression. To be obliged to procure a "pass" in order to go merely from the location to Graham's Town, without incurring the risk of getting a night's lodging in the *"tronk"*[34] on arriving there ; — and even when applying for one, to be flouted by petty official insolence, which had been fostered by the passiveness of slaves and Khoi, was a state of things that might accord with Russian serfdom, but it chafed the minds of Englishmen in a manner that soon gave a pledge of the downfall of the system. The voice of the people became too powerful to be silenced ; and in answer to reiterated representations of abuse, Commissioners of Enquiry were appointed, who arrived in Graham's Town during the year 1823.

I remember well, young as I was at the time, what enthusiasm their arrival excited. The general illumination of the town was not thought sufficient. The signal for an African welcome was given by a volley fired from the house where I was living. It was taken up at once, and the example spreading like wildfire, the hills soon resounded on all sides with a noise that might have been mistaken for the storming of the town, only that the importers of Xhosa muskets had not yet supplied the frontier tribes with firearms. As it was, however, this was a demonstration the authorities could not brook. The necessary orders were given, and we soon heard the bugles of the garrison sound the "assembly" at Scott's barracks, while the trumpets of the Mounted Rifles at Fort England sent squadrons of horse thundering up Bathurst street through the darkness, to assist in the terrible emergency, caused by blank cartridges and joyous hurrahs. Sergeants' parties of infantry patrolled the streets, making prisoners in all directions, among whom was my old master, — then young, and just married. The people, assembled in Church-square to see the illumination, were surrounded by troops; while the leading men among them, foreseeing the triumphant issue to their own cause that would be the result of such a style of repressing public opinion, bade them to be true to their principles and fear nothing. Of course the prisoners were set at liberty the next morning — the young bridegroom among the rest, — and the Commissioners of Enquiry were furnished with an additional and unforeseen item in the list of complaints.

Of the political reforms which resulted from the enquiries and report of the Commissioners, I was too young to know much. I believe that the recognition of

---

34. Jail

certain civil rights highly prized by Englishmen took place — trial by jury, and the modification of magisterial powers being among the changes introduced.

Various recommendations were made to the Home Government by the Commissioners of Enquiry. Some of them were adopted. Some half adopted and thus spoiled, and others rejected to be striven for again and again down to the present time.

While adverting to this subject it is but an act of bare justice to remember the public labours of one who has grown grey in the service of the Eastern frontier inhabitants; and who, from the first day of his appearance as a Journalist, has, with a perseverance un-wearied, though often single-handed, maintained the rights, and urged redress for the wrongs of his fellow settlers. This is not the place for a review of the editorial career of my honoured friend, the truly "Honourable" Robert Godlonton; but even in "a glance, at the early history" of our settlement it would be unpardonable to forget that the *Graham's Town Journal*, from the date of its first number, has been the British Settler's Advocate; and that the example of its Editor has taught many a man the value of the old motto, "Never despair!" I say this without any disparagement of the labours of others in the same field, because the scope of my lecture confines me chiefly to the period during which the *Graham's Town Journal* stood alone.

I hardly consider this a digression. If it be so, however, let me return to my subject. The visit of His Majesty's Commissioners seemed to have removed an incubus from many minds. The dawn of a brighter day seemed approaching, and men took heart. The settlement began to grow and prosper in spite of its drawbacks. If wheat could not be raised in Lower Albany, other grain could. The mealies did not take the rust, and they made very good porridge, and puddings too. If we had had in those days a few "American notions" on the subject, they might have been made more palatable still. And there were other things on which the children throve and grew fat. Bradfield's Clumber potatoes were renowned for their floury quality, and there was plenty of stuff to make good bacon of. And then by ones, and twos, and threes, the milk cows began to show themselves on the locations, and the fat hamels came with them, brought down by the young "Smouses"[35] from the inner districts.

Some of the cows were, it is true, sad unmanageable creatures, and made awkward work, not only with the milking pails and their contents, but with those who carried them as well. Horns and heels were often plied with perfect fury, and the astonished milk-man was chased round the kraal till he tumbled as he might

---

35. Traders

over the thorn hedge out of it. It was believed, and apparently with some reason, that the Boers had purposely weeded their milking kraals of the refuse, and palmed upon the ignorant Englishmen the most vicious brutes they had. "Ach! hy's maar een stomme Setlaar, gy kam hem zoomaar kulle, karl.[36]

But perseverance overcomes all difficulties. The cows were in due time either conquered or better understood. Lower Albany was found to be a noble pasture ground for cattle; the little herds grew larger every year, and Mrs. James' Green Fountain cheese became far-famed. It was not long before a span of oxen, large enough to plough with, could be made up by three or four uniting their cattle, each taking his turn in the lands of his neighbour. And it was not much longer before many a one had a little team of his own, and began to think that after all it was more pleasant to plough his own fields, with his own cattle, than to work as a labourer on a *Vaarm down along in Zommersetszhire*[37]. Home comforts gradually grew around them. The October rains taught the necessity for building more substantial houses, and the people built them. The furniture was both scanty and rough, it is true.

Those were not the days of horse-hair chairs, brass bedsteads and mirrored side-boards; — still less of pianofortes and harmoniums. But the Fathers of the settlement, and the mothers too, worked hard enough to enjoy their plain dinners and hearty suppers, although served up in tin dishes on yellow wood benches; and were weary enough at night to sleep soundly on their *riem-bottomed kaatles*[38] without either feather beds or curtains.

And then the children were growing up, acclimatised and naturalised; and it was soon found that the pure air, and the out-door exercise of South Africa, were making them bigger if they did not make them better men than their fathers. Sires of five feet six wondered to see sons of six feet five rising around them, and mothers had to look up to their daughters, even while their daughters were still looking up to them.

If longevity affords any test of the salubrity of a country's climate, we can bear the application of that test here. The fathers of the settlement have, I think, reached an average of nearly eighty years. The fathers of the Bowker, Biddulph, and Wainwright families were between eighty and ninety when they died. The patriarch of Glen Avon was not of the 1820 band, having come with the army in pre-settler times. But his family blended with the emigrant countrymen of their father, and

---

36. O he's only a stupid Settler, you can gull him, mate, easily.
37. Farm down in Somersetshire.
38. Leather strap bottomed beds.

when the iron-framed Robbert Hart sank into an honoured grave at the age of ninety, he left more than two hundred descendants behind him.

Then there are the names of Norman, Kestel, Warner, George Clayton, and others, averaging eighty-five. On the tombstones in some of our cemeteries, and in retired family burial-places, are names more hoary still. The venerable and venerated Mrs. Dold died at the age of ninety-three. Overy, Purdon, Foxcroft, Cooper, are names that will occur to the memory of many present. Father Purdon had served old King George the Third in the India wars of the last century, and had nearly completed his centenary when he passed away.

The Foxcrofts, husband and wife, were old people when they arrived; but the climate seemed to "renew their youth like the eagle's." They lived through the troubles of three Xhosa wars, and were both nearly, if not quite, an hundred years old when they sank quietly to rest, leaving behind them their children's great grand- children. Cooper of Bluekrantz walked Graham's Town streets and planned a voyage to England at a hundred. And just now, old Frank Allison, ("Old Frank" he was called when I was a boy) and Forbes of the Irish, party have gone, the one in his hundredth, the other in his hundred and first year.

The Jubilee year has proved the last to several who were hoping to see its completion. My old friend Joseph Walker among the number. Identified with the fortunes of the Settler's city for the best portion of his life, energetic and active in many a work conducive to the highest interests of his fellow townsmen, he has left to a goodly array of young representatives a name respected and honoured by men of all classes.

On the roll-call of names belonging to them that have departed there is another which I would not willingly let die, although I cannot place it on the centenarian list. It is something to be a man whose character individualises him amidst the general sameness of contemporaries. And dear little "Dr. Webb" was such a man. I see his slight figure now, "as straight," though not "as tall as a poplar tree," his short quick step, his prim keen look. And who does not remember his talent for mimicry and personification, his quaint humour, his power of acute observation, and quiet sarcastic retort? — always good-natured, but sharp enough to cut nevertheless. There is many a characteristic anecdote told of him which will keep him in remembrance.

Let me put on record two, the genuineness of which I will vouch for:

Working one day in his own line at a broken window, he saw Dr. Atherstone, (the Dr. Atherstone of former days) coming by. Dr. Webb — I am not sure that he then had his diploma — turned round on his heel with his characteristic abruptness, and said, "Doctor, do you know I think your profession and mine are very much alike."

"Indeed!" said the physician, eyeing the putty and the paint pot, "I don't see the resemblance."

"Well, you know, it's your business to take out old pains; and you see I am doing the same."

"Excellent!" said Dr. A., "I never saw the similarity before."

"But then," rejoined the other, "We always put new ones in their place you know."

The replication is not on record.

The other anecdote is of a different kind. A young couple just married, had come to live in Bathurst-street, directly facing his own house. It so happened that the position of the parlour windows, the back one being opposite the front, made it easy to see what was taking place inside. One day the bridegroom received a note in the little Doctor's hand-writing, and read the following lines : —

>Example is better than precept in life;
>The maxim I own very fine:
>I Saw you kissing your own dear wife,
>I immediately ran and kissed mine.

But the old settlers are not all gone. There was a muster of them on Monday; feeble and tottering some of them were, but others seemed to have years of life in

Figure 6: Probably Edward Turvey - Frederick Timpson I'Ons

them yet. The number might have been much greater, could we have brought together those who are at a distance. I hope no pains will be spared to complete the list of their names, not forgetting the wives and widows; and that a marble tablet bearing them all will stand conspicuously in the grand hall of the Jubilee Memorial, to tell succeeding generations who, among the fathers of the settlement, lived to see the Jubilee of 1870.

But I must go back again to resume my narrative. Health, long life, and growing prosperity make existence pleasant. But growing prosperity brought growing peril. The little flocks and herds of the settlers were at first tended by the sons and daughters of their owners; for Xhosaland was not yet thrown open, and the time for hiring native farm servants had scarcely arrived. The rapidly increasing stock, grazing in sight of the Xhosa over the border, soon began to tempt their cupidity; and depredators from the tribes of Eno, Botuman, Slambi and Gaika, began to make herding hazardous along the frontier.

Some of the children of the settlers were murdered while herding their parents' cattle: — Garbutt and Sloman for instance. Nor did the fathers themselves escape the frontier risks of the times.

The "Forlorn Hope" at the clay pits had its victims in Stubbs[39], and the Freemantles, father and son ; and the Irish party, with the rest of the frontier line, shared in its perils and its sacrifices, and added other names to the list of those who died for their adopted country in the early days of its history.

But all this was training a race of young frontier warriors, familiarizing the sons of the settlers with the dangers that a frontier life necessarily involves, and teaching them to unite African wood-craft with English courage. The men who were learning to cut off pauws'[40] heads with rifle bullets at two hundred yards distance, "that the body feathers might not be soiled," were likely to become dangerous to other heads as well, in a case of emergency. And frequent practice was training young English eyes to trace a spoor with the keen-sightedness of a Xhosa or a Khoi. The youth of the border were thus unconsciously preparing themselves for the crisis that was approaching, when, —

> The war cry echoing wild and loud,
> The war of the savage, fierce and proud,
> Would burst like the storm from the thundercloud,
>   Over Afric's southern wilds.

It must not be forgotten, however, that the first essay of the settlers in arms was not against the Xhosa, but in their defence.

---

39. Some of John Stubbs's son Thomas Stubbs memories are shared elsewhere in this volume. See page 131.
40. Directly translated a peacock. Probably however referring to an indigenous bird like the Gompou.

In the year 1828, a savage and very formidable horde under the chief Matinawa — an offshoot of the Zulu nation, entered the Tembuki country from the north-east, having skirted the Kwahlamba mountains, and crossed the upper sources of the Umzimvubu. They struck terror throughout the frontier tribes; for their warfare was an exterminating one that spared neither man, woman, nor child; while the tiger roar of their onslaught with the short stabbing spear, and the horrible "Tah! Tah!" which accompanied their death-dealing strokes in their hand-to-hand combats, were paralysing to the courage of men used only to the light-shafted and easily-evaded assegai of the frontier tribes.

The alarm they inspired threatened to drive the frontier [Xhosa] in upon the colony for refuge, or substitute for them, if destroyed, a more savage set of neighbours in their stead. To prevent general confusion, the Colonial Government deemed it best to help the Xhosa to repel their enemies. A body of troops was accordingly sent under the command of Major Somerset, to prevent the nearer approach of the Fetcani, as they were called.

A commando of Burghers was joined in the expedition with the regular troops, and numbers of active young men from among the English settlers eagerly came forward to swell their ranks, and share for the first time the excitements of a Xhosa campaign.

The tribes of Hintsa and Vusani (the paramount chiefs of the AmaXhosa and Abatembu tribes) mustered in force, and the young men of Albany obtained their first views of a Xhosa army, — in those days armed only with assegais[41], and carrying great lumbering shields of ox hide, five feet by three. I believe it was while awaiting the tardy gathering of these auxiliaries, that Major Somerset performed the feat of riding from the heights of the Umtata into Graham's Town in forty-eight hours.

The Fetcani army was met among the upper waters of the Umtata, and the Matiwana mountains, (as they have been called ever since) resounded for the first time with the musketry and cannon of the white men. Of course the Fetcani, though very numerous, were defeated. They had never seen fire-arms before. The Xhosa auxiliaries did little but look on till the fight was over; but an impression of British prowess was made upon the minds of the Tembukis, which the old men remember to this day.

Matiwana collected his scattered forces behind the mountains after the battle, and gave them a comforting harangue. "When we have fought with men," he said,

---

41. Spears.

"we have beaten them; but to-day we have had to battle with the thunder and lightning. It is no disgrace to be conquered by them."

When the commander returned, as many of the pressed horses as had survived the expedition were brought back to their owners by the men to whom they had been supplied. My old master, I remember, had contributed one, as he did not go himself. It was an ugly old mare, a "pas-ganger," that used to waddle along in most ungainly fashion. There were many handsome, high-fed horses on the commando, taken from the Graham's Town stables; and many a youth "spogh'd"[42] dashingly enough upon them at starting. But long after their curvettings had been exchanged for drooping ears and a footsore pace, and the carcases of some of them had been left for the aasvogels[43], old Bess waddled on as she had done at starting, and active Jerry Goldswain[44] (there's life in the old boy yet, I see!) brought back the old mare in triumph; and brought back this moral with her, that beauty, though lovely to look upon, is not always associated with strength of character, and that under a very plain exterior may exist very sterling qualities.

In looking back over the past of the Eastern Province, I have thus far confined myself to the Secular aspects of the subject. But it would imply a very unthankful heart not to recollect the means that were employed to keep alive, in the minds of the British Settlers, the Christianity of the Fatherland. The Sabbath bells of Old England were heard no longer. No steeple, rising from the midst of clustering elms, rocked to the joyous peal which invited high and low, far and near, to assemble in the sacred place where all meet on equal ground. There was much of secularising influence in the circumstances of the people. A new start in life in a wild country was likely to absorb the mind in the cares and enterprises relating to the present state of being, and there was danger of their forgetting "the life to come."

This danger was none the less from the fact that their lot was cast in close contact with barbarism. The reports that some of our own travellers bring us from the far North serve to prove that the families of a civilized, race may go down fearfully in social condition, where the elevating influences of Christianity are superseded by those of Heathenism.

To counteract these dangers on our frontier, one man organized an extensive scheme of religious visitation, reaching throughout nearly the whole Settlement. William Shaw had an eye and a heart that embraced all Albany, and gladly

---

42. Boasted
43. Vultures
44. Jerry, forty-two years after the occurrence started up in the audience when his name was mentioned, exclaiming, a midst great cheering — 'Here he is still!'

combined and guided the elements of usefulness wherever he could find them. The "locations" of the various "parties" had Sabbath Services, conducted by men who proved their own disinterested sincerity and earnestness by the long journeys they took (often on foot), without any remuneration but the satisfaction of knowing that they were conserving the Christianity of their fellow colonists, and enjoying a gladdening sense of the smile of God upon their labours. The names of Ayliff, Shepstone, Walker, Pike, Miller, Dukesbury, Gush, Oates, Roberts, Aldum, Sargeant, Booth, and others, are not all connected with one section of the Church of Christ; but they are all associated more or less with services that began fifty years ago, and have never ceased. They fed and fanned the flame of piety where it would have died out but for them; and they kindled it in many places where otherwise its light might never have appeared. They are remembered, as they ought to be, with gratitude ; but all, with one venerable exception,[45] have passed away from this scene of things.

It was in a very primitive style that worship was first solemnized among the Albany Settlers. The shade of a spreading tree, cleared of its underwood, formed in many instances the first place of public devotion for the population of its neighbourhood. Very plain sermons were preached by very plain men; but they were men who had the advantage of speaking from experience. What they had felt themselves they could tell with confidence to others. And what they aimed to tell related to those foundation principles of religion on the faithful application of which the Christianizing effect of all preaching depends.

As the circumstances of the people allowed, they began to build more substantial places of worship, here and there, in central situations. And so Green Fountain Chapel made its appearance on its little mount behind the sand-hills in Smith's party. And Reed Fountain had its house of prayer on the slope of one of its grassy hills. And Port Frances had one among the darkwoods on the banks of the Kowie. And Clumber's little knoll, that seemed as if raised by its Creator for the purpose in the midst of its beautiful vale, was crowned with its rustic temple for God, around which not a few of the fathers and mothers of the settlement were to find their last earthly resting-place.

"James' Party" Chapel, conspicuous on its high ridge, overlooked the woodlands of the upper Klein Monden. That of Bathurst stood in one of Nature's parks, where the capital of the settlement was to have been. It is needless to go on enumerating.

Later times have seen many others rise, to be means of blessing to both parents

---
45. The Rev. W. Shepstone.

and children, amidst the population around them. And thus the original Mother Chapel at Salem has had a large and overgrowing family, that is still spreading on all sides.

Let it not be supposed that in this enumeration I wish to ignore what has been done for the religious benefit of the Eastern Province by other denominations than my own. Much has been done by various branches of the Church Catholic, Roman and Anglican, Episcopalian and Nonconformist; but their exertions, and the results of those exertions, belong to a later period of Colonial history than that on which I am chiefly dwelling.

Though a Wesleyan myself, only a spurious modesty could induce me to hide the truth that for years the Wesleyans stood virtually alone in the work of preaching the Gospel among the rural population; while even in the towns and villages the Church of England did not disdain to avail herself of the proffered use of Wesleyan and Dissenting places of worship, which had anticipated her own. Zealously and energetically has that Church laboured since, to atone for the tardiness which some of her prelates and dignitaries have acknowledged and lamented. But all this leaves the honour of priority where the God of Providence saw fit to place it.

The dedication and anniversaries of these primitive places of worship were pleasant times. Gatherings of friends and neighbours from far and near made them occasions of hearty greetings and generous hospitality. Reminiscences of the "Dear Old Land" and its religious privileges were awakened in many a breast; and many a little group sat under the trees, talking of days of old, and scenes beyond the wide waters — called up afresh in the memory, though never to be visited again. All classes joined heart and hand to welcome the guests, and contribute to the general table, which was literally "spread in the Wilderness."

For those were not the days of spacious dining-halls, and the absence of pavilions was made up for by the shade of the wild-woods in which the dedicatory feasts were held. No boisterous mirth was needed to heighten the enjoyment. Hearty songs of praise, as befitted the occasions, ascended to God, both in the newly raised houses of prayer, and around the general board, which the green trees sheltered from the sun's rays. The people were refreshed in heart and mind at once, by the reunion of those occasions, and by the gladdening religious services which hallowed them. From these days of more advanced, though perhaps less natural social condition, many of the present generation look back with deep interest and glowing gratitude to those long gone by, in which the foundations of Christian character were laid in many a heart, and to which the colonial Christianity of the present day is deeply and lastingly indebted.

The circumstances of the Albany Settlers, in relation to Education, were very unfavourable during the early years of the settlement. The children were almost entirely dependent on the time, ability, and disposition of the parents to instruct them; and, situated as they were, "the pursuit of knowledge" was emphatically "under difficulties." Day schools were, as a rule, out of the question. With the exception of the Rev. Mr. Boardman, who, I believe, took a few private pupils for a short time before leaving Wilson's party, I do not remember to have heard of any person who was engaged in the work of teaching in any part of the Settlement between Salem and the mouth of the Fish river.

Little Sunday Schools were begun, as circumstances admitted, in connection with the small congregations that assembled in the country chapels ; and these, in many instances, supplied the only means of instruction within the reach of the children. The solitary Public School was at Salem, under the care of Mr. Wiliam Henry Matthews; and in that precursor of our later Academies, Seminaries, Institutes, and Colleges, not a few of the men who have since filled important public situations received their preparation for them. The teacher himself (the Father of Albany Education, as he deserves to be called) transferred his work in due time to other hands; but, a genuine "Settler," remained himself, rooted to the spot where he began his labours. And after living to a venerable age, — the Magistrate, Doctor, Adviser, Peacemaker, and Universal Referee of all the country round, — passed suddenly and painlessly away, not very long since, leaving a name as fragrant with true honour as any in the Colony besides.

Figure 7: Grahamstown (South Side), 1823 - Henry Foley

Part III

So the years rolled smilingly round. Despite of rust in the wheat, and occasional devastations from locust armies, such as we have seen again amongst us of late years, the people prospered.

Rural comfort and plenty were found in the country districts; commercial wealth was growing in the towns. The necessaries of life cost but little. The butcher who slaughtered an ox that weighed 1100 lbs., thought he had done a generous thing for his Christmas customers when he ventured to give thirty dollars for it. There seemed before the whole community a gradually but constantly brightening prospect of growing prosperity.

Meanwhile, however, a dark thunder-cloud was gathering among the Amatole mountains. From a course of reprisals, rendered necessary by incessant depredations along the border, had arisen a state of feeling among the frontier Xhosa tribes which needed but a spark to kindle it into a war-flame; especially as the acquisition of fire-arms had greatly raised their notions of their own prowess. That spark was struck in the wounding of a chief by a military patrol when recapturing stolen cattle; and the tribes of Eno, Botumane, Dushani, and Gaika, rushed over the frontier in a line of flame, — like one of our Queenstown grass-fires before an August wind — burning and blackening as they went.

The Christmas day of 1834 was a day never to be forgotten in the annals of Albany. Hundreds of families were preparing to spend it in the usual festive style, and were anticipating a brighter day of social gladness than in previous years, as their growing prosperity had raised them higher in the scale of comfort than they had ever been before. Friends were assembling for the brotherly-kindnesses of the season. Heads of families were calling in their scattered members for a Christmas gathering, that the dear old customs of the dear old Fatherland might not be forgotten in their African homes.

If they had not the bracing frost and snow of an English Christmas to exhilarate them, — if the holly with its bright berries was not there to deck the walls, — if the heat of an African December made the Yule log needless; — there was at least the beef to roast, and no stint of it either, for they could roast the sirloins of their own fat oxen, and there were plenty of materials for the plum-pudding, for there were plenty of Graaf-Reinet raisins in the land.

Ah! Only the grey-headed ones of the present time, looking back over the interval of six and thirty years, can remember their terrific revulsion of feeling, when a burst of barbarians, without an hour's warning, wrapped the whole frontier line in the fire and smoke of their own homesteads, and brought the unknown realities of savage war, with lightning suddenness, into the midst of their astonished family groups, met together for so different a purpose. Husbands, fathers, and brothers fell, while mothers, wives, and sisters looked helplessly and frenzied on. The frontier, utterly unprepared, was utterly defenceless. The families of the Settlers fled, as they could, to temporary rallying points, which had to he abandoned in succession for stronger places of refuge. Some three or four hundred men formed the military garrison of the frontier; and before any plan of resistance could be organized, or the Burgher force of the inner districts brought up, the plains of Albany had become a solitude.

The "cattle upon a thousand hills" had disappeared. The inhabitants first concentrated at Bathurst, moved in a body to Graham's Town as the only place of safety, and the smoked walls of the abandoned dwellings stood desolate. A sudden plunge from affluence into the depths of poverty was the lot of numbers of families, and some of them never rose again.

The aspect of Graham's Town, when made the central refuge, was such as it has never, in the same degree, presented since. Every tenement of every class was thronged with families of white, brown, or black, who had pressed in from every side for protection. The portions of the flocks and herds that had been saved from the Xhosa, crowded the vacant spaces in yards and gardens at nights, and covered the slopes of the hills around the town by day, exhausting very speedily the pasturage of the neighbourhood. Sad confusion and paralysing depression prevailed at first, and strange scenes, combining the pathetic and the ludicrous in about equal proportions, were presented, especially when St. George's Church, the present Cathedral, was occupied at night as the place of the greatest safety by the women and children.

At length, however, the fire-eating Sir Harry (then Colonel) Smith made his sudden appearance, having galloped overland from Cape Town in either five or six days. Breathing something of his own resolution into the desponding spirits around him, he speedily changed the face of things. He had come armed with plenary power from Sir Benjamin D'Urban, the new Governor, and instantly set about measures for arousing the people from their dejection. The change of feeling, when the attention of the people was diverted from themselves was, I heard, quite electric. Order soon sprang from confusion under the wave of Sir Harry's magic wand. Organizing right and left, with the energy of will, and the unforgotten energy of language for which he was distinguished, the adult population soon became a warlike-looking garrison. Gentlemen who had never dreamt of such honours before were placed in command of companies or battalions, and Major Wood, Captain Godlonton, Captain Wright, Captain Thompson, and Captains I know not who besides, marshalled their men and gave the word of command with newly inspired vigour ; while old Sergeants of pre-settler days — the Raffertys, Prices, Lucases, McDonalds, Featherstones — became prized acquisitions, and rose into quartermasters and adjutants at a bound.

Barricades were built across the streets, cannon planted in commanding positions; for the people remembered that in 1819, the same hordes who were now devastating the frontier, had boldly marched in thousands from the sugar-loaf hill across what are now the cricket grounds and cemeteries, to attack the infant town, while the war prophet Makanna stood invoking the promised thunder and lightning, that would not "come when they were called." A repetition of the old attempt on a more formidable scale was apprehended. In a short time, however. Sir Harry, ridiculing the idea of being "afraid of a lot of black fellows, armed with nothing but a knife stuck on the end of a long stick," had placed the town in a state of defence, which he said made it proof against the assault of seven thousand Frenchmen.

It soon became needful to clear the town of the refugee flocks and herds that were endangering the health of the crowded population. The open country at the head of the Meule river was selected as the safest place for them, and a cattle guard was formed of the men least qualified for active operations.

This was not deemed the most honourable branch of the service, for Colonel Smith was planning a grand combined attack on the fastness of the Fish River, and the Settlers, whose blood was now thoroughly up, were eager to turn the tables upon their enemies.

The attack proved a great success, and it was noted that some of the quiet Methodists, who because they did not curse and swear had been thought to have but little courage in them, could, when the war was *pro aris et focis*[46], (as Sir Benjamin said) bear themselves in action quite as coolly, and yet fight "for hearths and altars" quite as warmly, as their more blustering comrades.

I was not in the Colony, but in Xhosaland, when the war of '35 broke out. All our first tidings were from Xhosas. The plundering of the traders' stations was, to us, the first intimation of what was going forwards. The arrival at the Mount Coke Mission of such of the traders themselves as could affect their escape confirmed our worst fears. Some of them had barely saved their lives, and scarcely knew how

---

46. "For altars and hearths"

they had done it. One of them (as he told me himself) had, while the Xhosa were discussing the subject of putting him to death, given some of them lessons in shooting, that they might kill him with as little pain as possible.

The climax of triumph seemed to have been reached when the news was spread far and near that Fort Wiltshire (the impregnable, as the Xhosa had deemed it) was abandoned by the English garrison, and had fallen into the possession of Tyali and Macoma. And then return parties of warriors, laden with the spoils of the Settlers' dwellings, passed through the station, taunting us with our helpless condition, and telling us they could afford to let us alone for a while, as they intended to finish us at leisure. The suspense, arising from the cutting off of all intelligence from the colony, was horrible. The burning homesteads of Lower Albany lighted up the horizon night after night, and imagination was left to paint its most fearful pictures. Where the end was to be we knew not. Days seemed to grow into weeks; and week after week elapsed without any sign of aggressive movement from the Colony; till old Zetu, the chief who was protecting us, impatiently exclaimed, "*Akuseko 'm lungu ! inkomande ingavelinje, bapelile bonke!*"[47]

The first gleam of relief appeared in an extraordinary commotion that surprised us one morning. Herds of cattle suddenly made their appearance, driven in eager haste past the station, and towards the Kei, followed by troops of women and children, carrying loads of pots, mats, and baskets, and keeping company with the old pack-oxen that brought up the rear, laden with heavy milk sacks. A party of us at once mounted on horseback, and proceeded towards Wesleyville to find out the cause of the movement.

We saw that a sudden panic had seized the tribes which occupied the country between us and the Fish River. The whole upper basin of the Chalumna seemed alive with cattle, streaming down every bush-path from the ridges beyond, and all urged on in one direction — Eastward ho!

A night attack (as we learned afterwards), planned and carried out successfully under the command of the rosy-faced veteran, Major Cox, had surprised and destroyed the "Great Place" of the notorious old chief Eno, who himself narrowly and ignobly escaped disguised in the karos of one of his wives. The frontier Xhosa, who were securely revelling in the plunder of the colony, were confounded by the unlooked-for exploit. My escort, armed, and looking like a cavalry patrol, might have captured the flying cattle by hundreds; for the few men in charge of them, mistaking us for a part of the invading force, abandoned them, and took shelter in

---

47. "There are no white men left! No commando makes its appearance, — they must be all finished up!"

the bush as we crossed the path of their flight. If that attack had been at once followed up, it would have confirmed on the side of peace the coast tribes who were then wavering, and it would have shortened the war.

I have no intention, on this occasion, of bringing down my "Settler's Reminiscences" any farther than to this point.

Those who were old enough to shoulder their rifles in the wars of '46 and '51, have their own remembrances, and do not need mine. Such as were not, can ask their fathers and mothers to tell them of the struggles of those times, as their fathers told them of the struggles of the times before them.

But I have a word or two to say, before concluding, on the wondrous self-recovering elasticity displayed again and again by this Eastern Province of ours. The tide of war was rolled back, the homesteads were re-occupied, the houses rebuilt, and the fields cultivated anew. The old Anglo-Saxon energy had been stirred after a new style, and was not going to sleep again.

The men had found that though, like the Guards at Waterloo, it was the first time they had "seen service," there was stuff in them of the right sort; and the women had developed powers of endurance and fortitude unknown to themselves. They conquered prosperity a second time; and in a very few years most of the traces of war had disappeared. Struck by the energy they displayed, a keen observer said of them, "Why the Albany Settlers can afford to be ruined every ten years."

A more desperate conflict awaited them in '46, when both parties were stronger, and neither was taken by surprise. The inhabitants of the frontier districts, instead of abandoning them again to the enemy, formed themselves into camps, and defended their positions, often against fearful odds, in many an open day fight. Not a few of the settlers' sons made in those camps their first essay in arms, shoulder to shoulder with their fathers.

Had ten years, instead of three, intervened between that and the war of '51, it would have been seen that the self-recovering power of the Settlement had raised it from its second struggle to a firmer position than before. But the people had scarcely recovered breath when, for the third time, war without, aggravated now by rebellion within, tasked their energies to the utmost. It was hard to be hit again before they were fairly on their feet; but they stood the blow, and hit harder than ever back again.

The storming of Port Armstrong, the defeat of Hermanus, the battle of the Imvane, and, better than any of them, the hero-stand at Whittlesea, isolated, beleaguered, and assaulted week after week, till they had reached their last charge of powder, and were preparing to stake the last issue on the strength of their home-made battle-axes, when the welcome apparition of the "Cradock Bricks," suddenly dashing in to their aid, replenished their powder flasks, and turned despondency into triumph.

These were the tests which determined into what kind of men the little boys of '35 had grown. I do not forget that in these successive war struggles the Colonists had the aid of British troops; or that, without their aid, the issue might have been — probably would in those days have been — different from what it was. But it is only just to remember, that in many of the fiercest local conflicts there was not a single soldier present. And now that the troops are taking leave of us with the tune of "Paddle your own Canoe," it is not out of place to remind my young auditors that what their fathers did before them may be done again by themselves, if they are not degenerate scions of the old stock.

What have been the results of the '51 war ? One result has been, that eighteen years have elapsed, and the Xhosa have not ventured to make war again, although the previous eighteen years saw three of them. Another result has been, that the seeds of a civilizing community have been sown broadcast over British Kaffraria. And a third result is, the formation of the Queenstown Division (formed, I have heard, by Holden Bowker), and its settlement by men of youthful fire or middle age energy.

The feeble and the old are the very rare exceptions — the few venerable fathers and mothers whom the stalwart sons have brought with them to cherish in their old age. The staple of the community consists of men with strength for the present day, and the prospect of life for coming years in which to develop the resources of the inheritance they have won. They occupy the post of honour. They are the advanced guard of the Colony. God make them worthy of their position!

These results scarcely look like retrogression. And yet there are some who take gloomy views, and utter dark prophecies. They bid us think of our commercial depression, — as if there were no such thing as commercial depression at times even in wealthy England; — and forgetting how often in the history of a country the failure of superficial resources has led to the development of others, whose springs lie deeper indeed, and therefore require digging for, but which rise from permanent and exhaust-less reservoirs. They point to misgovernment as an incubus on our progress; — not remembering that with Englishmen misgovernment is an evil that has always wrought its own cure, and resulted in the establishment of rights fully proportioned to the wrongs they have overturned, though the process by which they have been established may not always have been a rapid one.

They tell us again of drought, and locusts; of rust in the corn, and murrain among the cattle. But locust clouds darkened the skies of Albany before the war of '36, and yet the people prospered. And corn has been "rusted" ever since '21, but there are districts nevertheless, without going into the West, that might be made to supply a whole province with wheaten bread. The elevated regions of the North-East know little or nothing of rust. Tell me not of droughts. They are the rod which the God of Providence sends to punish our reckless destruction of the wood we cut down without replacement, and our wilful waste of water; — and to teach us to take care of the water when it comes, — for come it does, (this season for instance) in quantities which might silver the surface of our landscapes with a thousand lakes, fringe their borders with groves of evergreen, and modify the climate of the whole land.

The first grand thunderstorm of the Queenstown district last season would have given us half-a-dozen square miles of water, if we had had a reservoir large enough to have received it.

There are individual farmers in the inner districts, who have made dams which render droughts a matter of comparative indifference to their crops, and have given them artificial lakes large enough for African college boat races. Why should not reservoirs such as those of Kidger Tucker, Carey Hobson, the Parkes', and others in the Albert and Colesberg districts, be multiplied a hundredfold, instead of allowing the water to run idly to the sea, sweeping with it the richest of our soils ? Or why (to come nearer home[48]) should we not see from the summit of Mount Tylden fifty sheets of water sparkling in the sun, fertilizing the fields below them, fostering the growth of wild fowl, and providing future sport for our duck shooters, like that which our energetic fellow-townsman, Mr. Ella, has spread before our eyes at Ashby Manor ? I know but of one reason why, and that is the want of fifty Ellas to resolve that the work shall be done.

"But there are Xhosa depredations." So there are, though fewer than of old; but have those who tell us so forgotten "The Blue Bonnets over the border" of the Old Country? Has Cumberland no tales to tell of Donald Beans, and Moss troopers, and black mail? Are the frontiers of our Indian empire free from depredators? Is the Indian border of the United States never disturbed by the Indigenous Tribes? And yet British India flourishes, and the Great Republic grows greater and grander every year.

---

48. The rest of the paragraph was a local application to Queenstown, at which place also the lecture was delivered.

Give all the weight you will to the obstacles, the trials, the disadvantages of our position. It will only place in bolder relief the progress that has been made despite those obstacles, and the energy and perseverance that have achieved it. We look back to 1820. Where then were the towns of Port Elizabeth, Colesberg, Somerset, Burghersdorp, Port Beaufort, Aliwal, Hopetown, Murraysburg, Richmond, Middleburg, Bedford, Alice, Adelaide, Queenstown, King William's Town, Bathurst, Port Alfred, East London? Must I go on to ask the same question in reference to Humansdorp, Alexandria, Pearston, Aberdeen, Hanover, Whittlesea, Dordrecht, Peddie, Seymour, Tarkastadt? There were none of them in existence. Even Graham's Town was not born — it was only in embryo. Some of us remember the transparency of it which we had at the half jubilee, some eighteen small thatched cottages!

I say nothing about the increase of towns and Tillages in the Western Province; though British immigration has had much to do with that. And I say nothing of the towns that are rising beyond the Orange river, though their commercial life owes itself to the presence of British energy, and the residence of not a few of the sons and daughters of the old settlers. Does any one ask for the rate of increase in these sons and daughters?

Take a couple of specimens. It is not very long since old Joseph Trollip died. There live among us today of his lineal descendants two hundred and seventy. The Cawoods came, a family of nine. The present number of the united generations living is three hundred and fifty-six. I wish I had the number belonging to the Hartley, Usher, Hart, and Bowker families.

They would supply figures quite as expressive, although the father of the Bowkers did not marry till he was forty, and said in after life that he had even then committed a juvenile indiscretion in doing so; for his sons increased till he had to name them by Roman numerals.

Does anyone ask again what sort of social positions are occupied by the old settlers' sons? They occupy magistracies and mayoralties; they fill seats in our Legislative Council and House of Assembly. There are settlers' sons members of the Government at Natal. A settler's son fills the second position in the government of the Cape. A settler's son ranks with the generals of the British army. The son of a British settler, knighted for his gallant deeds by our gracious Queen (God bless her!) has for years headed a force which might well bear the motto "Ubique" on its banners, for its detachments are seen everywhere; and if Sir Walter Currie's career has prematurely ended, it has been in his adopted country's service that he has wrecked his strength. Honour, all honour to the Brave! May they never lack successors worthy of themselves!

But to return to the question of difficulties and discouragements. The fact is, that, in our impatience of personal evils, we are apt to forget the inevitable conditions of a residence on the frontiers of barbarism, ignoring all past history; and in our estimate of progress, we are too prone to limit our view to the times we live in ourselves; forgetting that in all national prosperity, the safety, wealth and happiness of one generation, have been the fruit of the labours and struggles of the generations before it.

There was a little city in ancient Italy. It possessed a few square miles of territory — a territory, by the way, compared with which the Cradock, Colesberg, or Queenstown Division would be a kingdom. Its inhabitants, however, embodied the spirit of progress. But they were hemmed in by enemies on every side. Year after year, decade after decade, they battled for existence — now winning a few miles more — then driven back to their city gates. At length in the vicissitudes of the strife, the city itself was taken and ravaged — the citadel alone remaining uncaptured. Yes, and even that was saved by the cackling of a few geese! And yet that band of indomitable spirits held their own, beat back their foes, wrested city after city from them, won their way from strength to strength through the struggles of five hundred years, till Europe, Asia, and Africa crouched at their feet, and Rome, Imperial Rome, gave laws to the world!

But there is another lesson of later date. There was a time when Anglo-Saxon England was struggling for life with foreign foes; when the black ships of the Northmen brought their warrior swarms, that carried the Raven banner in desolating triumph over the land. And there was one Man who resolved that England should not be conquered. He wrestled with adverse fortune again and again, till, driven a solitary refugee to the shelter of his own Wildwoods, the cause of his country seemed lost for ever. And what became of him? Every schoolboy knows ; and every schoolboy can tell that the lad who let the woodsman's cake bum, and got his ears boxed for it; and the harper that wandered through the Danish camp, noting all its weak points; and the young King who rallied the scattered strength of England, and crushed the Danish power at Ethandune, were one, and that one the Royal Alfred, whose courage, wisdom, and piety combined, laid the foundations of England's constitutional liberty, and of England's naval greatness.

Are the lessons of the past to be lost upon us? Are the trials of a single generation to darken all the future to our view? A generation is but a step in the history of a people. And the history of advance. Every storm has left the English oak that has been transplanted to this Southern clime more deeply rooted.

As necessity forces our sluggish attention to fresh resources, they open up to our view. Mohair, Cotton, Silk, Coffee, Sugar, Coal, Iron, Copper, Ostrich farming, are offering themselves in succession for our acceptance, and asking only enterprise and perseverance. Look at our Jubilee Exhibition! Planned and carried out by men whose words are actions, — whose "silence" is eloquent. See what the Colony can do — is doing! If, with such a display before our eyes of Colonial products, incipient Colonial manufactures, and Colonial artistic taste and skill, my young fellow colonists do not go home with hopes brightened, energies new strung, and a fixed purpose to make the Jubilee a fresh starting point in an onward career, I shall only have to say that I have mistaken the character of the sons of the British Settlers.

The spirit of observation is at last shewing signs of waking up, and is finding treasures in the vegetable and the mineral worlds before unthought of "New fibres" are challenging attention one after another; and now the diamonds that have so long been reproaching the eyes which have been blind to their brilliancy, and the feet that have trodden heedlessly over them for so many years, are beginning a social revolution which will reach to the heart of the African continent. Nor do we know what is yet behind. When the work of research begins in thorough earnest, it opens many a hidden spring. I have long believed that the old "back-bone" of South Africa — the Stormberg and Quablamba range — contains a spinal marrow which will yet send a new nerve-force bounding through our social and commercial life system.

An old party war-cry in the world of politics was, "Agitate! Agitate! Agitate!" A better watch word for us would be, "Organize! Organize! Organize!" Organize for self-defence, and preserve peace by a readiness for war. Organize in the field of industry, and bring combined power to develop the resources of the country. Organize to increase our commercial facilities, and open safe harbours. Organize for the settlement of the wide fertile regions that would sustain in comfort the starving thousands of the Fatherland, and increase the wealth and strength of the colony at the same time. We have plenty of room for them. Our territory increases whether we will or no. Every war has added to it. The exceptions have been but the short waves of the flowing tide. Long ones rolled in when Queenstown and British Kaffraria were settled. And the destiny of Japhet is still "Enlargement." The Eastern slopes of the Quablamba will not always be a mere hunting ground.

Waving corn-fields will yet be seen among the uplands where the Eland roams, and the head waters of the Umzimvubu will yet turn mills to grind their harvests. A "New England" is rising on the Eastern borders of the Aliwal district. An

"Alfredia" is hailing it from the colony of Natal. A belt of civilization is fast encircling the tribes of Kaffraria. They may benefit by it, and rise in the social scale; or they may resist its influences and take the consequence. The might of civilization must absorb or annihilate all that comes into hostile contact with it. A solemn responsibility rests upon civilized nations as to how the process of annexation or absorption is carried forwards; but the destiny itself is providential and inevitable. Away then with the feebleness of despondency! And away with the short-sighted selfishness that narrows the horizon and fixes the eye on the present only. What was the song of our fathers ?

> Never Despair ! tho' the Harvests fail;
> Tho' the hosts of a savage foe assail.
> Never despair ! We shall conquer yet!
> And the toils of our earlier years forget.
> In hope's bright glory our sun shall set,
>   'Midst Afric's Southern Wilds.

Such, was our Father's song, and what is Ours ? —

> Our toilworn fathers have sunk to their rest.
> But their sons shall inherit their hope's bequest.
> Valleys are smiling in harvest pride;
> There are fleecy flocks on the mountain side;
> Cities are rising to stud the plains;
> The life-blood of commerce is coursing the veins
> Of a new-born Empire that grows and reigns
>   O'er Afric's Southern Wilds.

A Long and Tedious Voyage

by John Mandy[49]

He was the head of a small party who came with others by the Nautilus. He came from Foot's Cray, Kent, was a married man with two sons, John Wilkinson and Stephen Day, aged respectively six and five years. On the voyage another son was born to him named William. The location assigned to him was at the mouth of the Fish River, near Shaw Park, next to that of Mr. Rowles. In the war of 1835 he took refuge in Graham's Town, where he resided till his death on May 25, 1848, aged sixty-one years. The following letters are addressed to John Mandy's mother at Foot's Cray, Kent.

I take the opportunity of writing to you, as we expect in two days to put into St. Jago. I have the pleasure to inform you that we are all well and in good spirits. My letter of 5th December I suppose informed you of our disaster in the Downs; but as I hardly know what I wrote, I will give you more particulars.

Figure 8: Rolling to Windward - Thomas Baines

We left Gravesend on Thursday morning, had a fine wind to the Queen's Channel, where we arrived on the following day in the morning, and dropped anchor. It came on to blow tremendously hard, the sea running mountains high. We could not weigh anchor till Sunday afternoon, when our troubles began, the sea breaking over us in all directions, —tables, chairs, boxes, plates and dishes, men, women and children, all mixed together, tumbling over one another, and all dreadfully sea-sick, except myself and Smith, who was on deck working the ship; I below, basin-holder. In the midst of this the sea broke into our cabin windows, dashed glass and frame in, the things that were below rolling and sliding took to swimming. About three o'clock we had an alarm of fire. I ran into the captain's cabin; found the fire-place upset, which we soon put out.

At half-past eight our pilot informed us we were out of danger. When the ship

---

49. Cambell, Colin Turning (1897). British South Africa. John Haddon & Co. Pages 184-187.

struck on the sands, all was confusion and dismay; even the sailors seemed panic-struck. Every one only thought of self-safety. We lay in this situation one hour and a half, when a heavy sea set us afloat without much damage. During the time we had a light at the mast-head, and fired guns for assistance. We were much overjoyed at seeing five or six boats come to assist us, not without enduring a heavy sea.

One boat's crew came on board, and told us the whole town of Ramsgate was in confusion. We made a subscription of £5 or £6 for them. We passed the Lizard with a fine breeze in two days after, when we had a gale of wind which tossed us much about, but had plenty of sea-room. We have had plenty of amusement at fishing; saw several whales, one of which came alongside with its back ten or twelve feet out of the water. I shot at it three times with ball. It made a great noise and ran away at the rate of a mile in two minutes when wounded.

We had variable winds till we saw Madeira, which we passed on the 29th December. We saw the Peak of Teneriffe, had a good view of it, covered with snow, yet the weather was so hot we were obliged to throw off most of our clothes. On the 5th we had a storm, which lasted three days, the sea running as high as our mast-head, and two of the waves broke over us; the forepart of the ship had three tons of water in, which swamped almost every person in their beds. Joseph was washed out of his cot. The carpenters cuttled the decks, and pumped the water out. On the 8th we saw Palma, about ten at night, and a sail under land, but could not tell what she was till morning, when, to our great joy, we discovered it to be the Chapman—the first time we had seen her since we left the Queen's Channel.

At four in the after-noon we spoke her, all well, only lost four children, had nine births. We are now sailing in company, and shall continue to do so till we get to the Cape. We have now just arrived in sight of land—Salt Island, one of the Cape de Verde islands.

On the 13th we cast anchor in St. Jago, where we remained four days. Got plenty of refreshment: for an old coat, I bought 200 oranges, a fine goat and kid, and twelve coconuts. Mary Anne and the children were never in better health and spirits. We left St. Jago and had calms and contrary winds for a week. Got to the line on 1st February, where we saw a ship from England bound to the Brazils, that kindly offered to bring letters to England. We had a merry day in shaving old Neptune, who came on-board overnight. I have not time to describe the ceremony, which is not most polite.

Please to let Mr. Gower's family know that himself and family are well. Be so good as to let Mr. Whalley's know you have heard from us. We have had fresh beef ever since we left St. Jago. We brought six bullocks on board, which are just gone. I bought a fine sheep for a dollar, and a turkey of 14 lbs. for an old pair of shoes, and which we have killed this day. My goat gives milk for tea night and morning. I conclude in haste, as the boat is going to leave the ship. I hope, mother, to see you and the rest of our family with us in a short time.

From your affectionate son,
John Mandy.

Cape of Good Hope, April 13, 1820 :—

Dear Mother, — I have the pleasure to inform you I have arrived safe at Table Bay, after a long and tedious voyage. After leaving St. Jago on the 14th March, we had variable winds and calms till the 12th April, when we had a heavy gale of wind, which lasted till twelve o'clock at night, when the weather became moderate, and the clouds cleared off, and we saw, to our great joy, the Land of promise.

Mary Ann, Joseph and myself have been in the best health and spirits. I have the pleasure to inform you that on the 1st March, Mary Ann was put to bed with a fine boy in latitude 18°, longitude 6°. She never had a better getting up in England, and was able to go on deck in a fortnight. When within two miles of Table Bay, it came on a calm, which lasted three hours, when we had, without a moment's notice, one of the Cape gales we hear so much talk of in England, which carried away every sail we had standing.

The ship became her own master for a lime, which prevented our getting in that day. The next day we saw the Chapman, the first time for three weeks, standing in for the Bay, when we weighed anchor, and both got in together.

We were immediately put under quarantine for twenty-four hours, and then only the heads of parties allowed to land, which caused great dissatisfaction among the rest of the settlers. I have been on shore five days, and find it a very pretty place, about as large as Greenwich.

The country round about may well be called the garden of the world ; the graperies in the greatest perfection, and very cheap. The hedges in many parts are myrtles and geraniums, the aloe in high perfection in full bloom—many thirty feet high. I went into an orange grove; the grandest sight I ever saw. The farmers of the country came to town on hearing of our arrival, to try to get our people to come and live with them. One farmer offered to give Joseph £40 per annum, house, clothes and victuals, or a farming man £20 and sheep. We found mutton and beef cheap, — 2d. per lb.; fruit in great abundance.

We set sail on Sunday night for Algoa Bay, and have had a long and tedious voyage for nearly three weeks. We have this moment got the Bay in sight, which I hope to be to-morrow morning. We have to travel 130 miles by land. We are provided with wagons and camp equipage ; the heads of parties a marquee, and a tent to every three families.

Algoa Bay, 26th April 1820.—I finish my letter in haste. We expect to-set off for the country to-day. I have lain in camp eleven days. I landed on Sunday night, to get ready for Mary Ann and the children. When I had got all ready for them, a strong south-east wind set in, and stopped their landing for five days, the surf beating round the shore to the height of ten or twelve feet. They saw me, and could not get at me. Mary Ann and the children came on shore the 19th, very much frightened, the boat three parts full of water. We are now living on the fat of the land, —a fowl for 9*d*., beef 1 1/2d. Per lb., milk and eggs in great abundance. Joseph is well and in high spirits. Please to send to Gower's and inform them that you have heard from me.

They are all well.

From your affectionate and dutiful son,

John Mandy.

The following letter will be read with interest as showing how energetically the settlers proceeded in occupying their grants of land, and also giving a vivid description of the country in which they were placed. It is written by General Campbell's precursor, who was nearly sixty years of age, and who had only arrived in Albany a short time before (August 1820). It is dated, —

General Campbell's Location,
Albany, 28th January 1821.

"I like this part of the country very much. It is very pleasant, and capital land; all things seem to thrive well. It is like a gentleman's garden, decorated with clumps of all sorts of flowering shrubs, as if they had been regularly planted, and all parts covered with the finest grass as high as your middle. I never saw in England so much good land together. I have nearly an acre of turnips, which is doing well. My vines are nearly all dead; I shall want five or six thousand next season, as I intend to plant a large vineyard, and some fig orange and lemon trees.

I have plenty of melons, cucumbers and pumpkins, which are coming forward very fast. I have three huts complete, and a well that I sank at the top of the garden, which has plenty of excellent water. I have felled sufficient timber to build General

Campbell's house, and the men are digging stones for the walls. I have made a large kraal for cattle; all that have seen it say there is not its equal in the Colony.

I am sorry our parties have not come. I think they would have been well satisfied. There is nothing wanted but a good stock of cattle and industry. I wish I had four or five hundred head of cattle, a few quarters of corn, and sufficient rations for one year. I would be better off than with £5,000 sterling in England. I have set fire to more than 500 acres of grass to burn it off the land for the young to spring up. I see nothing of the wild tribe but monkeys and a few spring-bucks. Near our location we have a wood, I suppose two miles in length, where I fell the timber. I have been in all parts of the wood, but have not seen any snakes.

About four miles off, in a wood which I pass through on my way to Bathurst, are elephants, buffaloes, and many other different sorts of animals. I have not as yet met with any curiosities, having been very busy. I believe I have made more progress than most of the settlers. When any more settlers come out for me, I intend to form a town at the 'Reed Fountain River', as that is a suitable place, and the General will be a good distance from other inhabitants, as it was his desire, and will have a very pleasant place close to a wood, where I can with little trouble cut avenues for him and his family to walk in the shade all day, and will have the river running nearly all round his house.

My men have turned out as bad as I expected; they do not earn 8*d* each per day; they are too lazy to work. They go to the magistrate at Bathurst, eleven miles distant from home, who gives them encouragement, which causes me to go out of my employ almost every week as well as they. They have already lost fifty-one days at that fun. They are in hopes of getting off next week, as they have been offered two six-dollars[50] per day. They are getting on very fast with the magistrate's house at Bathurst. I shall be obliged to you to ask Captain Chissel for what strawberry roots he can spare, and send them by first conveyance.

If Mr. Bouri is not yet gone, he will have the goodness to bring them for me; and if he would likewise be so good as to bring a bushel or two of seed potatoes, for which I will pay him. Please tell Rock to send me five or six thousand vine cuttings, with a dozen of figs in sorts, and two dozen of orange and lemon trees.

Cypress Messer.

---

50. Probably Rix-dollars

The Cobblers Tale — A Disembarking Yarn

Gregory George Smith

Artisans of any variety including shoemakers like Christopher Webb[51] were highly sort after all around the globe in the 1800s. I long pondered their courage and sense of adventure in choosing an unknown shore of the Eastern Cape of South Africa. I depend upon the oral tradition of folk tale telling circulated among such 1820 yarn-smiths in a 'cobbled' tale of the excitement & adventure of the day of arrival in Algoa Bay in 1820. This is the story of the Webb's as told within my line of Webbs and Smiths. My paternal grandmother was Hazel Mary Smith, née Webb[52] and this 'yarn' was told to me as a young boy by a number of family members connected to the Smith clan including my great grandmother Mary Lovedale Webb, nee Dell [nicknamed Girlie] who lived to the ripe old age of 95 years old. At 80 years of age my grandfather, Geordie—George Smith fulfilled his promise to take her in as ageing family member were and I recall him joking about the length of that commitment saying—"Always be careful of what you promise!" She was a treasure, and I am always reminding myself of how lucky I was to spend time with her in the 1970s when my grandparents moved out the Transkei, from their Cofimvaba trading store, to Berlin. A little hamlet between East London and King William's Town in the Eastern Cape. This is the folk tale great-granny Girlie fondly spun to me as pint-sized 'pickaninny' on a veranda in Berlin.

Christopher Webb was 36 years old and a cobbler married to Mary Evans (26) in 1815 in St Mary's Church, London. They'd been blessed with a son in 1817 and when they embarked on their journey to Africa, Mary was already 6 months pregnant again. They joined the Sephton Party specifically on-board with Richard Gush group on the Brilliant.[53] I've little in-depth detail of them prior to this epic adventure except Christopher Webb was a shoemaker and judging by his age he was demobilized back to his native Berkshire at the end of his service in the Napoleonic War [18 May 1803 – 20 November 1815]. This, however, is unverified and as such fits the folk tale nature of the yarn itself. I imagine, as I have read, post-War times were tough in England—finding people of equal religious

---

51. Family Tree Christopher Webb https://www.1820settlers.com/genealogy/familychart.php?personID=I91251&tree=master&

52. Mary Hazel Webb showing Mary Loveday Webb—nee Mary Loveday Dell https://www.1820settlers.com/genealogy/familychart.php?personID=I64709&tree=master&

53. Sephton Party https://www.1820settlers.com/genealogy/settlershowparty.php?party=Sephton

persuasion for a mission to an unknown shore must have resonated with both Christopher and his young brave wife—Mary Webb. The true hero of this tale.

So, like this, it came to pass that Christopher and Mary Webb came to hold the distinction of having one of only four recorded births at sea en route to the Eastern Cape in 1820.[54] Joseph Webb making his rude appearance mid-voyage apparently as the Brilliant approach the Cape of Good Hope.

Mary Webb, it is told, and I am sure, was bravely putting on a stiff upper lip as they approached Algoa Bay. Great Granny Girlie was clear in reminding me of what stern stuff we're made of. Imagine she said: A three-year-old son in tow plus nurturing her newborn second boy — born just 2 weeks ago, that approaching prospect tugged at her natural survival instincts, she was a mixed bag of emotion in terms of disembarkation day and surely contributed to her mix up of the day. Christopher Webb, Great Granny Girlie romantically assured me, was always near, a man of devote religious conviction but ever doting on his Mary. High esteem clearly oozing from my stoic great grandmother and evident from the number of repeats of Mary found in the family tree.

Anyhow, luckily the voyage passed without much further cause to panic after the smooth but awkward childbirth at sea near Table Bay. The Brilliant had left Gravesend on the 15th of February and now on the 15th of May they skirted the final corner approach of Cape Recife point to see the wide calm arms open of the beautiful Algoa Bay. Long yellow beaches with dunes stretching as far as you could see. On a calm day an impressive sight with the dotting islets of St Croix and Bird Rock.

That night the thirty-five families aboard the Brilliant sang hymns and bolstered their spirits for docking with a ferry boat to bring them to shore. The final step to their ship bound adventure, disembarkation. All aboard were a little restless and eager to get off the ship that had imprisoned them for the last three months voyage. It had taken them through calm & rough weather but luckily that night was calm.

As the sun rose on the day of disembarking. The wind picked up, as it so often does in the now famous Windy City — the nickname so often connected to the soon to emerge Port Elizabeth. The pond-like tranquillity of Algoa Bay changing to a choppy see-saw ride of cresting white horses. Not far from the Brilliant's

---

54. Birth's en route—Joseph Webb
https://www.1820settlers.com/genealogy/getperson.php?personID=I41711&tree=master
"Brilliant left Gravesend 15.2.1820 carrying Erith's and Pringle's parties and Gush's division of Sephton's party. ...four children were born at sea: Joseph Webb, James Temlett, WB Jenkinson and Frances Maria Searle"

anchorage in the bay, Bird Rock was teaming with wildlife. Seals and birds buzzed around visibly interested in the novelty of the visitors. Undersea, as anyone who has fished or dived off St Croix Island can attest, the ragged-toothed sharks swirled, always on the lookout for a seal that wasn't keeping a cautious eye. The circle of life. Hunter & prey.

Figure 9: Going ashore in Table Bay - Thomas Baines

The Aurora and Brilliant lay 300 meters abreast of each other in Algoa Bay on the adventure filled 15th of May 1820.[55] The ferry boats made there way out to meet them and the Brilliant was first to disembark — a mere 500 meters to the yellow sands of their new home. The very first of those aboard to disembark would be Mary Webb with her baby.

A basket contraption was used to swing the passengers over to the rowing boats to ferry them ashore. Mary and Christopher embraced and carefully entered together with two infants.

The ship rode the waves and the job of keeping the basket steady was complicated by infrequent white horses crashing into the ferry vessels and swells bobbing & jostling. The conditions, at best, Granny Girlie said with her typical unperturbed tone, could be best summed up as "a little rough."

Undaunted and without much option, Christopher Webb transitioned from the basket to the little rowing boat and accepted the handing over of three year old Christopher (jnr.) without issue or incident. That's where things rapidly turned for the worst.

As an anxious Mary aimed to pass the two-week infant over to her reassuring

---

55. The Aurora https://en.wikipedia.org/wiki/Aurora_(1808_ship)

husband, a rising swell clashed the basket into the row boat. Mary narrowly averting mashing her leg between the two colliding boats grazed her thigh falling short of the row boat and into the sea (with child).

With swirling blood in the water and chaos reached fever pitch as four men including Christopher instantly dived in to the rescue. One grabbed the baby, two dragged Mary away from any clashing danger between the vessels and Christopher drawing his "cobblers knife" on a group of ragged-tooth sharks that had flocked, in a wink into the scene.

The screaming from aboard the Brilliant had reached such a pitch that the passengers aboard the Aurora we alarmed and sent their rowing boats out to the escalating calamity.

The tiny infant being a top priority was plucked safely to the arms of a rescuer on-board the rowing boat while Christopher turned to the protection of and rescue of mother Mary. Unfortunately a swell had driven her 50-meter clear with two men keeping her afloat in her soaked heavy outfit. The struggle was immense. (Granny Girlie grew tense.)

The ragged tooth sharks darting in between them. Christopher, our hero, slashed his trusty shoemakers blade over a nasty raggy heading into the group and joined Mary. The second raggy was poked in the eye just before they were raised by a tumbling breaker and pushed onto shore. Exhausted and soaked, a little battered and bruised — they made the beach.

That's the folk tale of how Christopher & Mary Webb first set foot in Africa.

* Christopher Webb and Mary Webb went on to Salem. They had nine children which became the bedrock of future generations of the evolving Eastern Cape, including mine—Gregory George Smith

Very much vexed that no one could go on shore

by Sophia Pigot[56]

Sophia Pigot was born at Foxearth in Staffordshire on 9 May 1804. She was from a reasonable well off family and came to South Africa as a young lady with her father[57]. Her journal sketches a very different life from the average settlers but is unique in that it is one of the few accounts from a woman that have been published. Sophia later married Donald Moodie in 1824 with which she had 14 children. Sophia died in Pietermaritzburg in October 1881.

March 1820

Wednesday 1st March. A very rainy squally day. Making patterns in the morning. Sea very rough. Ship rolled much. In a very droll humour. Captain Charlton stiff neck; wanted him to have it ironed. Mama[58] rather poorly. Disturbances with Mr. Clark.

Thursday 2nd. Fine day. On deck a little. In our Cabin a short time. Playing the Bagpipes, with Mr. Dalgairns at night. Putting our Clothes in bundles to be put in the hole.

Friday 3rd. Very nice day. In my Cabin all day working handkerchiefs, curtain — the Ship rolled and pitched very much, on deck at night. Great disturbances with the Irish people, sharpening both sides of their knives. Rather frightened. Rose at 5 o'clock to see the sun rise — too late — walking on deck with Miss Dalgairns. They were threatening to put a sentinel at Mr. Mahoney's Cabin door.

Saturday 4th. Very fine windy days— the Ship rolled very much indeed. Writing my 'Journal'. In my cabin almost all morning —in a very odd humour.

Figure 10: Dick at the Wheel - Thomas Baines

---

56. Rainer, M. (Ed) (1974). The Journals of Sophia Pigot (1819-1821). A.A. Balkema, Cape Town
57. George Pigot died 1830 in South Africa.
58. Elizabeth Tomkinson married George Pigot in 1819 shortly before leaving for South Africa. They had no children.

Sunday 5th. Fine day. The Ship rolled too much to have prayers on Deck. Read them in our own Cabin. Sat in almost all forenoon, Did not… Miss Dalgairns dined with us in the Cuddy — Sat on deck with us all evening, Miss O'Connor offended.

Monday 6th. Fine day — holding consultations about Mr. Mahoney. In my Cabin all morning working muslin work. Did not… Mr. Brown and a number of people ill after drinking at Mr. Mahoney's Cabin the other night — Eliza Dalgairns slept in our Cabin with us. Not well at night — they were getting in at our window.

Tuesday 7th. Fine day — In my own Cabin all day; began a bit of muslin work after dinner. Mr. Smith and a number of the people forward were making matlocks etc. whatever they thought they should want — did not. Mr. Mahoney was sent off the weather side of the Quarter Deck. On deck at night — very dewy — Magdalene slept with us; looking at her pictures and naming them.

Wednesday 8th. Very rainy day, could not go upon deck — finished my bit of muslin work — Eliza slept with us. Going 9½ Knots an hour in the morning — fair wind — The two little Dalgairns with us all day—Making patterns in the Cuddy in the morning, I made Mamma's. Kate[59] and Eliza Dalgairns were sitting on the pump by the main Mast. I was walking about. A certain person very troublesome — The Doctor walking on our side — salmon fell down the Hatchway. Tacked. Saw an Albatross.

Thursday 9th. Fine day. In my Cabin all day till just before [word omitted]. Magdalene working with me. I began Mamma's muslin work. They all sat with me after dinner. Walking on Deck at night — Mr. Baikie poorly. The Doctor very silent all day —Kate and I making a noise in bed. Eliza slept with us. Mama making a Pelisse, very pretty. Wished to be at Cape Town.

Friday 10th. Very fine day, did not go in to Breakfast. In my Cabin all day, working, writing etc. Went on Deck at night. Very bad headache. Papa would not let me sit on Deck. Came in, could not work, went out again with Kate, cried — Magdalene could not sleep with us. Latitude 34 degrees 9, Longitude Noon. The two little Dalgairns in our Cabin all day.

Saturday 11th. Very fine day. The wind changed very suddenly to [word omitted]. Not very well — Kate poorly in Bed till 11 a.m. On Deck walking with Papa before Breakfast, low. Very little rain. Not in my Cabin all day scarcely. Walking on deck after dinner with Captain Charlton trying to get behind Papa and Kate, laughed a great deal — fun — A disturbance on deck between Mr. Clark and Mr. Elley — fighting, the latter in fun at first — did once — Eliza D., Kate and I

---

59. Her sister Catherine Mary Pigot died 1863 in Pietermaritzburg, unmarried.

were naming the people who were generally on the Quarter Deck. Dropped my Scissors on deck last night, someone found them, gave them to me.

Sunday 12th. Very nice comfortable weather — Saw two Ships at a distance — wanted to lay to — did not. I got the 3rd Mate to measure how long the Quarter deck that I might see how long was a Mile. I walked two Miles by myself then 1 with Miss Dalgairns and Miss O'Connor — Walked an hour and a half with Miss D. afterwards, liked her more than ever I did, very nice Girl. Sitting by the Captain at tea, the (Doctor?) sitting by me talking. Eliza D. trying how far she could walk the while. Had prayers in our own Cabin. A fuss in the Cuddy the while. Poor Mr. Elley was sent into his own Cabin — very sorry for him. Went down to see Mrs Comfield.

Monday 13th. Very nice day but almost a Calm. Saw the two ships plainer, they were sending a Boat to one another. Walked almost a mile before Breakfast, finished it after. Worked at Mamma's muslin work — Captain Charlton said this day two years he was tried by a Court Martial. Expect to be at the Cape this time next week. Saw a very large Albatross and some Cape hens. Walking on deck with Miss Dalgairns all evening after tea. Mr. [name illegible] one of the Settlers, trying to shoot the Albatross — brought some riddles on deck in the evening, Miss O'Connor looking at them —laughed.

Tuesday 14th. Very fine morning. An Eclipse of the Sun at Noon very beautiful — Writing all morning in the Cuddy, poetry from my Manuscript [Book] for Miss Dalgairns. Made a little. Miss O'Connor sitting in the Cuddy at work a short time. Quite a calm. Saw the Ship astern very plain, one coming towards us very fast noon, lost sight of it in the evening. Went down to see Mrs. Comfield, gave me a pattern, showed us old-fashioned work etc. — writing in our Cabin in the evening — gave Miss D. [word omitted]. Walking with her all evening and the Doctor by us, laughing very much about first coming on Board. Eliza Dalgairns slept with us. Latitude 35 degrees 33. Longitude 7 degrees 44 West. 1248 Miles from the Cape.

Wednesday 15th. Very nice fine day — Saw the Ships much plainer, did not know whether it was the same — thought it was the Minstrell. On deck after Breakfast. They were taking Papa's cases out of the hole, and looking at them — putting some things by. The Doctor returned More's 'Essays' after having had them about a month. Asked Mr. Comfield to write my name — he did. Mr. Smith shooting at an Albatross swimming on the Water. Saw some porpoises, worked in my Cabin etc. — Obliged to have tea in the Cuddy, working and reading (in) our Cabin all evening.

Thursday 16th. Very fine day. Got up, went on Deck not half Dressed to see the

Sun rise — two minutes too late. In my Cabin reading two hours before dinner — on Deck after breakfast — the Ship rolled very much. Miss Dalgairns and I sitting in the Port-hole. On deck after dinner. Mr. Mahoney said he thought the Cape was 523 miles to the N.W. of us, by his calculation — they would tell him we were going 16 Knots when we were going 4 or 5. On deck very little after tea.

Friday 17th. Fine day. Sorting all our things for the wash at the Cape. On Deck reading 'Maternal Solicitude'. Sitting on the floor. On deck after dinner reading my Manuscript Book. Very rainy after and at tea. In our Cabin all night — dreadful motion and foul wind. Kate had the soup on her lap at dinner all the things tumbling about fun.

Saturday 18th. Fine day. Been a very dreadful night — a great deal of motion. Kate out of Bed 3 times — did not get up till 12 o'clock. Papa brought Breakfast to us in bed, went into the Cuddy at 2. Writing in my Cabin all the rest of the morning, felt rather sick. Fair wind — Kate sat by me at dinner, all the things tumbling about very oddly on deck in the evening. Made a little bet... Miss Dalgairns. Kate and I were learning poetry.

Sunday 19th. Altogether fine in the morning. Going to have prayers on deck. A Squall came and prevented us. Reading all forenoon. On deck in the afternoon, rained a little. Looked at Captain Charlton's chart, only 600 miles to go, very glad — Miss O'Connor, Miss Dalgairns, Kate and I learning poetry at night. 739 Miles from the Cape.[60]

Monday 20th. Fine and cold morning. Went on Deck after breakfast, soon came in. They began to bend the Cable, very happy indeed to see that Mr. Mahoney talking to someone and saying he did not think Captain Charlton knew where we were, or something of that sort. Went into my Cabin, writing etc. all morning there, very happy, In my Cabin and on deck in the evening. Walking with Kate — Mr. Baikie telling us very odd tales about his friends. Kate tired, walking by myself, talking to Bootes now and then. Very delightful day. Making poetry in the morning with Kate — Evil (genius?). Going sometimes 10 and 11 Knots an hour — longing to be at the Cape. A fuss with (word illegible) about the poor Cow. Scarcely anyone on Deck, no Ladies, too busy. Walking. Bootes said I should get home before the Ship. 549 Miles from the Cape.

Tuesday 21st. Very delightful day indeed, just warm enough. Looked at Captain Charlton's chart, very glad to see we had such a short way to go. In my Cabin all morning working — Mamma with me some of the time. Went to Sleep with her

---

60. The difference is likely due to her being given two different distances at different times during the day.

after dinner on their bed, Papa came, soon went. Mamma Tickling me, made a great noise, fine fun — On deck after tea a— learning 'The Daisy'. In very high spirits all day little — singing. Up very late in the morning. Talking to Mamma of old times — Learning poetry at night with Miss D. and Miss O'Connor, Walking and laughing very much — fine fun making poetry. 412 miles from the Cape.

Wednesday 22nd. A very fine day, rather warmer. Could do nothing but talk of the Cape. On deck a little after Breakfast. Came in, writing in my Cabin — making patterns etc. working— making poetry with Kate, laughing very much at it. L.P. On deck at night walking with Miss Dalgairns, did not learn much — talking — laughed till our heads ached — wild Beasts. Latitude 37 degrees 4 minutes — Longitude 12 degrees 12 minutes — 340 Miles from the Cape.

Thursday 23rd. Very fine day — did not go very fast — Writing poetry in the Cuddy all morning from a book of Miss Brown's. On deck after dinner reading — walking with Miss Dalgairns at night, playing at "how, why and where do you like it?" — laughing very much. 296 Miles from the Cape.

Friday 24th. Very fine in the morning. Rained at [word omitted] a little, came in off deck, writing in the Cuddy all morning, poetry. On deck after dinner reading — Walking at night with Miss Dalgarins on the Lee side — they sounded. I took a bet with the Doctor— won — was told something (code: Kate poetry) Mr. Elley walking with us. Latitude 36 degrees 17 Longitude 16 degrees 30 minutes Noon, 140 Miles from the Cape — fine breeze. 9 Knots. Talking very seriously with Miss Dalgairns; did not know something about the first (Code: man).

Saturday 25th. Very fine day — Mr. Elley called at ½ past 4 in the morning to say we could not see land — got up at 6, went on deck, they all saw the land but me — I could not — Saw it very plain indeed just after Breakfast — first saw it standing at the Cuddy door by the Doctor, very happy to see it — Very unhappy at something my young friend told me about Cubit. Come into my Cabin, writing. Papa looking into his Boxes— our Chest of Drawers got up out of the hole. Making poetry a little — copying some for Miss Dalgairns, walking about with her at night, very unhappy both of us — The Doctor came and walked a little with us. Saw the land very plain, walked on the other side. The ropes of the Wheel got foul, very much frightened — cried — did not leave the deck till past eleven, did not turn in soon.

Sunday 26th. Very fine day — Let go the Anchor in Table Bay at about 10 Minutes past one in the night — did not completely turn in till two. The first thing we saw (in) the morning was Cape Town — could not see it very plain therefore did not like it much —almost the first Ship arrived the Mountains looked very barren at first. Could not do anything all day a Sheep and some fruit came off. Could not get on Shore, in quarantine. No one allowed to come on Board of us. Miss O'Connor, Miss Dalgairns, Kate and I on the round house after tea, Captain came to us, all got into the boat astern, admiring the beauties all around us very much. Papa said it was time to walk, did a little then turned in. Saw Henry Monckton while at dinner, he came (on board?), very fat, the Doctor came with him. Struck with the red coats.

Monday 27th. Very fine noon, very hazy in the morning, could not see the Shore — wrote to our friends in England. Henry Monckton came. Looking at the Shore through a glass, liked it very much indeed — very much vexed that no one could go on shore.

Tuesday 28th. Very fine day — Papa went on Shore in the Afternoon. The Signal was made about noon. They all went on Shore after Colonel Monckton and the Doctor were gone. Henry M. sent us an immense basket of fruit, Grapes, Pomegranates, Gooseberries, Figs, etc.

Wednesday 29th. Very fine day, Looking at the Shore through a glass, the Gig went two or three times — liked the appearance of the land more than ever, more every time we looked at it.

Thursday 30th. Fine day. Papa on Shore all day.

Friday 31st. Very fine day. Papa came on Board with Cousin Henry, brought two very pretty horses, brought a very odd pair of shoes, Bengally stayed a little time, went again. Two dogs came, not for us. Good Friday, Spent very oddly — talking with Kate and Mr. Elley in Captain Charlton's Cabin — on eternity. Captain C. came for a short time, dined with Captain. A number of things came from the Shore, wanted to go very much.

Editors note: Sophia would have to wait till Algoa Bay to go ashore on 2 May 1820.

Travel to Our Wild Domain

Thomas Pringle[61]

He was the head of a small party from Scotland, who were located on the Baviaan's River, beyond Albany, after successively planting his little band of relatives and followers in this remote corner of the Frontier, he removed to Cape Town, where he intended to devote himself to literature. He returned to Scotland and then died, December 5, 1834. He wrote an account of the settlement of the British immigrants, and a volume of poems, which are prized for their simplicity and description of African scenery from which this section is taken describing their trip from Algoa Bay to their settlement.

Another week elapsed, after our destination had been fixed, before the commissariat could furnish wagons to convey us and our "stuff" to our location among the mountains. These carriages were the common country wagons used by the Dutch-African colonists. They were called out by a Government order in a

Figure 11: Thomas Pringle - Unknown Artist

certain quota from each field-cornetcy, or local subdivision of the eastern districts; and were to be paid for at a stipulated rate, out of the money deposited by each party of emigrants in the hands of Government. The distance from Algoa Bay to Baviaan's River, whither we were bound, was estimated to be about 170 miles by

---

61. Pringle, Thomas (1835). *Narrative of a Residence in South Africa*. Edward Moxon.

the route which it was necessary for us to follow; and as there was no place by the way where provisions could be procured (excepting sheep), until we reached the military post of Roodewal, we stored our carriages with an adequate supply of all necessaries for the journey.

Figure 12: Andries, A Khoi. Celebrated wagon Driver in Grahamstown - Henry Foley

We struck our tents on the 13th of June [1820], which is about the middle of winter in the Southern Hemisphere. The weather was serene and pleasant, though chill at night— somewhat like fine September weather in England. Our travelling train consisted of seven wagons; all, except one which was driven by a slave, being conducted by the owners or their sons, Dutch-African farmers. These vehicles were admirably adapted for the nature of the country, which is rugged and mountainous and generally destitute of any other roads than the rude tracks originally struck across the wilderness by the first European adventurers; and which are repaired by merely throwing earth and faggots into the gullies and beds of torrents, which during heavy rains sometimes render them impassable. Each wagon is provided with a raised canvas tilt to protect the traveller from sun and rain; and is drawn by a team of ten or twelve oxen, fastened with wooden yokes to a strong central trace ("trektow"), formed of twisted thongs of bullock's or buffalo's hide. The driver sits in front to guide and stimulate the oxen, armed with a whip of enormous length; while a young Khoi, running before, leads the team by a thong attached to the horns of the foremost pair of bullocks.

Having forded the Zwartkops River, we unyoked, and dined on its farther bank amidst a clump of mimosa trees. In the afternoon, on resuming our journey, I induced the drivers, by a little present of tobacco, to deviate a few miles from our direct route, in order to visit a remarkable salt lake, which I knew from Mr. Barrow's account to be in the vicinity. After travelling about a couple of hours through a dense jungle, or forest of shrubbery, we reached its southern bank about sunset.

This lake, which lies in the midst of an extensive plain, elevated considerably above the level of the sea, is of an oval form, about three miles in circumference, and has on one side a sloping margin of green turf; in other parts, banks of greater elevation and abruptness are covered with continuous thickets of arboreous and succulent plants.

At the time of our visit the whole of the lake round the margin, and a considerable portion of its entire surface, was covered with a thick rind of salt sprinkled over with small snow-white crystals, giving the whole basin the aspect of a pond partially frozen and powdered over with hoar frost or flakes of snow. This wintry appearance of the lake formed a singular contrast with the exuberant vegetation which embowered its margins, where woods of beautiful evergreens and elegant acacias were intermingled with flowering shrubs and succulent plants of lofty size and strange exotic aspect, —such as the *portulacaria afra* (favourite food of the elephant), the tree *crassula*, the scarlet *cotelydon*, with several species of the aloe some of them of large size, and in summer crested with superb tiaras of blood-red blossoms; and, high over all gigantic groves of *euphorbia*, extending their leafless arms above the far-spread forest of shrubbery. The effect of the whole, flushed with a rosy tinge by the setting sun, was singularly striking and beautiful.

I did not attempt to examine the saline incrustation, which is said to extend over the whole bottom of the lake; but I tasted the water, and found it as salt as brine. Of the various theories suggested by naturalists to account for the formation of this singular Salt Pan (as it is called by the colonists), that which ascribes its origin to saline springs in the bottom appears the most probable.

Having obtained from this natural reservoir a sufficient quantity of excellent culinary salt to supply our party for a twelve-month, we continued our journey through the wilderness of jungle until the twilight closed in upon us; when, selecting an open space among the bushes, we unyoked, or, according to the colonial phrase, out-spanned the teams.

Our encampment this night was to our yet unexperienced eyes rather a singular scene. Some families pitched their tents, and spread their mattresses on the dry ground; others, more vividly impressed with the terror of snakes, scorpions, tarantulas[62], and other noxious creatures of the African clime, of which they had heard or read, resolved to sleep as they had travelled—above their baggage in the wagons. Meanwhile, our native attendants adopted due precautions to avert surprise from the more formidable denizens of the forest. Elephants and lions had formerly been numerous in this part of the country, and were still occasionally, though but rarely, met with. Two or three large fires were therefore kindled to scare away such visitants; and the oxen, for greater security, were fastened by their horns to the wheels of the wagons.

The boors unslung their huge guns (or *roers*) as they called them) from the tilts of the wagons, and placed them against a magnificent evergreen bush, in whose

---

62. Tarantulas are not native to South Africa although there are similar indigenous species like the baboon spider.

shelter, with a fire at their feet, they had fixed their place of repose. Here, untying each his leathern scrip, they produced their provisions for supper, consisting chiefly of dried bullock's flesh[63], which they seasoned with a moderate *zoopjé* or dram, of colonial *brandewyn* from a huge horn slung by each man in his wagon beside his powder-flask. The slave men and Khoi, congregated apart round one of the watch fires, made their frugal meal, without the brandy, but with much more merriment than their phlegmatic masters. In the meanwhile our frying-pans and tea-kettles were actively employed; and by a seasonable liberality in the beverage 'which cheers but not inebriates' we ingratiated ourselves not a little with both classes of our escort, especially with the coloured caste, who prized 'tea-water' as a rare and precious luxury.

It was not a little amusing after supper (as I sat in the front of my wagon jotting down in my notebook the day's memoranda) to contemplate the characteristic groups which our rustic camp exhibited. The Dutch-African boors, most of them men of almost gigantic size, sat apart in their bushy *bield*, in aristocratic exclusiveness, smoking their huge pipes with self-satisfied complacency. Some of the graver emigrants were seated on the trunk of a decayed tree, conversing in broad Scotch on subjects connected with our settlement, and on the comparative merits of long and short-homed cattle (the horns of the native oxen, by the way, are enormous): and the livelier young men and servant lads were standing round the Khoi, observing their merry pranks, or practising with them a lesson of mutual tuition in their respective dialects; while the awkward essays at pronunciation on either side supplied a fund of ceaseless entertainment.

Conversation appeared to go on with alacrity, though neither party understood scarcely a syllable of the other's language; while a sly rogue of a Bushman sat behind, all the while mimicking, to the very life, each of us in succession. These groups, with all their variety of mien and attitude, character and complexion, — now dimly discovered, now distinctly lighted up by the fitful blaze of the watch-fires; the exotic aspect of the clumps of aloes and euphorbias, peeping out amidst the surrounding jungle, in the wan light of the rising moon, seeming to the excited fancy like bands of Xhosa warriors crested with plumes and bristling with *assagaais*; together with the uncouth clucking gibberish of the Khoi and Bushmen (for there were two or three of the latter tribe among our wagon leaders), and their loud bursts of wild and *eldritch* laughter; had altogether a very strange and striking effect, and made some of us feel far more impressively than we had yet felt, that we were now indeed pilgrims in the wilds of savage Africa.

---

63. Known as Biltong.

By degrees the motley groups became hushed under the influence of slumber. The settlers retired to their tents or their wagons; the boors, sticking their pipes in the bands of their broad-brimmed hats, wrapped themselves in their great coats, and, fearless of snake or scorpion, stretched their limbs on the bare ground; while the Khoi, drawing themselves each under his sheep-skin *caross*, lay coiled up, with their feet to the fire and their faces to the ground, like so many hedge-hogs. Over the wide expanse of wilderness, now reposing under the midnight moon, profound silence reigned, —unbroken save by the deep breathing of the oxen round the wagons, and, at times; by the far-off melancholy howl of a hyaena, the first voice of a beast of prey we had heard since our landing. With the nightly serenade of the jackal and hyaena we soon became familiar; nor did any more formidable visitors disturb us during our journey.

Having thus detailed our mode of travelling and bivouacking in the wilds, I shall pass rapidly over the ground which we traversed during the ensuing eight days, and which has been repeatedly described by travellers. Suffice it to say that we crossed successively the Kuga, the Sunday, the Bushman, the New-year, and, the little Fish rivers. None of these rivers contained any considerable stream of water: some of them were quite stagnant, and almost dry. Nevertheless, the great depth of their beds, and the abruptness of the banks, rendered the crossing of them with our heavy-loaded vehicles a task sometimes of no ordinary difficulty.

We passed also over an extensive tract of mountainous country near the Zureberg, where the roads appeared to us most frightful and perilous. Certainly wheel carriage used in England could have survived them; but our African charioteers jolted us along with great sang-froid, and without any material disaster. Sometimes we had two teams of twelve oxen each yoked to one wagon, to drag our loads of iron-ware up the steep hills; and then there was tremendous shouting, and barbarous flogging of the poor animals. But these are ordinary occurrences in Cape travelling.

We saw but few inhabitants of any class, and few wild animals, except antelopes and quaggas in the distance. The features of the country changed alternately from dark jungle to rich park-like scenery, embellished with graceful clumps of evergreens; and from that again to the desolate sterility of savage mountains, or of parched and desert plains, scattered over with huge ant-hillocks and flocks of springboks. Here and there a solitary farmhouse appeared near some permanent fountain or willow-margined river; and then again the dreary wilderness would extend for twenty miles or more without a drop of water.

At length, on the 21st of June, we reached Roodewal, a military post on the

Great Fish River, estimated to be upwards of 130 miles from Algoa Bay by the route we had followed, and about 40 miles distant from the spot allotted for our location.

Here we were received by the officers of the garrison and their ladies with the utmost kindness and hospitality. They insisted on our abandoning our tents and wagons during our stay, and establishing ourselves in their quarters, where some of them resigned their own apartments to accommodate our females and children. 'Roughing it, as we had been doing for the last four weeks, in tents and wagons, and after a journey of nine days over such execrable roads, and through a country so waste and lonesome that it seemed almost devoid of inhabitants, we felt the sudden and unexpected transition to the cordial hospitalities and English comforts of our agreeable hosts altogether delightful. We had not entered a house since we left Algoa Bay, except one or two comfortless boors' cabins, and indeed had scarcely seen above a dozen farm-houses during our whole journey; the route we'd followed having necessarily led us through one of the wildest and least inhabited tracts of the frontier districts.

On the following day we received a visit from Mr. Hart, a Scotch gentleman residing in the vicinity, and father-in-law to Lieutenant Stretch, one of our kind entertainers. He had formerly been an officer in the Cape Corps (a Khoi regiment raised for the defence of the colony), but was now superintendent of a great agricultural and commissariat establishment belonging to government, called the Somerset Farm, lying at the foot of the Boschberg mountains. Haying resided altogether upwards of twenty years in Southern Africa, he was extremely well informed respecting the capabilities of the country and the character of the inhabitants. His information and advice, therefore, in regard to many points connected with the successful prosecution of the enterprise we were engaged in, were highly important, and were communicated with much kindly feeling, and with a certain shrewd sagacity which we found to be one of his characteristic features.

A numerous party of us were assembled at tea in the officers' dining hall, when Mr. Hart joined us. The Scottish accent, seldom entirely lost even by the most polished of the middle ranks of our countrymen, was heard from every tongue; and the broad 'Doric dialect' prevailed, spoken by female voices, fresh and unsophisticated from the banks of the Teviot and the Fields Lothian. Hart, a man of iron look and rigid nerve, was taken by surprise, and deeply affected. The accents of his native tongue, uttered by the kindly voice of woman, carried him back forty years at once and irresistibly, as he afterwards owned, to the scenes of his mother's fire-side; and recalled freshly before him the softened remembrances of early life—

those tender and sacred remembrances which, though apparently buried beneath the cares and ambitious aims of after years, are never, in any good heart, entirely effaced. Our Scottish poet Graham, has beautifully described this natural sentiment —not unallied to lofty virtues— in one of his neglected pieces. '

"How pleasant came thy rushing, silver Tweed,
Upon my ear, when, after wandering long
 In Southern plains, I've reached thy lovely banks!
How bright, renowned Sark, thy little stream,
Like ray of columned light chasing a shower,
Would cross my homeward path! How sweet the sound.
When I, to hear the Doric tongue's reply,
Would ask thy well-known name!
And must I leave.
Dear land, thy bonny braes, thy upland dales,
Each haunted by its wizard stream, o'erhung
With all the varied charms of hush and tree;
Thy towering hills, the lineaments sublime,
Unchanged, of Nature's face, which wont to fill
The eye of Wallace, as he musing planned
The grand enterprise of setting Scotland free?
And must I leave the friends of youthful years,
And mould my heart anew to take the stamp
Of foreign friendships in a foreign land?
Yes, I may love the music of strange tongues,
And mould my heart anew to take the stamp
Of foreign friendships in a foreign land,
But to my parched mouth's roof cleave this tongue.
My fancy fade into the yellow leaf,
And this oft-pausing heart forget to throb,
If, Scotland! thee and thine I e'er forget."
Graham's British Georgics.

On the 23rd of June, after spending two days at Roodewal, we proceeded on our journey. We were now provided with a new train of wagons, drivers, and attendants from the sub-district of Cradock, in lieu of those that had accompanied us from Algoa Bay; and at the residence of the field-cornet Opperman, where we arrived the same evening, we were joined by an escort of armed boors under his direction, who had been called out to accompany and assist us during the remaining part of our journey, and to place us in safety upon the ground allotted to us. The distance we had still to travel, after reaching Opperman's did not much exceed twenty-five miles, but it proved to be by far the most arduous portion of our journey. We had now crossed the Great Fish River, and, though still within the old boundary of the colony, were upon its utmost verge to the eastward. The country beyond, for a distance of seventy miles, to the new frontier at the Chumi and Keisi rivers, had been the preceding year forcibly de-peopled of its native inhabitants, the Xhosa and Ghonaquas, and now lay waste and void, 'a howling wilderness' occupied only by wild beasts, and haunted occasionally by wandering banditti of the Bushman race (Bosjesmen), who were represented to us as being even more wild and savage than the beasts of prey with whom they shared the dominion of the desert.

Figure 13: Train of Wagons at Karreebergen Poort - William John Burchell

The Baviaans' River, or River of Baboons, (now the Lynden,) on the banks of which we had arrived, is one of the smaller branches of the Great Fish River, flowing from the north-east, and watering a rugged mountain glen of about thirty miles in extent. The upper part of this glen could scarcely be said to have ever been permanently settled, but had been formerly occupied chiefly as grazing ground by a few Dutch-African boors, among the most rude and lawless of the whole colony. These men had been dispossessed, and some of them executed for high treason, about four years before, in consequence of their having taken a prominent part in an insurrection against the English government; and a portion of the lands thus forfeited were now to be assigned as the location of our party.

Having waited a day at Opperman's for some part of our escort, and a free black, formerly in the British army, who had been sent for to act as an interpreter, we moved forward on the 25th. After travelling a few miles, we entered the poort or gorge of the mountains, through which the River of Baboons issues to the more open and level country where it joins the Great Fish River. In the very middle of this poort, we passed the residence of a substantial African boor; a gigantic fellow, six feet five inches in height, and corpulent withal, who had been one of the leaders in the late insurrection. His name was Prinsloo; but from his remarkable size even among a race of very large men, he was usually known by the name of Groot Willem, big William.

This African Goliath, however, in place of gnashing his teeth, like old Pope and Pagan in the Pilgrim's Progress (as would have been but natural), came forth very good humouredly to shake hands with us, his new neighbours, as we passed; and drank to our better acquaintance out of his flask of home-made brandy. And 'as we went on our way,' like old Bunyan's Pilgrims, we received, on passing the corner of the orchard, a present of excellent vegetables, and a basket of lemons and pomegranates; a testimony of good will, which we repaid by distributing among the family a few Dutch tracts and hymn books. Groot Willem's house and farm offices, were constructed in a nook of the glen, with tremendous precipices of naked rock rising above and around, so as barely to leave on the bank of the river sufficient space for the houses and cattle-folds, together with a well-stocked garden and orchard, enclosed with quince and pomegranate hedges, and a small plot of corn land below.

A couple of miles or so above this spot, we came to a point where the Lynden is joined by a subsidiary rivulet, called Bosch Fontein, —now the Plora. This little stream waters a valley of seven or eight miles in length, containing fine pasturage, and rich alluvial soil capable of being extensively cultivated by the aid of irrigation; without which, in fact, little or nothing can be raised in the arid climate of South Africa, at any considerable distance from the coast. Looking up this valley, which extends eastward behind the back of the Kahaberg, we observed the skirts of the magnificent timber forests, which cover the southern fronts of this range, stretching over the summits of the green hills at the head of the glen. In those hills are the sources of the Flora, which being fed by more frequent rains than most other parts of the adjoining country, and protected from evaporation by the dense woods, furnish a perpetual supply of pure water; an advantage which in this country is quite invaluable, and for the want of which nothing else can compensate. To this valley, and the wooded hills which bound it, we gave the name of Ettrick Forest.

Leaving this subsidiary glen on our right, we proceeded up the River of Baboons. To this point the wagon track, wild and rugged as it was, might be considered comparatively safe and in good repair; but it now became difficult and dangerous to a degree & exceeding anything we had yet encountered or formed a conception of; insomuch that we were literally obliged to hew out our path up the valley through jungles and gullies, and beds of torrents, and rocky acclivities, forming altogether a series of obstructions which it required the utmost exertions of the whole party, and of our experienced African allies, to overcome.

The scenery through which we passed was in many places of the most picturesque and singular description. Sometimes the valley widened out, leaving space along the riverside for fertile meadows, or haughs (as such spots are called in the south of Scotland), prettily sprinkled over with mimosa trees and ever-green shrubs, and then clothed with luxuriant pasturage up to the bellies of our oxen. Frequently the mountains, again converging, left only a narrow defile, just broad enough for the stream to find a passage; while precipices of naked rock rose abruptly, like the walls of a rampart, to the height of many hundred feet, and in some places appeared absolutely to overhang the savage-looking pass or poort through which we and our wagons struggled below; our only path being occasionally the rocky bed of the shallow river itself, encumbered with huge blocks of stone which had fallen from the cliffs, or worn smooth as a marble pavement by the sweep of the torrent floods.

At this period the River of Baboons was a mere rill, gurgling gently along its rugged course, or gathered here and there into natural tanks, called in the language of the country *zeekoe-gats* (hippopotamus pools); but the remains of water-wrack, heaved high on the cliffs, or hanging upon the tall willow trees, which in many places fringed the banks, afforded striking proof that at certain seasons this diminutive rill becomes a mighty and resist-less flood. The steep hills on either side often assumed very remarkable shapes—embattled, as it were, with natural ramparts of freestone or trap rock—and seemingly garrisoned with troops of the large baboons from which the river had received its former Dutch Appellation. The lower declivities were covered with good pasturage, and sprinkled over with evergreens and acacias; while the cliffs that overhung the river had their wrinkled fronts embellished with various species of succulent plants and flowering aloes. In other spots the freestone and basaltic rocks, partially worn away with the waste of years, had assumed shapes the most singular and grotesque; so that with a little aid from fancy, one might imagine them the ruins of Hindoo or Egyptian temples, with their half decayed obelisks, columns, and statues of monster deities.

It were tedious to relate the difficulties, perils, and adventures, which we encountered in our toilsome march of five days up this African glen;—to tell of our pioneering labours with the hatchet, the pick-axe, the crow-bar, and the sledge-hammer, —and the lashing of the poor oxen, to force them on (sometimes 20 or 80 in one team) through such a track as no English reader can form any adequate conception of. In the upper part of the valley we were occupied two entire days in thus hewing our way through a rugged defile, now called Eildon-Cleugh, scarcely three miles in extent.

At length, after extraordinary exertions and hair-breadth escapes—the breaking down of two wagons, and the partial damage of others—we got through the last poort, of the glen, and found ourselves on the summit of an elevated ridge, commanding a view of the extremity of the valley. "And now, *mynheer*," said the Dutch-African field-comet who commanded our escort, "*daar leg uwe*", —"there lies your country."

Looking in the direction where he pointed, we beheld extending to the northward, a beautiful vale, about six or seven miles in length, and varying from one to two in breadth. It appeared like a verdant basin, or cul-de-sac, surrounded on all sides by an amphitheatre of steep and sterile mountains, rising in the background into sharp cuneiform ridges of very considerable elevation; their summits being at this season covered with snow, and estimated to be about 5000 feet above the level of the sea. The lower declivities were sprinkled over, though somewhat scantily, with grass and bushes. But the bottom of the valley, through which the infant river meandered, presented a warm, pleasant, and secluded aspect; spreading itself into verdant meadows, sheltered and embellished, without being encumbered, with groves of mimosa trees, among which we observed in the distance herds of wild animals—antelopes and quaggas—pasturing in undisturbed quietude.

"Sae that's the lot o' our inheritance, then?" quoth one of the party, a Scottish agriculturist. "Aweel, now that we've really got till't, I maun say the place looks no sae mickle amiss, and may suit our purpose no that ill, provided thae haughs turn out to be gude deep land for the pleugh, and we can but contrive to find a decent road out o' this queer hieland glen into the lowlands—like ony other Christian country."

Descending into the middle of the valley, we unyoked the wagons, and pitched our tents in a grove of mimosa trees on the margin of the river; and the next day our armed escort, with the train of shattered vehicles, set out on their return homeward, leaving us in our wild domain to our own courage and resources.

By Flood and Field – The Life of a Post-Holder

by Isaac Dyason[64]

Isaac Dyason came to South Africa with the British settlers. In the two parts in this book he recounts some of his experiences in the early years of the settlement. He continues to recount his life through several subsequent parts that had originally been published in the Anglo-African newspaper in twelve parts in total.

> "There is a tide in the affairs of men,
> Which, taken at flood, leads on to fortune."

Part I

There is a deal of truth in the above oft-repeated quotation from Shakespeare. Such tides I have experienced more than once in my life, and by some unaccountable fatality, have allowed them, when just at the flood, to ebb from me; so that I am left, at this day, in a less favourable position than when I started, with a fine flowing stream, forty-six years ago. At that time I was entering upon all the vigour and energy of healthy and sanguine manhood. Full of hope for the future; prompt at all times to do a good turn to others; ready for any enterprise that might be presented, and in the sequel it will be seen that I have had my share of adventure. Now 'Father Time' is fast taking hold of me, reminding me that decline and age are rapidly advancing; but I am thankful for the health and vigour I still retain, and have faith that the protecting arm of Omnipotence will shield me to the last.

Figure 14: Boer Huntsman, c1802 - Samuel Daniell

In the outline I intend to trace it will be

---

64. The sections of the 'Rough outlines' appear in the Anglo-African, printed in Grahamstown, as follows: -
Part I   23.6.1866.
Part II   30.06.1866

found that my colonial life has been a very chequered one, and that about twenty-seven years of it has been engaged in public service, in which I did not make very much progress, and then I suddenly disappeared from it altogether, causing an impression, on some minds, not altogether favourable on my reputation. But, however much it may appear that I have wanted decision of character, and however much it shall be seen that I have neglected to take advantage of several propitious positions I have been placed in; yet, it is with much satisfaction I can prove, that in the various portions of South Africa it has been my lot to be placed, I have been respected by the inhabitants, and have had their good wishes. It was even so with me in my boyish days, and during my course of education in England. At Chatham House Academy I obtained a silver medal, still in my possession, having my name engraved on one side of it, and on the opposite, the 'Reward of Merit.'

I was born on the 1st of November 1803, at Ramsgate, in the Isle of Thanet, Kent, England. My father's father was an enterprising and an eminently successful man there. His projects and means added much to the improvement and advancement of the place. His sister was married to Capt. Strivens, harbour-master of Ramsgate. My grandfather's family consisted of four sons and a daughter.

My father was the eldest child, and my mother was the daughter of a farmer in Kent, named Lily. After my grandfather had given his sons a fair start in life—two engaged in business, one sailing-master in the navy, and another in Commissariat Department—and saw his daughter settled in marriage to a sea Captain, he retired with a good competency to a pretty villa in St Thomas's Hill, in the vicinity of Canterbury. He also rented a portion of the estate of the late Lord Rokeby, in Kent.

Years passed on; and in the interval many splendid achievements were attained by British troops on the Peninsula, and then followed the Battle of Waterloo, which we now know resulted in the success of the Allied Powers and the downfall of Bonaparte. Soon after a general peace was proclaimed, followed by many reductions in the war department. This caused a considerable stagnation in several branches of business, and at Ramsgate, being a seaport town, it was much felt, even by my own kindred.

In 1819 Government proposed a scheme for emigration to the Cape of Good Hope. It was eagerly embraced by the public, and so numerous were the applications -far beyond what was anticipated—that numbers were disappointed. Those who did succeed had to obtain the recommendation of influential individuals for a favourable result; and in our case, we procured the interest of the Hon. Mr. Lushington, a member of parliament for Kent, and Sir William Curtis.

The result of the emigration movement was, twenty-six vessels successfully sailed for the Cape, having emigrants on board, including women and children, to the number of about four thousand. The Isle of Thanet party, of which I was one, consisted of seventy-two, old and young. Mr. George Dyason was the acknowledged head of it, but there were five others—namely, Messrs. Isaac, Joseph, and Robert Dyason, Hougham Hudson, and Samuel Bennett —who had, by agreement, equal power. In December 1819, (and some of the party, with other emigrants, in the early part of January 1820,) we embarked on board the fine tight little ship Zoroaster, about 400 tons, Capt. Thompson, lying in the Thames.

The parties on board besides our own were Messrs Thornhill's, Weight's, and Barker's, altogether numbering between three and four hundred, exclusive of the ship's crew. It was a very severe winter, and the vessels in the river were frozen fast for weeks, but as soon as a thaw had set in, several of them, including the Zoroaster, our ship, and the La Belle Alliance, the ship appointed to sail in our company, dropped down to Blackwall, and after a short detention, all arrangements for the voyage were completed. We next made the Downs, where we cast anchor, and were detained a day or two by contrary winds. At last the breeze was propitious; we got ship under weigh; sailed down Channel in fine style; experienced it a little rough in the Bay of Biscay; called at Palmer, one of the Canary Islands; and after a pleasant passage of about four months, anchored in Simon's Bay on the 30th April 1820.

Our ship was a fine vessel, — high between decks, — good accommodation, — a pleasant gentlemanly captain, with civil subordinate officers and crew; so that most of us were very comfortable on board, and I was a favourite with the captain. But there was an inconvenience connected with this ship, and that was, as she belonged to the East Africa free trade service, she was charted to take us no further than Simon's Bay. The emigrant ships Brilliant and Albury were then at anchor in the bay, and arrangements were made to transfer us, with our stores, to them. Our party was appointed to the Brilliant, a ship nothing equal to the Zoroaster for accommodation. I remember I was impressed at the time with the feeling that it must have been a source of great inconvenience and annoyance to all on board the ships to which we had been transferred, to have an addition of some four hundred persons crowded upon them; but happily they took it with a tolerably goodwill.

On getting on board the Brilliant, I was informed that my berth was to be with Messrs Pringle's, or Scotch party, and by whom I was received with kindness. Dr Caldercott and family were also on board this vessel. Our ship and the Albury being ready for sea, we set sail in company, in May, and in about thirteen days arrived in Algoa Bay, and were safely landed at Port Elizabeth. We found, besides the fort, only a few huts there.

Captain Evatt was the commandant of the fort. From thence we were, with our baggage and stores, conveyed in ox-wagons to the spot allotted as our location, and where we arrived early in June 1820. We pitched our tents, and had to live under canvas for months. In the meantime we were busy, when not engaged in farming avocations, erecting dwellings of a more substantial nature. The bushy country in our vicinity was full of wild animals, especially wolves[65], which made sad havoc at times amongst our sheep. Tigers[66] and elephants would occasionally pay us a visit.

We were located in a valley, having a stream running through it called Braak river, the Kowie bush forming one of its borders. It is situated about four miles from Bathurst, and twenty from Grahamstown, and to which we gave the name of Lushington Valley. I remained there for about three years, and had a hand in all the branches, fatigues and privations, of a Settler's life in the wilderness. I witnessed the successive failure of the crops by rust; the heavy and destructive flood; the occasional plunder of our stock by Xhosa, and, to crown all, a settler or two had already been murdered by them.

This decided the Government to raise a levy from amongst the settlers, of five hundred infantry and one hundred cavalry, as a protective force. The whole levy was commanded by Harry Rivers, Esq., Landdrost of Albany, who was termed Colonel; and the different divisions by half-pay officers, who came from old England with the body of British Settlers, as well as pensioned non-commissioned officers. The latter performed the duty of drill-sergeant, and Mr. George Dyason was the adjutant. I had the honour of being a private in the Bathurst troop of horse. The commanding officer of our troop was Lieut. Charles Crause, formally of the Marines, on half-pay. He was a fine, good-natured, merry fellow.

Divisions of the Levy used to assemble monthly in various parts of Lower Albany, for drill, presenting a most ludicrous appearance in dress and accoutrements. The place of muster for my troop was at Mount Donkin, not far from the locations of Messrs Cawood and Bowker, both of whom had some fine promising sons. This levy was, however, by no means in favour with the people; and with several of the heads of families it was detested, as they could not conceive why their sons should be required (as was done) to take the Oath of Allegiance, the same as in the regular army, and thus in a manner become a soldier. The musters did not long continue well attended, and the force therefore did not arrive to anything like perfection, nor long exist.

---

65. Hyenas
66. Leopards

Part II

In the early days of the settlement it was considered that Bathurst would be the capital of the district of Albany. Grahamstown was, however, ultimately fixed upon. At the time Bathurst had only just sprung into existence, and Grahamstown could only boast of some half-a-dozen houses, with a few military huts. This year, 1866, gives evidence of the progress of the settlers.

On arrival of the British settlers at the Cape, Sir Rufane Shaw Donkin was the Acting Governor, during the absence of Lord Charles Somerset to England. He did all in his power to have the settlers located satisfactorily. Lord Charles returned in December 1821, and resumed his government.

The Dutch law was then in force, and all the appointments of government were conducted therewith. This state of things was very distasteful to the settlers, who had been brought up under the laws and glorious free institutions of their native land; and although, as a body, truly loyal, yet no great time had elapsed, before it was determined that a move should be made, in a constitutional way, for a remedy.

Meetings were convened, and petitions were drawn up which were numerously singed, and forwarded to the Imperial Government, representing their wants and grievances. This resulted in the arrival of His Majesty's Commissioners of Inquiry in 1824, who, after due investigation, recommended in their able report, that the Civil and Judicial Establishments of the Colony be remodelled and framed somewhat in accordance with the British Constitution. The report was mainly adopted, and hence we now have Judges, Civil Commissioners, Magistrates etc.

The first few years of the settler's life, were those of continued trial, disappointment, and failure; but with that intrepid spirit, so famous in the Anglo-Saxon race, nothing could daunt them in their exertion and faith in ultimate success, and if unsuccessful in one sphere, a trial would be made in another. Many of the settlers determined to follow up their agricultural and grazing pursuits at all hazards, and others, such as business men, mechanics and clerks resorted to towns and villages in the Colony to seek for employment, but Grahamstown was the chief point of attraction, it being the headquarters of the few troops then stationed on the frontier.

The mechanics soon obtained employment of started on their own account, and several of the other classes accepted situations of the most humble description, either under government or with private individuals, and a few became Xhosa traders.

I find I am entering too much upon generalities, and have lost sight of my own adventure. Were I to describe all the incidences, with which I am acquainted, connected with the settlers, it would fill three or four volumes. This is foreign to my purpose, and, besides, has been done by others, and amongst whom there is not one stands more prominent than Mr. Robert Godlonton, who so long and so ably edited the *Grahamstown Journal*. This gentleman was always on the alert for the defence of the settlers, whenever their acts or character were wrongly assailed. Mr. J C Chase was another able defender of the settlers.

Prior to the arrival of the Commissioners of Inquiry, the mails were conveyed to and from Cape Town to the Post Offices in the interior, once a week, by land-holders, residing at convenient distances, on the post route, and were by government terms Post-holders. They were required to have trustworthy riders to take charge of the mail-bags, which were then conveyed on horse-back, and sufficient horses for the due performance of the duty, and they were moreover directed to perform it, whether agreeable to themselves or not. The amount of remuneration was fixed by the government, but such a low figure, but it barely defrayed the outlay required, and in the seasons of the horse-distemper, when so many died, it was found to be a losing game, and by a deficiency of horses, the post was frequently conveyed very irregularly.

In 1820, and for some time thereafter, the post was conveyed from Grahamstown to Bathurst by the military, but on the opening of the Kowie, a Post-office being established there, I was appointed Post-holder from thence to Bathurst and to Grahamstown; and, mark, this was my first appointment under government. Most of the Post-holders employed native servants, or slaves, to convey the post, but, as I was without anything of the kind, I had to perform the duty myself for upwards of a year, and, although it a little touched my pride, yet, it was not very repulsive to my feelings. I was fond of change, light of weight, young and active, and upon the whole, (although I say it myself) made a smart post-boy.

Besides riding the post, I had to convey all extra posts and expresses on the route, and sometimes expresses to different parts of lower Albany. I have been on the road day and night for weeks, in darkness, storm, and rain, and many are the narrow escapes I have had by my horse falling with me, and 'by flood and field', as well as when the day has been drawing to a close, by avoiding marauding Xhosa, making for the road I had to pass.

I believe that the post was conveyed by me satisfactorily, but I should want in candour if I omitted to record one sad mishap that I had. The post-bag was out of repair, and I had started from Port Francis in the evening, with the mail secured in a strong cotton handkerchief, which I slung over my shoulder. The horse I rode was young and fiery, and not well broken in. I reached Bathurst all right, received the post there, and placed it in the aforesaid handkerchief, and took my departure for Grahamstown. It was a starlight night. I had passed Lushington Valley; reached the 'Blue Flag,' Wilson's party, which I did not hail; crossed Dyason's Flat; got through Blauw Krantz; and was riding at a smart pace on the heights beyond, approaching the Zigzag, when my horse suddenly started at full gallop, to the left of the road, down to a Kloof, and I came in contact with some thorn trees, which tore me from my saddle, and brought me to the ground with great force. I was not only considerably hurt and bruised, but was stunned for a time.

On recovering myself in some measure, I found I had fortunately kept the bridle-rein in my hand, and my horse was standing by me. I again mounted, got into the road, and had ridden some distance, when I placed my hand behind my back, to feel if my packets were all right, but, to my consternation, found they were gone, having burst through the handkerchief with the force of my fall. I retraced my steps, and searched diligently for a long time for them, but without success. Early morn was drawing near and as I must be in town by a certain time, before the mail was despatched from thence to Cape Town, I had no other alternative but to proceed, and report my mishap to the Postmaster of Grahamstown. It is satisfactory for me to be able to state that the packets were soon afterwards recovered, all safe.

Had I faith in the doctrine of fatalism, I should say that there was an evil fatality attached to the horse that caused my accident. The same horse, some time afterwards became the property of Thomas Lawson, Esq., Magistrate for Albany. He was one day riding it at Fort England when he was thrown from its back, and sustained so much injury from the fall, that the unfortunate gentleman died a few hours afterwards.

It was part of the years 1823 to 1824 that I personally conveyed the post. Afterwards it was conveyed by others under my supervision. My residence was in Lushington Valley, but when in Grahamstown waiting for the arrival of the Cape Town post, I was put up at the Postmaster's and when at Port Frances[67], at the Postmaster's, Lieut. Cowderoy, formally of the 21st Light Dragoons. This gentleman was somewhat eccentric, but I experienced from him the greatest kindness and hospitality. Lieut. Bisset, R.N. was the postmaster at Bathurst. I held the appointment of Post-holder to the end of 1826, when, upon the new order of things coming into force, consequent upon the report of the Commissioners of Inquiry, I received a circular from the Postmaster-General, of which the following is a copy:-

---

67. Now Port Alfred.

{CIRCULAR} Post Office, Cape Town,
15th December, 1826.
Mr. I Dyason, Post-holder, Grahamstown.
Sir, I have to acquaint you that you are to convey the Mails to and from the Interior at your present allowance of pay, and three months notice will be given to you at any intended change in its transmission.
I am, Sir,
Your obedient servant,
(signed) R Crozier,
Postmaster-General.

I had previously become aware that it was in contemplation to call for tenders and to enter into contract for the transmission of mail throughout the colony; therefore the above quoted letter only indicated what was about to take place, which did immediately result notwithstanding that it stipulated that three months notice would be given of any intended change, as tenders were directly called for, and I sent one for the Kowie route for the year 1827, which was accepted, and so were my tenders for the same route till 31st December, at the expiry of which another party sent a lower tender for 1832, which was accepted, and the duty fell into other hands.

Having described my career as a Post-holder and Post-contractor, I find it necessary to advert to the year 1824, at which period I entered upon a new epoch in my life, by taking up my residence in Grahamstown. My uncle, Mr. George Dyason was Postmaster and Field-cornet there then, and the duties of Field-cornet required him frequently from town, it was arranged that I should assist him in the Post-office. Grahamstown was rapidly increasing in inhabitants, and buildings were being erected in all quarters of it.

Harry Rivers, Esq., the Landdrost, who afterwards became Treasurer-General, was relieved by Major Dundas, R.A. – D.J. Cloete, Esq., was the secretary; Mr. Wills was the Vendue-Master. There were besides several subordinate appointments. I continued as an assistant in the Post-office till 6th March 1828, when urgent private affairs required my uncle's presence in England; he obtained leave of absence, and I was appointed Acting Postmaster, and so continued till 2nd July 1830. I have testimonials to prove that I performed the duty to the satisfaction of the Postmaster-General, and it would seem that the public were satisfied with me from the circumstance of my having had some time after the Postmaster resumed his duty, a handsome and valuable snuff-box presented to me, with the following words engraved on the lid:-

> *Presented to Mr. Isaac Dyason, by a few of the inhabitants of Grahamstown, as a mark of their approbation of his conduct while acting Postmaster.*

December 12th, 1830

Figure 15: Grahamstown (North Side), 1823 - Henry Foley

Satisfied with their Situation and Prospects

by George Thompson[68]

He was born on 8 April 1796 and was a sailor in his early life. He came to South Africa in 1818 as a clerk to a solicitor. He became a partner and ultimately the head of the firm. He was a resident at the Cape for about 40 years and later returned to England where he died on 29 January 1889. He travelled widely in South Africa at various intervals between 1821 and 1830. Thus extract from the two volume book he published about his travels pertain to the very earliest years of the settlement in Albany.

11 May 1823. — Crossed the Bushman's River, which, on account of continued drought, had not been running for two years, and consisted merely of a chain of pools. At 8 o'clock reached Mr. Daniel's at Sweet-Milk Fountain. Here I stopped to breakfast, and was much delighted to see the very great improvements that had been effected since my visit in January 1821. Mr. Daniel is a lieutenant in the navy, and one of the British emigrants of 1820. He, and his brother, who lives near him, are generally allowed to be among the most enterprising and industrious of the settlers.

Figure 16: A black man leading two oxen - Henry Clifford De Meillon

A great extent of arable land had been brought under cultivation, and divided into neat fenced enclosures; and their wheat crops were already about a foot high,

---

68. Thompson, George (1827). Travels and Adventures in Southern Africa. Volume 1. Henry Colburn, London.

while the African boors in the vicinity had only commenced sowing.

Proceeded on to Assagai-Bush, where, since the arrival of the settlers, a sort of inn has been established. Here I left the Graham's Town road, and turned off towards the coast, it being my intention in the first place to visit the mouth of the Kowie River. On my way I called at Captain Butler's, an Irish settler, abounding in hospitality, but at that time, poor fellow! But ill supplied with the means of exercising this liberal disposition, so general among his countrymen. We dined upon a little dry cheese and butter-milk; but it was his best, and given with cordiality.

A short time before, his only daughter, a child about three years old, had died of bite of a serpent, which she had trod upon while playing in the garden. Poor Mrs. Butler appeared very disconsolate, and her mind in a morbid, disordered state, in consequence of this distressing event. Venomous snakes abound in every part of the Colony, and it is wonderful that fatal accidents are not more frequent. Since leaving Cape Town, I had heard of the death of two women on my route, by these reptiles.

After leaving Captain Butler's, a plain of about twenty miles extent lay before me, over which we galloped at a good round pace, and soon reached the small river Karrega, near which were the locations of several settlers; and the pretty village of Salem, inhabited entirely by Methodists, lay a little to the right. I did not stop at any of these locations, but observed as I rode along a good deal of land cultivated and enclosed, and numerous herds of cattle.

About an hour's ride from the Karrega, I arrived at Lombard's Post, a farm belonging to Colonel Fraser, commandant of the Cape Corps, to whom I had a letter of introduction. This officer has been long stationed on the frontier, and is universally beloved by all classes of the inhabitants; and even the Xhosa, against whom he has served in many a harassing campaign, respect his name, on account of the exemplary humanity and good faith he has displayed in all his dealings with them. Unhappily his health, which had long been in a declining state, has obliged him to retire from active duty, and leave the defence of the frontier in other hands.

After partaking of a second dinner with Colonel Fraser, and his brother and surgeon, who resided with him, I proceeded forward to Theopolis, a missionary institution belonging to the London Society, near the mouth of the little river Kasouga. This place had been repeatedly attacked by the Xhosa during the late war, but had been successfully defended by the vigilance and intrepidity of its Khoi inhabitants; who, for the security of their numerous cattle, (the principal object of Xhosa cupidity) had industriously fenced the common kraal of their village with a very strong and lofty palisade. The stakes of this fence, consisting chiefly of Coral tree (*Erythrina Caffra*) (which grows abundantly in the neighbourhood, had in numerous instances struck root, and thrown out flourishing branches, which gave the palisade an uncommon and agreeable effect. The missionaries were now occupied in removing the establishment to a more favourable site, about half a mile down the river. The new village is to be laid out in regular streets, and the houses of the Khoi to be substantially built of stone or brick, in place of their old, irregular, and uncomfortable wattled cabins. The new parsonage and school-room had been already erected. Here I spent the night, and received very hospitable entertainment from Mr. Barker, the missionary.

12. — Proceeded onwards towards the Kowie mouth, which is only about twelve miles from Theopolis. Passed the location of the late General Campbell, (one of the heads of the settlers) which is now occupied by his widow, an elegant and accomplished lady. The natural features of the country are here exceedingly beautiful, and Mrs. Campbells neatly ornamented cottage, though constructed only of wattle and plaster, had a most pleasing and picturesque appearance, surrounded by luxuriant woods and copses of evergreens, in the disposal of which the wanton hand of Nature seemed to have rivalled the most tasteful efforts of art.

As I travelled along through this rich and smiling scene, now enlivened by the dwellings and improvements of civilized man, and saw the flocks of sheep pasturing on the soft green hills, while the foaming surge broke along the beach on my right hand, I could not help recalling to mind the fate of the Grosvenor's shipwrecked crew, who traversed this beautiful country in other times and far different circumstances.

It was not far from this very spot that the poor boy, Law, after surmounting incredible hardships, lay down to sleep upon a rock, and was found dead in the morning. At that time the boundary of the Colony extended only to Algoa Bay, and the wretched wanderers had still innumerable toils and perils to endure before they could reach the residence of Christians, — and but few survived indeed to reach them.

A skeleton, which was lately found by my friend Mr. Thornhill, in one of the sand-banks, a few miles farther to the eastward, in a sitting posture, may not improbably be the remains of one of those unfortunate wanderers; for many instances are related, in the journal of the survivors, of individuals exhausted with hunger and fatigue, sitting down to rise no more; and a corpse left in such a situation would be covered up by the drifting of the sand in a few hours, if the wind happened to blow strong from the south-east.

This coast has been rendered but too remarkable by many other disastrous shipwrecks. Many years ago the Doddington, Indiaman, a fine large vessel, having struck upon a rock near Algoa Bay, was totally wrecked, and all on board perished.

In February 1796, a vessel from India, under Genoese colours, was wrecked between the Bushman and Sunday Rivers. The boors flocked from all sides to plunder; and one person, who alone attempted to assist the unfortunate crew, was, on this account, as it is said, murdered by his barbarous countrymen. Very different was the conduct of the Xhosa 'savages', when the American ship Hercules was stranded in 1797, between the Fish River and the Keiskamma. They treated the crew with the utmost kindness and hospitality, and conducted them safely into the Colony.

After a very pleasant ride I reached the mouth of the Kowie River. Here I found the tide running out with great rapidity, and as the stream can only be safely forded at low water, I was obliged to wait some time.

At length, two soldiers, employed on the opposite side, pushed off for me with a small boat; and having discharged my guide with the horses, and taken my saddle and other accoutrements into the boat, I crossed over, and proceeded on foot to the residence of my friend Mr. Thornhill, which is about a mile from the landing-place.

Figure 17: Thornhill near Port Frances - H Coburn (1827)

The location of Mr. Thornhill, which lies in the angle formed by the left bank of the river Kowie with the sea, is one of the most beautiful spots in all Albany, with lawns and copse woods, laid out by the hand of Nature, that far surpass many a nobleman's park in England. In fixing his dwelling, the proprietor, and his son-in-law, Lieut. Gilfillan, have not failed to avail themselves of the most favourable situations.

The cottage of the latter especially, which, with its little garden, crowns the summit of a small green mount, commands a prospect scarcely, I think, to be rivalled in Africa for rich and romantic scenery: while the village of Bathurst, in the back-ground, about eight miles distant, gives animation to a landscape, which, at the time I visited it, appeared to a European eye somewhat too lonely amidst all its loveliness.

But the probability of the Kowie mouth be coming available as a harbour for small vessels, is a matter of far higher importance to the prospects of Mr. Thornhill's family, than the fine scenery on their grounds: and on this subject, interesting not alone to them, but to the great majority of the Albany settlers, I heard much conversation, without, however, being able then to form any very decided opinion myself. At that time, the hopes of the Albany settlers were high, and their prospects on this point very flattering; a small vessel called the Good Intent, of twenty tons, having made several successful trips from Cape Town to the Kowie, and landed her cargo in good order.

13. — This morning I set out, accompanied by Lieut. Gilfillan and Mr. J. Thornhill, to visit the mouth of the Great Fish River, about eighteen miles distant.

On our way we passed through several locations of settlers, with the appearance of which I was much pleased. The hedges and ditches, and wattled fences, presented home-looking pictures of neatness and industry, very different from the rude and slovenly premises of the back-country boors.

A small river, called the Kleine-Montjes (Little Mouths), crossed the line of our route; but its outlet to the sea being entirely filled up with drift sand, we passed it perfectly dry.

This bar is at present elevated very much above high-water mark, and gives to the mouth of the river the appearance of a small lake. The scenery at this spot is very beautiful. A range of sand-hills, places overgrown with tall brushwood, in many extends along the whole of the Albany coast. These hills have been evidently formed by the drifting of the sand from the beach at low water, by the strong south-east winds, though sight their great elevation and apparent antiquity render this at first supposition scarcely credible.

As we rode along, Mr. Gilfillan amused us with a story of two settlers, a man and his wife, who, when recently passing through this part of the country, were terribly frightened by a troop of elephants. Seeing those enormous animals suddenly emerge from an adjoining copse wood, they fled in the utmost alarm, and to aid their speed, popped their infant child, which they were carrying, into an anteater's hole.

The elephants, however, fortunately took a different direction, and the selfish parents recovered their poor child uninjured from its dismal bed.

We reached the mouth of the Great Fish River about noon, and, It being then low water, we had a fine opportunity for inspecting it. The bar, on which the surf breaks with great violence, will, I much fear, forever prevent vessels from entering; but could this obstacle be by any means permanently removed, it would form a most excellent harbour. Within the bar, the mouth of the river opens out into a magnificent sheet of water, extending eight or ten miles into the country; and which is wide and deep enough to afford safe anchorage for a large fleet. We could perceive no vestiges of the Portuguese fort said to have been erected here in former times. Other travellers, who possessed no means of crossing the river, may possibly have been deceived by some rocks on the left bank, which at a distance certainly have a striking resemblance to the ruins of a fort.

On our return we called at Captain Crause's residence, a few miles from the mouth of the Fish River; and, varying our route, we also visited a number of other locations on our way home. Altogether, the country I had passed through since leaving Theopolis, was the most beautiful and pleasing I have seen in Africa.

On reaching Mr. Thornhill's, we learned that the little schooner, Good Intent, was arrived off the mouth of the river, and that the harbour-boat had taken a pilot on board, but in returning had been upset by the surf on the bar, and the boatmen had with difficulty saved their lives by swimming. As I had intended to have gone out in the pilot-boat to meet this vessel, and examine the bar more narrowly, I could not but congratulate myself on my accidental absence; for had I not been at the Fish River, I should in all probability have been upset in this boat, and, being no swimmer, most likely drowned.

I spent the two following days with Mr. Thornhill's family, conversing of former days which we had spent together in Cumberland, and listening with interest to the detail of their past adventures and future plans in South Africa. Whatever regrets might be blended with the retrospect of the past, I found them on the whole satisfied with their situation and prospects— and that, in the comparative estimate of human circumstances, is all that in general can be reasonably hoped for.

16.— Took leave of my kind friends, except the elder Mr. Thornhill, who accompanied me to Graham's Town. At noon, we reached Bathurst, a village founded by Sir Rufane Donkin, the late acting governor, and designed by him to be the seat of magistracy for the English settlers.

For this its situation, near the centre of the locations, rendered it much preferable to Graham's Town. Its vicinity also to the Kowie mouth and to the moist sea air, which renders irrigation unnecessary, and many other local advantages which it possesses above Graham's Town, as well as the general concurrence of the settlers in its favour, appear fully to justify the selection of this spot.

Graham's Town has, however, been ultimately re-established by Government, as the Drostdy[69] town of Albany. Had Lord Charles Somerset been accurately informed, or fully aware from personal inspection of the comparative advantages of the two villages, I think he would scarcely have directed the removal of the Drostdy; particularly as many individuals had been induced to expend considerable sums of money in building houses and establishing themselves at Bathurst, upon the presumption that the village would enjoy, in addition to its other advantages, the benefits naturally resulting from being the seat of the local magistracy; a Drostdyhouse having been already built at a considerable expense, and other indications shown of the intentions of Government on the subject.

Among this part of the community, therefore, I found, as might naturally be expected, many persons loud in their complaints against his Lordship, and not slow in ascribing the ruin of their prospects to this sudden and unlooked-for change. Whether in a newly-settled country, contiguous to such trouble some neighbours as the Xhosa, it may not have been expedient to place the military and civil powers upon the same spot; and whether, in such a case, Graham's Town is not better situated for a military station, is a matter upon which I do not pretend to decide; but it may, in some measure, perhaps, account for the change.

Leaving this deserted Drostdy, we soon reached the residence of a settler, commonly known by the name of 'Philosopher Bennet', and celebrated for his indefatigable industry. In spite of the blight in the corn, this eccentric but enterprising old gentleman appeared to be sanguine of the ultimate success of all the settlers whose exertions deserved it. He had himself shown a most laudable example, and his exertions had not been unrewarded, for he had a profusion of vegetables of almost every sort fit for the table, and had planted a vineyard which looked thriving and beautiful.

Having procured fresh horses here, we continued our journey, passing many locations on our way, and arrived at Graham's Town about 10 pm. The distance from the Kowie to this town is about forty miles.

The route I had followed from the Bushman's River to the Kowie mouth, and

---

69. This is essentially the government building from which an area was governed.

from thence to the Fish River, and again by Bathurst to Graham's Town, enabled me to survey, though somewhat cursorily, a large proportion of the locations of the settlers.

But as their distresses were much aggravated after the period of my visit, by the effects of a dreadful deluge of rain, which destroyed many of their dwellings, gardens, and corn-fields;[70] and as the capabilities of that part of the country, and the prospects of the emigrants, have been since more clearly developed, I consider it better to reserve my observations on this interesting subject for a subsequent chapter; when, without anticipating the thread of my narrative, I may bring down their history to a much more recent period.

The calamitous effects of this hurricane are vividly described in a letter by Mr. Philipps, in Mr. Pringle's tract on the "State of Albany" (1824); where, among numerous other disasters, it is stated that poor Bennet had lost his labour for three years; and that "not a vestige of his beautiful garden and vineyard remained." I am happy to add, however, that the indefatigable 'philosopher' has subsequently re-planted them with success in a safer situation.

May 17. — Spent this day in Graham's Town, where I transacted some commercial business, and called on the landdrost, Mr. Rivers, and several of the principal inhabitants. I found this town much increased in size and population since I was here in January 1821.

At that time it contained only about eighty houses; now there were upwards of 300. A drostdy-house of large dimensions was erecting; extensive barracks, and a large tronk (or prison) were also in progress, and the foundation of a church was laid.

These public buildings, together with a number of private houses constantly erecting, furnish employment to a great number of mechanics and labourers at high wages; — but whether this demand for workmen may be permanent seems extremely problematical. The present prosperity of Graham's Town seems to rest almost exclusively upon its being the seat of magistracy, and the head-quarters of the military stationed for the defence of the frontier.

18. — I had intended to have prosecuted my journey this morning at an early hour, but on calling for the horses I had, found they had been put in the schut-kraal[71] or pound. This is an inconvenience very much and justly complained of at Graham's Town, and arises chiefly from a considerable portion of the public

---

70. In January 1826, the population of Graham's Town amounted to about 2,500 souls, the great majority of whom were English.
71. Pound

grounds formerly belonging to the town having been inconsiderately granted to private individuals, so that the instant cattle on or horses are turned out the common, they are sure, if not carefully tended, to trespass on some of the adjacent ill-fenced fields, and are hurried off to the schut-kraal till the damage is adjusted.

At length, after waiting several hours, we got the horses relieved from durance, and I started about ten o'clock, directing now my course north-ward towards the source of the Fish River.

Figure 18: Zak River 04/09/1811 (2) - Willliam John Burchell

The memories of James Samuel Reed

First 1820 Settler to land in Algoa Bay.

As imagined by Karen Cross, based on historical records

I, James Samuel Reed am an old man of 90 years. I was born in 1813 in London, England and am the oldest resident of Port Elizabeth in this year, 1902. I reflect with regularity as I get older, back on those days when we came out as settlers to the Cape in 1820. The memory clear in my mind, as I was then 7 years old.

Figure 19: James Samuel Reed

My father:

William Reed, a Naval Officer Served under Lord Howe, and was on Board the Frigate 'Thunderer'[72] and was in Battle on the Glorious 1st of June[73] and Severely wounded by the French, had his windpipe Cut, also many old wounds by the French while Boarding."

He was later a carpenter and farmer from Kent. Father's first wife, Sara, had died, and they had had 6 children[74]. My mother Elizabeth, née Gough, was his second wife, and they had 2 children, myself and my baby brother George Thomas[75]. She was a widow and had been previously married to Mr. Mansel Powell.

My Father had applied to take 10 families to South Africa to accompany his

---

72. HMS "Thunder" was a 74-gun frigate built in 1783 and broken up in 1814.
73. Battle of Ushant 1st June 1794. Lord Howe defeated a French fleet.
74. Mary Reed b 3 July 1797; William James Reed b.13 Jan 1799; Sarah Eliza Reed b 20 Nov. 1799; Henry John Reed b. 7 Mar. 1802; Charles Proctor Reed b. 24 Aug 1807; Louisa Reed b.21 Nov 1810.
75. James Samuel Reed b. 25 May 1813; George Thomas b. 1818/9

own family as a private party, as he had capital to fund the venture. These are some of the letters he wrote applying to take a party of 10 families.

4 Oxford Court
Cannon St.
20 July 1819
My Lord,

In the event of not being able to secure 10 able-bodied persons, would his Majesty's government have any objection of my emigrating to the Cape with my family, 8 in number (three of whom are of the age required, provided I make the same deposit as would be required by 10 persons or families?

Trusting your Lordship would excuse this liberty.
I remain your Lordship's humble servant.
Wm Reed[76]

4 Oxford Court
Cannon St
23rd July 1819
Sir,

The day before yesterday I took the liberty of addressing Lord BATHURST for permission to emigrate to the Cape with a family of 8 children on depositing the same sum as would be required for 10 families – but since when have been informed that my request was not like to meet with success. I now humbly request permission to emigrate with 10 persons or families under my charge on the conditions required by His Majesty's Government.

I am Sir very respectfully
Your most obed't humble serv't
Wm. REED
PS Will the settlers be allowed to take articles for their use freight free.[77]

4 Oxford Court
Cannon St
28th July 1819
Sir,

In reply to your letter of the 24th inst I beg permission to be allowed, with 10 able bodied persons, to emigrate to the Cape of Good Hope on the terms & conditions required by His Majesty's Government.

---

76. National Archives, Kew CO48/45,440
77. National Archives, Kew CO48/45, 458

> I have the honor to be Sir
> Your most obed't serv't
> Wm. REED[78]

My father, fearing that his application would be unsuccessful decided instead to join Mr. John Bailie's[79] party on the *Chapman*.

There were 600 applicants and only 256 chosen. Fortunately, our family was one of them.

As I sit in my old rocking chair made years ago in Kragga-Kamma where we had a business building wagons, I remember the smell of the sea, tar and mustiness of the unventilated hold of the *Chapman*. I hear the wind whistling in the rigging and the flogging of the sails being unfurled.

How excited we were when we boarded the *Chapman* in Gravesend to commence the voyage.

For a few days, we young ones jumped up and down on the ice which encircled the ship, to try to break her free, so we could leave. The children squealing with pinched cold faces and icy hands.

Before we left on the 3rd of December 1819, we did not realise what a moving ship felt like. Suddenly there was a lurch and our chests with all our possessions in them slid to the lee side. All the children screamed and even the moms let out vocal sounds or words of anxious fear.

Little did we realise what a long voyage it would be, nor how meagre our rations. Sometimes I wished that I had had something to do as I was an extremely energetic lad with an impulsive spirit who wanted to try my hand at anything I could. We had to be on deck during the day, with our quarters tidied before 8 am. Heads of parties were placed in the saloon on the upper deck and slept in bunks arranged around it. We had a tiny cabin leading off the saloon which had curtains drawn around the bunks. Early in the voyage my mother wanted to get some items out of her chest, but she was so seasick at that stage, that she called on Charles and Louisa my half-brother and sister to help her. It was so difficult that after taking out some plates and cutlery, for Frans the cook to ladle our food into, we sealed up the chest again.

My mother was very busy with my baby brother George Thomas, my only full sibling. She had to get over the seasickness but as she was breastfeeding, she

---

78. National Archives, Kew CO48/45, 484
79. Lt. John Bailie, (1799 – 18520. A member of an Anglo/Irish land-owning family and a former Lieutenant in the Royal Navy.

recovered quickly as mothers had to have great resilience.[80]

I remember the early days of the voyage being terrifying. The noise of the sails, the pounding of the ship hitting into the waves, the smell of seasickness of many passengers, children crying and some merely softly whimpering. As the days passed, and we reached warmer latitudes I began to feel at home as I got my sea-legs. One day Louisa came crying to my mother. She had got in the Frans's way in the kitchen, and he had accidentally slopped boiling water onto her, and she had been badly scalded. The ship's surgeon, Dr Daniel O' Flinn[81] was called to attend to her and dress her burns.

We sailed in company with the "Nautilus" under the command of Lieut. Cole, who had been fellow officer with my father in the navy. He gave me some naval buttons to sew on to my canvas suit. We had been given rolls of canvas from which to make wet-weather-gear which was standard procedure, and I was mighty proud of the buttons. The suit became disgracefully dirty and greasy, but I refused to remove it and became known as the 'dirty agent'.[82]

We were often thirsty as the water was foul and even boiling did not improve the taste. We were given rations of biscuits, salt beef, rum, tea, sugar salt and soap. I loved to sit on the deck and feel the sun on my small body and sometimes even hid behind a coil of rope to listen to the men who sat in groups on the deck and discussed the dreams they had of a better future in a land that sounded so beautiful, in fact like paradise itself.

On the 17th March 1820, our ship reached Table Bay with the majestic Table Mountain wrapping around it.

My half-sister Sarah Eliza had fallen in love with the dashing ship's captain John Milbank and in our excitement on imminently reaching land he proposed to her. She accepted. Talk on board was of a marriage. My father and the couple got permission to disembark so that they could get married in the Dutch Reformed Church,[83] by Special License, even though the ship was under quarantine, flying the yellow flag, due to whooping cough which had taken the lives of 3 infants.

We set sail again on the 26 March, bound for Algoa Bay.

---

80. Rivett-Carnac, Dorothy E.; "Thus came the English in1820"; Howard Timmins; 1961; Cape Town
81. Schoeman, Karel; "Baillie's Party, The new Land, 1820 – 1834"; Protea Book House; 2019; Pretoria.
82. Settler's Memories transcript of manuscript in the Cory Library, Rhodes University. Copy supplied by Mrs MD Nash. Notes by A. Porter
83. Settler's Memories transcript of manuscript in the Cory Library, Rhodes University. Copy supplied by Mrs MD Nash. Notes by A. Porter

There was great excitement as we approached at sunset on the 10th April 1820, almost exactly 5 months since we had left England.

> We descried a coast lashed by a broad belt of angry breakers, threatening, as we feared, death to a large proportion of our numbers. The shore girted with an array of barren -looking sand-hills, behind and close to which appeared a series of rugged and stony acclivities, and is the distance behind these the dark and gloomy range of the Winterhoek mountains frowned upon us—shutting us out, as it seemed from that Paradise of which we had so often and so fondly dreamed while on our long and perilous voyage.[84]

Government surf boats came out to meet us under the supervision of Captain Evatt[85]. Caution was required as capsizing with all the settlers' worldly wealth could have been tragic. We were the first to reach the beach and "my father jumped out of the boat taking me in his arms he placed me on dry land" so that I, James Samuel, was the first to land. I was always quite proud about that.[86]

> On arrival, we got our rations from old De La Harpe. His store was part of Store know as Blaine & Coin Jetty street behind the Phoenix Hotel, Old James Dagleush was Govt. Storekeeper and lived near Fort Frederick.[87]

The breakup of the Baillie's group began almost on arrival.[88]

Father, William Reed, who has been described as "a man of some capital and much industry" elected to stay behind with his family at Algoa Bay. He saw commercial possibilities, receiving three building lots in the fledgling settlement in lieu of a farm and buying a fourth. Governor Donkin was liberal in giving grants of land, and we received several.

Father built a store on the property owned by J A Holland[89]. This was encouraged in order to have a point of export for produce from Albany.

---

84. Schoeman, Karel; "Baillie's Party, The new Land, 1820 – 1834; Protea Book House; 2019; Pretoria
85. Settler's Memories transcript of manuscript in the Cory Library, Rhodes University. Copy supplied by Mrs MD Nash. Notes by A. Porter.
86. Schoeman, Karel; "Baillie's Party, The new Land, 1820 – 1834; Protea Book House; 2019; Pretoria
87. Settler's Memories transcript of manuscript in the Cory Library, Rhodes University. Copy supplied by Mrs MD Nash. Notes by A. Porter.
88. Schoeman, Karel; "Baillie's Party, The new Land, 1820 – 1834; Protea Book House; 2019; Pretoria
89. Settler's Memories transcript of manuscript in the Cory Library, Rhodes University. Copy supplied by Mrs MD Nash. Notes by A. Porter.

Father was contracted by Sir Rufane Donkin to build the Donkin Memorial, in memory of his late wife Elizabeth, after whom Port Elizabeth was named. I helped my Dad build the pyramid and the monument on the Donkin reserve. I led the oxen and brought the stone even though I was only 10 years old. It was very hard work. The foundation stone was laid in 1825. When it was finished, I was apprenticed to old Buffery[90] as a blacksmith for 5 years.

My father built a stone mansion for the family with twenty rooms. The garden was never cultivated and remained covered in bush, as it was too expensive to remove the stones. It later became known as Pullen erf after his estate was sequestrated.

He was an entrepreneur and went to Cape Town where he purchased merchandise and chartered a schooner to bring it to Algoa Bay. He never insured it and came home crestfallen as the schooner had sunk. He had lost everything. Not giving up easily he invested in a salt boiling facility at Smelly Creek. However, when the duty was taken off salt in England, he had to close the operation. In 1827, soon after this shock, father died. We were devastated and mother was heartbroken as she had now lost a second husband. Later my mother married Mr. Brown, that is a name reflected on the Reed family gravestone.[91]

Figure 22: Reed family gravestone

Figure 20: Elizabeth Elliot

Figure 21: James Samuel Reed

I married Elizabeth Elliott when I was 21 on the 18 February 1834 at St Mary's church Port Elizabeth. She was the daughter of Joseph and Cecilia Elliott from Cumberland and was born in 1818. Elizabeth and I had 10 children 5 boys and 5

---

90. Settler's Memories transcript of manuscript in the Cory Library, Rhodes University. Copy supplied by Mrs MD Nash. Notes by A. Porter.
91. Settler's Memories transcript of manuscript in the Cory Library, Rhodes University. Copy supplied by Mrs MD Nash. Notes by A. Porter.

girls. What a strong able woman I married. She supported me through thick and thin and was truly a pioneer, putting her hand to whatever was needed.

Besides running a blacksmith shop from 1835, Elizabeth and I, owned a butchery in partnership with my brother, George Thomas, and James Williams. From 1840, we ran the little Pier Hotel which later became the Palmeston and which is now the Campanile Hotel.[92] Here our eldest son William was born on 5 November 1840.

Many a game of whist was played there.

> I with old Charles Gurney,[93] our old Market Master, challenged to play 10 games of Whist against Mark Norden[94] and Dale, the pianoforte tuner, 10 Games for 100 pounds on PE versus G Town. Which was played in Hope Hotel Military Road & kept by Nathaniel Randal. PE won 1 out of 10.

Once I remember WB Frames made a bet, he would attend church with head shaved and one whisker, he won the bet. He was a Liberal Man. His store was on the Spot the Custom house Stands. The rendezvous for Captains. Kept the best liquor. One day took in his Head after attending a Temperance meeting, told his wife who was one of old J Berry's daughters to place on the table a Bottle of Water with glasses & when the captain came as usual all drink was stopped. From then WB Frames was a Strict abstainer.[95]

We chartered ships to take horses and bullocks to Mauritius, where they were exchanged for sugar. George was the buyer of stock and I the bookkeeper so when the chartered boat was loaded I had to take off my butcher's apron and go to Mauritius. The worst job was catching these wild oxen and getting them on board

---

92. 1840—James Samuel Reed opened the Pier Hotel in Jetty Street, it later became known as Dreyer's Hotel. From November 1848 Francis Wasley took over the hotel and ran this as the Palmerston Hotel and it became known as Wasley's. There was a hotel on this site for 150 years. The original house was considerably extended over the years and became known as the Palmerston. A new hotel, the Campanile was built in 1924/5 McCleland Dean;"Port Elizabeth of Yore:The Palmerston, its predecessors and successors"; http//thecasualobserver.co.za;2015
93. Charles Gurney, born in 1778, was the leader of the party from Deal Kent which arrived aboard the Weymouth. He established a fishing settlement near the mouth of the Swartkops in the area now known as Deal Party Estate. Later on, he was appointed market master. He died in Port Elizabeth on 12th July 1853. A son, Charles, came with him in 1820. McCleland Dean;"Port Elizabeth of Yore: Charles Gurney"; http//thecasualobserver.co.za
94. Marcus or Mark Norden was born probably around 1791. Sarah, his sister married to John Norton, Benjamin and Joshua Davis were all amongst the earliest British Jews who settled in the Cape. Hazel Duikers family history . www.hazeldakers.co.uk;
95. Settler's Memories transcript of manuscript in the Cory Library, Rhodes University. Copy supplied by Mrs MD Nash. Notes by A. Porter.

with slings.[96]

The firm had a contract to feed the convicts. Large pots of soup were cooked by my old mother, who used to walk down Main Street to see me every morning. She would pick up all the iron horseshoes she could find and put them into a black bag under her dress.

People she met would ask her, "Why are you picking up that old Iron?"

Her reply was "On the instruction of my son Jim".

This cargo was off loaded in my smithy shop. On her return, she picked up all the rats thrown onto the street the night before and into the black bag they went. Some questioned her as to why she did that?

She would reply' "On the instructions of my son George and to fatten those rascals, the convicts".

Into the pot they went, so strengthening the brew![97]

The Brig, *Blackaller*, was driven ashore in a South Easterly gale on the 26th March 1846. Fortunately, no lives were lost[98]. Our firm purchased it. There was a need to break her up and I being a blacksmith was elected to do it with the help of 6 men. It was difficult backbreaking work and we needed a boat to get out to her. I would leave early after breakfast and generally came home at one o'clock for dinner. My bookkeeper, P M Williams, was an inquisitive man and while I was having dinner he decided to go and investigate the wreck. He wandered down to the beach to find a drunken sailor who offered to take him out to the ship in our punt.

They came alongside the wreck, but the sailor was too drunk to throw the rope. None on board heard any call. The boat sliding past and drifting out to sea, the man singing "Brittannia". One of the men, swam to the shore to report. I rushed down, undressed Jumped in and swam about 2 miles, before I reached the boat. It took longer than I write this you bet, to get to the boat, only to find Williams in a feint from fright and the sailor, still singing, dousing Williams with salt water. Then I was in a fix to take both oars in order to get the Boat back to the Ship. I heard it was 4 pm when I landed. Many people Congregated.[99]

---

96. Settler's Memories transcript of manuscript in the Cory Library, Rhodes University. Copy supplied by Mrs MD Nash. Notes by A. Porter.
97. Settler's Memories transcript of manuscript in the Cory Library, Rhodes University. Copy supplied by Mrs MD Nash. Notes by A. Porter.
98. Settler's Memories transcript of manuscript in the Cory Library, Rhodes University. Copy supplied by Mrs MD Nash. Notes by A. Porter.
99. Settler's Memories transcript of manuscript in the Cory Library, Rhodes University. Copy supplied by Mrs MD Nash. Notes by A. Porter.

In 1846 I had a blacksmith's shop and wagon makers establishment at Kragga-Kamma. I was ordered to the front with my brother George who was the wagon maker. We had to leave our wives and children on the farm, 6 new wagons in the shop, 50 horses and mares and about 170 head of cattle. We had hardly got to the Fish River, when a band of Xhosa (War of the Axe refers)[100], shifted our stock, drove our women from the farm, and burnt everything.

Six months later we returned penniless. We succeeded in getting another wagon and oxen together and had to start from scratch, ploughed the land and re-established the shop.

The wagon and oxen were then commandeered. My wife and two children, Eliza Anne and William James, along with twenty other wagons were on the way to Grahamstown along the Addo when the Xhosa attacked and took all the oxen. My wife and children were obliged to walk back to Kragga-Kama almost dead from fatigue and hardship.

No person of today can have any conception of what those brave pioneers, the 1820 settlers went through.

We had come from England to what we believed was a land flowing with milk and honey and, found in reality an exceedingly difficult terrain.

> Then we had besides the enemy, wolves[101], Jackals, wild dogs and Tigers[102]. No poison was available. Every beast not in [a] good Krawl[103] was one less the next morning. Horse sickness started in October 1854. My son William, with help, shifted about 200 mares and foals to Schoenmakerskop. Tragically 70 died.[104]

In 1852 the Reed firm was given the contract to deliver post for the western area for 100 miles from Port Elizabeth.

Later the partnership in the firm was dissolved, and I became an auctioneer. I bought Thornhill in 1854 for £3500, the Zwartkops pontoon in 1855. In 1858, Reed Capper and Company established a service of passenger carts between Port Elizabeth and Grahamstown.[105] The Sunday's River punt was bought 1859 for

---

100. Rivett-Carnac, Dorothy E.; "Thus came the English in1820"; Howard Timmins; 1961; Cape Town
101. Hyenas
102. Leopards
103. Paddock
104. Settler's Memories transcript of manuscript in the Cory Library, Rhodes University. Copy supplied by Mrs MD Nash. Notes by A. Porter.
105. Rivett-Carnac, Dorothy E.; "Thus came the English in1820"; Howard Timmins; 1961; Cape Town

£4750. The right of way to operate the punt was leased from the Uitenhage Council for £300 p.a. The punt was operated successfully for 10 years, then in a dispute, the Uitenhage Council sued me to deliver the right of way and remove my punt. We fought to keep the right of way, both by preventing a successor to operate it as well as a Supreme Court action. As Capper my partner, had died, I had no redress which caused my surrender.[106] My son William, then made an offer to the principal creditor W.R. Metlerkamp through JS Kirkwood to pay an amount and my estate was then released from insolvency.

My brother George and I served on Port Elizabeth's Municipal Council for 5 years from 1860.

In the same year George arranged a hunt for Alfred, Prince of Wales, who had arrived in Algoa Bay aboard the *HMS Euraylus*.

> "This gentleman (George), who was one of the best hearted of plain-spoken burgesses of Port Elizabeth was the life and soul of all manly sports. On meeting the Prince, he explained, 'I am a rough chap, Your Highness. My name is George Reed.'"[107]

They shook hands and became firm friends. A successful hunt ensued during which the Prince and George bagged two fine buck and three hares.

In 1856 My eldest son, William, who had been a difficult boy had played truant from school, ran away on a ship bound for Mauritius because he had been severely punished for truancy. We were beside ourselves with worry and did not know where he was for many months.

In his words:

> I played truant about 10 years. Was So Severely punished that I ran away to sea on the brig *Emperor*. Nobody knew I had cleared. This brig sailed to Natal, Mauritius and India. I was away 18 months. When Capt. Scorgie, commander of the Barque *Shepherdess*, which was struck on the rock at Receife all hands lost, happened to come aboard the *Emperor* and recognised me. He reported to the Governor, who to my surprise came on board and brought me home. Had Captain Scorgie not seen me. I would not have come on shore . . . parents or no for I was punished too severely for this truant playing. ,

---

106. McCleland Dean (2018). "Port Elizabeth of Yore: The Macay Bridge over the Sunday's River". http//thecasualobserver.co.za.
107. Redgrave JJ MA; "Port Elizabeth in Bygone days."; The Rustica Press Ltd.; Wynberg Cape; 1947

and I was happy on board the *Emperor*.[108]

We had lots of sadness too. We lost sweet Louisa in 1841 she was only 3 years old. She was also interred in the Reed Family Grave. Years later Emily Jane was born in 1854 and died 6 years later.

On the 5th November 1900, I arranged to meet William my eldest son and two of his brothers at the Palmeston Hotel at 11am. William was unaware that we were to celebrate his 60th birthday. Once we had assembled I, James S Reed ordered the waiter bring a bottle of the best Champaign. Glasses were filled. I raised a toast and said to my boy:

> I wish you many happy returns of the day. We will drink to your 60th birthday. What happens this day will never happen again, that after 60 years, a father, toasts the health of his son in the very hotel in which he was born.[109]

So much happened in the last thirty years of my life. My children have grown up and I have grandchildren and great grandchildren. My daughters: Eliza Anne, Louisa, Anne Elliot, Emily Jane and Amy Flora have all sadly passed on before me. My five sons, William James, James Joseph, Henry John, George Thomas and Arthur Clarence have been very strong. The blacksmith shop and butchery remained financially viable.

I recovered my finances and when I die, I hope to leave an inheritance to my boys. Elizabeth was an amazing companion and faithful wife to me and only passed away in 1895. I miss her dearly.

Our settlers' community in Albany has changed completely.

> They are now no longer the outer bastion of the colony and are themselves leaking out into the wide world of Southern Africa. [110]

My son George Thomas married Fanny Ledger[111] in St. Pauls church, Port Elizabeth on the 27th February 1871. After 11 years of marriage, Fanny gave birth to Cecily Emily Mabel Reed on the 14th May 1881. She was born in an ox-wagon on the banks of the Sand River, where George was trading guns and horses with the

---

108. Settler's Memories transcript of manuscript in the Cory Library, Rhodes University. Copy supplied by Mrs MD Nash. Notes by A. Porter.
109. Settler's Memories transcript of manuscript in the Cory Library, Rhodes University. Copy supplied by Mrs MD Nash. Notes by A. Porter.
110. Redgrave JJ MA; "Port Elizabeth in Bygone days."; The Rustica Press Ltd.; Wynberg Cape; 1947
111. The Ledger family arrived in Port Elizabeth on the "Warwick" In September 1858. Fanny Ledger was 7 years old. Bull, Esme; "Aided Immigration from Britain to South Africa"; HSRC; Pretoria; 1991

Boers. They now live on a farm in the Cradock area called Goia. Being an only child, she was a very lonely little girl, and she told me how she played with black children making oxen and wagons of clay. She was educated at a convent school in King Williams town and became an accomplished equestrian. Cecily aged 19, George and Fanny have recently returned from Australia where George had an interest in an opal mine and the trading of horses.[112]

So, bye for now and farewell; I need to rest.

The Last of the Settlers

James Samuel Reed died on 25 May in 1902.

He was son of Lieutenant W. REED, R.N. who arrived in South Africa in the *Chapman*. The party was located at North End, an area which subsequently became known as Chapman Gardens. He it was who so 'largely assisted in building the monument on the hill' stated his obituary. He is also credited with having established a post cart service from Port Elizabeth to Grahamstown. He was associated with Capper in the establishment of the pontoon at the Sundays River. The pontoon became known to early travellers as Capper's Ferry. At the time of his death, Mr. Reed was living at Pine Cottage, North End.[113]

Post Note

Cecily Emily Mabel Reed was the writer's grandmother.

Figure 23: Ceclily Emily Mabel Reed

Figure 24: Elizabeth Elliot

Figure 25: George Thomas and Fanny Reed

---

112. Memories as told first-hand by Cecily Emily Mabel Reed to her daughter and granddaughter Edel Johnson and Nanette Townsend.

113. Newspaper cuttings from the Eastern Cape. Newspaper unknown. www.1820Settlers.com

Norton I, Emperor of the United States and Protector of Mexico

(Joshua D. Norton, 1819-1880)

By Robert Ernest Cowan [114]

Joshua Davis Norton (1818-1880) was one of the three sons (Philip and Lewis or Louis being his brothers) of John Norton and Sarah Norden. Sarah was one of the two daughters of Abraham and Abigail Norden (of Smithfield and Hammersmith in London). They came to South Africa on the *Belle Alliance*. Joshua attended John Hancock's school in Grahamstown. In 1844, he owned "Gingerbread Hall" near the Baakens River. He failed in business in Port Elizabeth and joined his parents in Cape Town. Following the deaths of his parents and brother Louis, Joshua joined the rush to find gold in California, landing at San Francisco in 1849.

"Every age has its peculiar folly; some scheme, project or fantasy into which it plunges, spurred on either by the love of gain, the necessity of excitement, or the mere force of imitation." Thus has a gifted writer laid down a human law as universal as the human race itself.

Figure 26: Joshua A. Norton

All cities have had that singular class of eccentric individuals commonly and generally known as 'characters.' Of these San Francisco has had perhaps more than her share. The years from 1860 to 1875 were generously prolific of these freaks.

Some were impoverished, soiled and ragged; some were hopelessly woebegone and pathetic; some in their personal appearance were fantastic or picturesque; some were noted for sheer strength of character and vitality of obsessions; others, less few in number, were those who retained the gentility of their happier days and bore themselves with consistent and conspicuous dignity to the end.

In San Francisco in the sixties, the popular promenade was through the streets Montgomery and Kearny from Jackson to Sutter. Here in the late afternoon might

---

114. Printed in the Quarterly of the California Historical Society, October, 1923.

be seen as in a rapidly shifting kaleidoscope, a most unusual procession relieved here and there by the injected 'characters,' who lent life and colour to the warp and woof of that most strangely variegated tapestry. A small army they were, each member living his own life and absorbed in his own mysterious schemes. Here were 'George Washington Coombs,' known also as the 'Great Matrimonial Candidate'; 'Old Rosey'; 'Money King'; 'Robert Macaire'; the 'Gutter-Snipe'; 'Old Crisis,' and others, all of whom long since have passed into oblivion. And in this motley throng though never of it, appeared 'Emperor Norton.'

Joshua A. Norton was his real name. He was of Hebrew parentage, born February 4, 1819, probably in Scotland. Of his earlier life nothing is known as he rarely spoke of it. Before coming to California he had been for some time at Algoa Bay, Cape of Good Hope, where he was a member of the Cape Mounted Riflemen. He finally reached San Francisco in December 1849, having come from Rio de Janeiro on the Hamburg vessel *Franzika*.

Norton at once engaged in business. He was occupied in extensive transactions in real estate, and many tremendous operations in importation commissions. His native shrewdness was even unusual; his intelligence was wonderfully clear, and his business judgement was remarkably accurate. To this acumen were added the rarer attributes of a sound and inflexible moral and financial integrity. Some of these commissions involved transactions to the extent of several hundreds of thousands of dollars weekly, and Joshua Norton rapidly became wealthy. He had brought with him to California, $40,000, and towards the close of 1853 he had amassed a fortune of a quarter million of dollars.

Figure 27: Joshua A. Norton

In 1853, in association with one Thorne and others he attempted to control the rice market. Earlier he had operated heavily, had been uniformly successful, and was applauded for his daring and foresight; co-operation was offered and accepted from other large firms and an immense quantity of rice was secured and held. Everything was promising for yield of immense fortune as profit, as rice was then thirty-six cents per pound in bulk, unloaded. Almost the last pound of rice in this port had been purchased by the combination. The profits were being calculated when two unexpected cargoes of rice arrived, which the combination could not take up nor control. The market was drugged and prices fell much below cost. To add to the general disaster, in order to protect themselves, some of the associated firms sold out and Norton was financially ruined. He contended stoutly to his closing days that one well-known firm owed him $60,000.

Extensive litigation followed. The first of these cases was that of Ruiz Hermanos vs. Norton, et al. In this contention Norton was sustained in the lower court, but upon appeal this decision was reversed by the Supreme Court. This was in November 1853. Other serious embarrassments followed, and the sacrifice of his extensive holdings of real estate, principally around North Beach, was the last chapter of his unfortunate disaster. The previous excitement of false expectation and shock of these disappointments coupled with the legal troubles constituted a severe blow to Norton's sanity. He retired into obscurity, and when he emerged in 1857, he gave palpable and distinct evidence of an overthrown mind.

His obsession took the form of a belief that he was the Emperor of the United States.

He claimed that by an act of the legislature of 1853, he had been made Emperor of California. With this he was dissatisfied, and not unreasonably so, for he argued that California was but one of a union of states, and as such could neither loyally nor logically create an emperor. Further, as he would not renounce what he styled the 'national cause,' the act was accordingly suppressed.

The earliest printed proclamation of the self-created Emperor appeared in 1859.

> At the peremptory request and desire of a large majority of the citizens of these United States, I, Joshua Norton, formerly of Algoa Bay, Cape of Good Hope, and now for the last 9 years and 10 months past of S.F, Cal.[115], declare and proclaim myself Emperor of these US.; and in virtue of the authority thereby in me vested, do hereby order and direct the representatives of the different States of the Union to assemble in Musical Hall, of this city, on the 1st day of Feb. next, then and there to make such alterations in the existing laws of the Union as may ameliorate the evils under which the country is laboring, and thereby cause confidence to exist, both at home and abroad, in our stability and integrity.

---

115. San Francisco, California

NORTON I, Emperor of the United States. 17th September 1859.

Having assumed the sword and the plume, Norton I actively entered upon the many duties that pertained to his royal station. It is of interest to note that the pretensions of Norton were early recognized by the public of San Francisco and as speedily humoured. His name had temporarily disappeared from the city directory, but in Langley's issue for 1862, we find the following: "Norton, Joshua, (Emperor), dwl. Metropolitan Hotel." His empire was established and Norton I, Emperor of the United States had begun to reign.

One day at this period, some important news was received from Mexico, and in this as in all such matters, the Emperor was greatly interested. In a spirit of levity some joker stated that Mexico needed a protector, and suggested that Norton was the logical choice. Thereupon 'Protector of Mexico' was added to the official title and retained for almost a decade. It was dropped during the unhappy career of Maximilian, for, as Norton sanely and even prophetically observed: 'It is impossible to protect such an unsettled nation.'

The imperialistic duties were manifold, comprehending grave affairs both national and international. The civil war gave him deep concern. On July 12, 1860, he declared the Union dissolved. Early in the war he declared a blockade, and in 1862 he issued a mandate to the Protestant and Catholic churches to publicly ordain him as Emperor, that he might more efficiently bring order out of the chaos into which the country had been plunged by the violent conflict and fierce dissensions of its rebellious people.

Some of the proclamations to be found in the contemporary journals were jokes which originated with the graceless wags and inspired idiots of the day. Others, of which one or two are extant, were the inspiration of Norton alone. They are couched in terms of sanity and composed in superior English. Most of them are national in purport and bear upon relations with Great Britain, Russia, Mexico and other foreign countries.

Others relate to the affairs of the civil war. One has survived which is entirely personal. In February 1860, the Emperor desired to visit Sacramento where the legislature was then in session. The Steam Navigation company denied him transportation. Norton issued an order to the commander of the revenue cutter to blockade the Sacramento River until the offending company could be brought to terms.

The proclamations which were issued as jokes are easily to be recognized. Norton had no part in them as they were the work of the conscienceless wags and amiable villains of the times. One of these fictitious documents was issued in observance of the forty-sixth birthday of the Emperor:

> Owing to unsettled questions between His Majesty Maximilian I, El Duque de Gwino, The Tycoon, the King of the Mosquitos, the King of the Cannibal Islands, &c.;, the usual display of bunting on foreign shipping and on public buildings, in commemoration of our 46th birthday, will be omitted. Feb. 4, 1865.

Another proclamation was to the effect that the Emperor contemplated marriage, but to avoid arousing jealousy among the fairer sex, he played no favourites, and they were to decide for themselves which one of them should be Empress.

Falsified telegraphic news was also a source of great amusement for the versatile wits.

In 1864, Jefferson Davis telegraphed to inquire if it were true that Norton was in sympathy with Lincoln, also the request that $500 be sent, as Davis had but one pair of trousers, and even that was worn out. Another telegram was from Lincoln. The President thanked the Emperor for his support, and said he had a good story to tell but at present was too busy settling accounts with a seedy individual named Davis.

Norton was instructed to proceed to Petaluma, there to remain until further official notice. What the Emperor thought of these effusions will never be known. But interlinear reading is not altogether difficult, for in many directions the mind of Norton was unusually clear, and at all times he was remarkably philosophic.

During his long reign the equanimity of the Emperor was never seriously disturbed except by the actions of two individuals.

The first of these was D. Stellifer Moulton, formerly New York correspondent of the Boston Traveler. In 1865, he proclaimed a monarchy and styled himself, 'Stellifer the King, Reigning Prince of the House of David, and Guardian of Mexico.' Stellifer was of fine education and possessed luxurious tastes, but unlike Norton, was entirely insane. He had lived at the leading hotels in New York and Boston, and when dunned by them had agreed to pay upon receipt of his claims against the United States Treasury for $3,500,000, which was to be his semi-annual allowance. In a republic such regal ambitions are not always appreciated, so the authorities apprehended Stellifer the King, and promptly sequestered him.

This state of affairs was too much for our Emperor. He, himself, was of the House of David, and also was he not Protector of Mexico? He purged his soul of its bitter resentment which flamed forth in the following:

PROCLAMATION.

Down with usurpers and impostors! Off with his head! So much for cooking other people's goose! The legitimate authorities of New York are hereby commanded to seize upon the person of one Stellifer, styling himself King or Prince of the House of David, and send him in chains to San Francisco, Cal., for trial before our Imperial Court, on various charges of fraud alleged against him in the public prints.

NORTON I Emperor of the United States and Protector of Mexico.
S. F. 6th day of Nov. 1865.

The other member of the grossly offending duo was Denis Kearney, famed for his sand-lot statesmanship and anti-Chinese oratory. For Denis, the Emperor favoured speedy judicial extermination. At the same time the new Constitution also exasperated him, and he denounced it as high treason. He would have destroyed it but was willing to have the eminent attorney, Hall McAllister legally annul it.

In personal appearance the Emperor was always a picturesque and striking figure. He was of medium height, heavy-set, with hair that was inclined to curl, heavy eye-brows under a massive forehead, moustache and beard that became a royal personage, and clear and penetrating eyes. His garb was of navy blue cut in military style and profusely adorned with brass buttons. The shoulders were surmounted with massive gilt epaulettes, sometimes tarnished from exposure. In the earlier years of his reign he had worn a military cap embellished with red trimmings, which is quite familiar in the cartoons of that time. About 1865, one of his loyal subjects presented the Emperor with a tall beaver hat, which was thoughtfully decorated with a cockade of feathers and a rosette. The cap had outlived its usefulness and was laid aside forever. The hat, replaced from time to time, continued to be the regal headgear until the close of the Emperor's reign. In 1867, one of his subjects had sent from Oregon a large and unusual specimen of grapevine intended for a walking-stick. It was shod with a ferule and gold-mounted, and thereafter constituted his sceptre. He was never without it, but in inclement weather he carried also an umbrella, knowing wisely that royalty may be drenched and that his kingly authority was no greater than that of his illustrious predecessor, Canute.

He bore a sort of resemblance to Napoleon III, which fact when commented upon brought forth the ridiculous rumour that Norton was the son of that ill-starred monarch.

This misstatement, so obvious in its utter absurdity, was hatched in the scattered brains of some irresponsible contemporary, whose living prototypes, loud with vacant volubility and rich in historical misapplications, are yet in our midst.

The private life of the Emperor was simple. For seventeen years he had lived at the Eureka Lodging House, and the regal apartment was not palatial. It was a room of 6 x 10 feet in dimensions, with threadbare carpet and disabled furniture. The chief mural decorations were portraits of the foreign rulers and his collection of hats. His familiar figure was seen and known everywhere. He was a constant attendant of churches, theatres, musical affairs, civic gatherings and school commencements. He was deeply interested in higher education and in the earlier days of the University was a frequent visitor. He was fond of children and to them he was always gentle and courteous.

There was at that time a Lyceum of Free Culture of which he was a member, and there he sustained many debates most intelligently and logically. It is said that he had some interest in spiritualism, but in which direction is not known. For sustenance, he had the freedom of nearly every restaurant in the city, as also of every saloon. He was unusually abstemious, and if he frequently appeared in the popular saloons of Barry and Patten and 'Frank's,' or in the famous 'Bank Exchange' and the 'Pantheon,' it was not in quest of liquor, but of 'free lunch.'

It was his custom to visit the markets and the docks, and to view buildings in process of construction. This was not from idle curiosity but from genuine interest, for in all these and kindred matters he was keenly informed. From time to time visits were made to men of affairs, and the Emperor had that rare discretion that never permitted himself to be regarded as a nuisance. He was even welcomed, for his own business training had taught him to appear at a suitable time and to retire at a proper moment.

He had never met with royalty but once, and that distinguished personage was Dom Pedro, Emperor of Brazil.

No sketch of Norton would be entirely complete without some reference to 'Bummer' and 'Lazarus,' the two dogs that enjoyed the freedom of San Francisco in the sixties. Lazarus was a wretched beast of low degree, and Bummer was but little better. But in some of his long gone ancestors there must have been a strain of nobility, for it was Bummer who sniffed this in the Emperor, and thereafter associated himself with the royal presence, with the miserable Lazarus as a humble retainer. This was not of Norton's choice, but-nobleness oblige. [116][117]

Figure 28: Emperor Norton, Lazarus and Bummer - Edward Jump

---

116. Bummer and Lazarus went everywhere with him. No theatrical performance opened in San Francisco from 1855 to 1880 that three complimentary tickets for the first row of the balcony were not put aside for Bummer and Lazarus and Norton I, Emperor of the United States. Samuel Dickson—San Francisco is My Home

117. The old vagrant 'Bummer' is really dead at last; and although he was always more respected than his obsequious vassal, the dog 'Lazarus,' his exit has not made half as much stir in the newspaper world as signalised the departure of the latter. I think it is because he died a natural death: died with friends around him to smooth his pillow and wipe the death-damps from his brow, and receive his last words of love and resignation; because he died full of years, and honor, and disease, and fleas. He was permitted to die a natural death, as I have said, but poor Lazarus 'died with his boots on'—which is to say, he lost his life by violence; he gave up the ghost mysteriously, at dead of night, with none to cheer his last moments or soothe his dying pains. So the murdered dog was canonized in the newspapers, his shortcomings excused and his virtues heralded to the world; but his superior, parting with his life in the fullness of time, and in the due course of nature, sinks as quietly as might the mangiest cur among us. Well, let him go. In earlier days he was courted and caressed; but latterly he has lost his comeliness—his dignity had given place to a want of self-respect, which allowed him to practice mean deceptions to regain for a moment that sympathy and notice which had become necessary to his very existence, and it was evident to all that the dog had had his day; his great popularity was gone forever. In fact, Bummer should have died sooner: there was a time when his death would have left a lasting legacy of fame to his name. Now, however, he will be forgotten in a few days. Bummer's skin is to be stuffed and placed with that of Lazarus. — Mark Twain

Edward Jump, then a young man, was the popular cartoonist of the sixties. In numerous of his cartoons he had introduced the well known figure of the Emperor. In one of these, Norton is depicted at a free-lunch table satisfying the royal appetite, and beneath him are the two dogs awaiting the crumbs. Bummer as usual is alert and confident; Lazarus stands meanly, looking even more dejected than he did upon the morn of his resurrection. This caricature was displayed in a local shop-window where it was seen by Norton. It was the only time throughout his long reign that he was known to exhibit signs of violence. He savagely growled, "It is an insult to the dignity of an Emperor!" and crashing his stick through the window, destroyed the offending print.

Figure 29: The funeral of Lazarus

Once only was he arrested. In 1867, a newly-appointed, young and zealous deputy apprehended Norton and took him before the Commissioner of Lunacy. The next day when brought before the proper authorities he was promptly discharged with an apology. The verdict was, "that he had shed no blood; robbed no one; and despoiled no country; which is more than can be said of his fellows in that line."

There were returned to him the key of the palace, and the imperial funds amounting to $4.75 lawful money. For these the Emperor gave his royal receipt. During all of these years the Emperor had lived. From June 15, 1858, he had been a charter member of Occidental Lodge, F. and A.M., and the Masons, it is said, had paid his room rent. Voluntary subscriptions were made by the faithful among his subjects, and when the treasury was depleted he was accustomed to levy a tax of varying but small amounts. For these he invariably gave or offered a receipt in the form of a promissory note. This was a printed scrip which bore a vignette of the Emperor and was payable in 1880. It had been his purpose to exchange these for a new series, payable in 1890 at 4%.

The last hoax played upon him was also the crowning effort of the graceless, witty scamps of his realm. Norton was induced to believe that by marriage with Queen Victoria, he could bind closer the ties of the two great nations. Telegrams of congratulations upon the approaching happy event were found among his effects.

These purported to be from Alexander of Russia, Beaconsfield, Grévy, former President Grant, and others.

The close of the Emperor's life and the end of his long reign came on January 8, 1880. Early in the evening while standing at the corner of California street and Grant avenue, he was observed to fall. Assistance was rendered immediately, but ten minutes later the Emperor was gone. Death had been caused by sanguineous apoplexy. An autopsy by Doctors Stivers and Douglass, made with special reference to the brain, disclosed the fact that that organ was quite normal, and the more unusual fact that it weighed 51 ounces. The costs of the funeral were provided by Joseph G. Eastland, R.E. Brewster, and the members of the Pacific Club. The final ceremonies were conducted at the Morgue, and the eulogy was delivered by Rev. N.L. Githens, Rector of the Church of the Advent. It is estimated that 10,000 people of all walks in life came to view that silent figure, which rested in a wilderness of flowers. A lady, well-known and of high social station, with her own fingers pinned upon the lapel of the sleeping monarch a beautiful boutonnière of hyacinth and a spray of fern, remarking quietly that Norton had been kind to her when she was a child, and he was in the heyday of his success. He was interred in Masonic Cemetery.

For twenty-three years the Emperor had reigned in his fantastic realm. His were the best-known features in San Francisco, and many hundreds of citizens yet live who vividly remember him. A striking portrait of him, painted by Benoni Irwin, was formerly in the chess-room of the Bohemian club, and a familiar little Terracotta figure, possibly by Mezzara or Wells, may yet occasionally be seen.

The question of the insanity of Norton has been debated, but the evidence would appear to be in favour of the entire sincerity of his belief. At the time of his disaster he was but thirty-five years of age, and with his great abilities might easily have regained his fortune or created a new one. But that single, twisted convolution lay uppermost and for twenty-three years dominated his purpose. Poor, sometimes soiled and shabby, pathetic and philosophic, but always with a noble mind, he bore himself with dignity amid his squalid surroundings with one fixed and unvarying purpose, and that was consistently the welfare of his people. The heritage of honour and integrity that he had handed down while in his affluence, was never squandered nor dissipated, and so he bore the respect and goodwill of the best of his people to the end. The jokes played upon him had been harmless, and the merriment that he sometimes excited had been without the bitter venom of ridicule.

If sincere, his was a career of long heroic sacrifice; if an impostor, he must be ranked as one of the most extraordinary of that class who has yet lived. He left no successor.

The emoluments of an unattractive throne and an empty royalty were not alluring; there was none strong enough to follow him; and finally the world was entering upon an epoch of materialism in which there is no provision for such a monarch. From that strange stage through the doors of oblivion, thus passes forever Norton I, Emperor of the United States, and Protector of Mexico.

L'Empereur est mort.

In the same month, at a Low Jinks of the Bohemian club, a gifted and beloved member, the late Dr. George Chismore, presented this beautiful tribute:

NORTON IMPERATOR
No more through the crowded streets he goes,
With his shambling gait and shabby clothes,
And his furtive glance and whiskered nose--
Immersed in cares of state.
The serpent twisted upon his staff
Is not less careless of idle chaff,
The mocking speech or the scornful laugh,
Than be who bore it late.
His nerveless grasp has released the helm,
But ere the Lethean flood shall whelm
The last faint trace of his fancied realm,
Let us contrast his fate
With other rulers and other reigns,
Of royal birth or scheming brains,
And see if his crazy life contains
So much to deprecate.
No traitorous friends, or vigilant foes,
Rippled the stream of his calm repose;

No fear of exile before him rose,
Whose empire was his pate;
No soldiers died to uphold his fame;
He found no pleasure in woman's shame;
For wasted wealth no well-earned blame
Turned subjects' love to hate.
No long and weary struggle with pain;
One sudden throe in his clouded brain
Closed forever his bloodless reign,
With every man his friend.
For Death alone did be abdicate.
What Emperor, Prince or potentate,
Can long avoid a similar fate
Or win a better end!

Figure 30: Emperor Norton

Fetcani command (1827-8)

By Thomas Stubbs[118]

He came to South Africa as a boy with the 1820 Settlers. He spent most of his life in the border area. The reminiscences were written between 1874 and 1876. They recount a short episode in his long life when he participated in the Fetcani command as a young rascal.

A report was brought to Graham's Town, that there was a nation of cannibals destroying the Xhosa in the neighbourhood of the Bashee. The whole frontier was in an uproar. Orders were issued by Major Dundas, then Commandant, for preparations for defence and attack. The troops were to march to Xhosaland, the outposts to be occupied by civilians who could not muster a horse, the mounted men to go to the front. There was only one man to be left in each house in Graham's Town.

Figure 31: Thomas Stubbs

I was apprenticed at the time, but as my brother John, Richard Southey and others of my friends were going I asked to go also. I mustered a horse, and we were served out with guns and ammunition, that had been taken from the Dutch, at the

---

118. Maxwell W.A & McGeogh, RT (1978). The Reminiscences of Thomas Stubbs. AA Balkema, Cape Town.

taking of the Cape. Mine was a carbine about two foot six inches long mounted with brass, with a lock large enough for a cannon; it took a strong arm to pull it off. The powder was so bad that if you fired at anything at forty yards it went click — then fizz for some time —and then pop, about as loud as the grunt of a middling sized pig; the bullet which was split into four fell about half way.

Well, such were the arms we had to fight the cannibal with! The troop I was attached to was about one hundred strong under the command of Captain Crause, a half-pay officer. The force were ordered to Fort Beaufort, and started in the morning.

I and Mr Rafferty were not quite ready as we had to make up our pack, for we had a pack horse. We got away four o'clock and reached the brave army sometime after dark. Of course Rafferty joined his mess of middle-aged men, and I joined mine some distance from him. They were all young men. After some time talking, I proposed we should open a bottle of wine, as I knew Mrs Rafferty had two bottles packed up for him. One was a glass bottle the other a stone one, there were also a lot of sandwiches and cakes done up in a cloth.

We emptied the glass bottle and put it into a pack and broke it. The next morning on the top of the Koonap Rand, I and some of my friends remained behind where we emptied the other bottle and finished the cakes. We off-saddled at the Koonap river — Rafferty and Stringfellow (he is just now dead, 1875) were sitting together when I was called to get the wine and cake out. "Oh lor! How now Tom?" I put my hand into the pack; of course I kept my back to them and pulled it out quick, and said the bottle was broken.

"Try the other one it is stone that will not be broken," said Rafferty, I said, no, but here was another misfortune, the cork had come out and it was empty. Poor Rafferty swore a bit and then said, "Get out the cakes." This was almost too much for my gravity. I pulled out the cloth, at the same time telling him they were all smashed to pieces. He said with an oath, "Pitch them to the Devil."

I was glad when the word saddle-up was given, for I felt vexed with myself for what I had done. But there it was— it was no use crying over spilt wine. We next off-saddled at Leeuw Fontein for the night. William Stanton was on horse guard but left his post as he said he heard a lion. The next morning there a report that old Bill Clayton had stolen his comrade's rations, Stanton was also reported. But Captain Crause said he would leave it to the men themselves. Donald McDonald, father of the McDonalds in the Queens Town district was Sergeant of Guard. The two prisoners were brought up to the Guard House—alias a Xhosa hut. I shall never forget Stanton, who was a very young man at that time refusing to go in, when McDonald, who was as strong as a giant, said "Gang in we ye" and just took him by the breeches and the neck and put him as easy as I could a cat.

A court was duly formed, and old Mr Thomas Nelson, merchant in Graham's Town was Judge. The prisoners were each sentenced to a dozen cuts with a double bridle riem[119]. Stanton threatened all sorts of actions at law. So to give him an opportunity of having plenty of it, it was arranged for one out of each mess to give a cut. After he had received his share, poor old Bill was brought. It was the fashion to wear leather crackers at that time. Old Bill had a pair on that had been wet and dried on his breech in a sitting position; so when he stood upright they formed a large bag behind, and a small one on each knee. When the cut was made, he drew himself in, the riem fell harmlessly on the bag behind, which sounded like a drum.

The old fellow giggled and laughed to himself, until old Pote, who was a Portuguese, and had been in a man-of-war, came to give his cut. He swung the riem round his head, and gave a grunt. Old Bill drew himself in, but unfortunately for him, Pote reserved the blow until old Bill filled the bag with his posterior, when down it came fit to cut him in half. "Oh! my G-d!" he cried, "I aye gotten."

This was the last, so we saddled up, and started for Fort Beaufort — which consisted of about a dozen huts — which we took possession of. The next day I was ordered to join a patrol to look for spoor and on my return to camp I found rations of grog had been served. I asked Rafferty if he had received mine, he said, "Oh yes; but the one bottle is broken, and the cork has come out of the other." That was enough for me.

The next night there were a great many of the men having a spree. There was one mess, called Gilbert's party. He had brought most of them from Cape Town to build the Cathedral in Graham's Town for which he had the contract, (and out of it made his fortune). One man of the party named Dennis Cary was put on sentry above the drift to see no one passed. About 9 o'clock Joe Buller came to me and said, "Let us have a bit of fun with Dennis Cary, he is on sentry." All right. When we got pretty close to him he called out, "Who comes there?" "Friend" "Advance Friend". "Ah! be the power, is that your-self?" Joe told him he thought it, very hard he sentry all alone while his comrades were having a spree, if he liked, he would take his place while he went and got a drop.

He embraced the opportunity, gave Joe the gun and off he started. He had not been gone long when Joe said "You go tell him I have bolted with the gun." I found him about half screwed, told him that fellow had gone with his gun. Off he started

---

119. Leather thong.

to the place, and called out all sorts of names without effect. At last, he took a piece of old rafter, and marched up and down with it over his shoulder. Joe had hidden himself behind an old wall some little distance off. I started for the guard house and found old Mr John Mandy, sergeant of the guard. I told him the man above the Drift, was walking sentry without a gun.

He called out two men and went to make Dennis prisoner on their arrival, Dennis called out, "Who comes there?" "Guard" said Mandy. "Where is your gun? Men make him a prisoner."

As the two men advanced, Dennis brought the pole to the charge and then brought it round with such force, that he felled one of them to the ground. The others rushed in and made him prisoner; marched him off. But when they came opposite the hut where Gilbert's party were drinking and singing, Dennis said, "Be the powers, Mr Mandy, let's be going in and, have a wet before we go to the guard house" — which they did, and remained there until the morning: the guard house had to look after itself. After a week's spree, we were ordered back to Graham's Town. I believe the whole thing was got up by the frontier Xhosa—to draw the troops out of the Colony, for them to make a rush in.

But finding the whole frontier on the alert and outposts occupied by the civilians they 'funk't' it, and so ended the great Fetcani War.

Figure 32: Grahamstown, 1827 - H. Coburn

The Loss of a good Wife

by Thomas Shone

He was born on 6 August 1764 and emigrated to South Africa in 1820 on the *Nautilus*. He had lost his wife on 26 December 1837 leaving him with six children to care for. This loss seems to have increased his drinking. On 30 June 1838 he resolved to mend his ways. This extract from his diary gives a look into the day-to-day struggles and life of a settler 18 years after coming to South Africa.

1838[120]

Saturday 30 June. Resolved to drink no more Spirits for the space of twelve months, if I live so long, with God's help.

Figure 33: Two men drinking at a table - Frederick Timpson I'Ons

Saturday 30 June. Went to Bathurst. I Called at two Canteens. Resolution[121] wanted a glass, but I gave him none. Came home. Went to George Bager for the newspaper, meets Hodgkinson on my return. He tries to pull me off my horse, we fight, he proves a Coward.

---

120. Please note this diary is not a direct transcription of the diary. Some parts have been left out and wording standardised for ease of reading. For the direct transcript see: Silva, PM (1982). The diaries of Thomas Shone. MA Thesis, Rhodes University. Available at: http://hdl.handle.net/10962/d1005799

121. Resolution seems to be his want of alcohol.

Sunday 1 July. Sunday PM went to Bathurst to see James Armstrong. Took tea with Mr & Mrs McCarty. Asked to take some brandy three times by James Armstrong: Resolution wanted a glass, I gave none.

Monday 2 July. Went to Mr Hartley's. Resolution wanted a drop: I gave him none, as he had been treated so many times.

Tuesday 3 July. Worked on the land; no temptation to drink.

Saturday 7 July. Mended a boot for Pikes, 2 Sk[122]. The same day went to Bathurst for meat, to Mr Hartley's. Resolution said "Give me a glass," I said "No, you will want more, so I shall give you none."

Sunday 8 July. At home all the day; wrote a letter to my son George.

Saturday 14 July. Finished harrowing and picking up potatoes, pulled some thatch off the old house, and went to Bathurst for meat. No desire to. . .

Sunday 15 July. At home all the day.

Monday 16 July. Loaded the wagon with six muids[123] of potatoes and two hundred of forage for Town[124].

Tuesday 17 July. Left home with the wagon for Town, spanned out at Cooper's place. Treated James Armstrong with a glass of brandy. Resolution I treated with a glass of water, but he wanted a glass of wine as it would do him good. I told him if I gave him a glass of wine he would then want a glass of Brandy, and he must be contented with a glass of water. James Armstrong likewise found an Iron Vice, which he gave to me. We again spanned out for the night at Mrs Heley's place. Got supper and went to rest.

Wednesday 18 July. Inspanned for town. Called at Jolly's Canteen. Treated James Armstrong with a glass of brandy. Gave Resolution none. Sold two muids of potatoes for 20 Rix dollars, and three camp kettles for three half-crowns, and some pig potatoes for three Shillings. We then proceeded to Town and out spanned at my Son's place, and went to Mr Pinnock to breakfast. He charged me half a crown, for my breakfast and James Armstrong's.

Thursday 19 July. Inspanned for the Market and sold two hundred of oat hay for Eight Rix dollars. No person would buy my seed potatoes in the Market. Likewise, I sold to my Brother-in-law 12 Camp Kettles of Potatoes at 10 rix dollars per muid, and the two muids of seed potatoes to Mrs Dixie for 2. Check shirts, 2/6 each; 2 pair worsted Stockings, 1/- each; a piece of calico, 16 Ells, for 7/6; and 3/ 6

---

122. Skillings
123. A weight measure.
124. Presumably Graham's Town.

in money. Bought at Howse Sale 10 Quire of paper, 5/6; twelve pair socks, 6/6; one dozen of lucifer matches, 1/6. Bought from my brother-in-law Meal, 5/-; Sugar, .., Cwt, 10/1; coffee, 10 Ib, 8/4; Tar 1/6; a pair of Spectacles, 2/-; one piece Calico, 16 Ells, 6/9; two sacks, 2/-; one pound pepper, 1/-; Steel pens, /6. Meat from Mr Simpson, 45 Ib, 5/7t; three sheep heads /9. Bought at Temlett's store 5 lb of fat, 2/6; Bread, 1/-. At Mr Pitt's half a paper of hemp, 3/9; Pitch and rozin, 1/-. At Yarrington's, black lead pencil, /4; slate pencil, /3; cases for pens, /4. Went and in spanned for home. Out spanned at Carlisle's for 4-hours. Inspanned for Cooper's. Out spanned at Cooper's, took supper and went to rest.

Friday 20 July. Took breakfast, inspanned for home. Arrived safe, delivered my cargo, shaved, took dinner, mounted my horse and returned to town. Inquired for German, heard he was at William Cockcroft's, took supper at my Son's (George), and Slept with John.

Saturday 21 July. Rose early, went in search of Thomas German, found him at William Cockcroft's house. Waited on him all day. Gave Resolution a glass of beer, took my meals at my son's house and slept with John.

Sunday 22 July. Took breakfast and went to find my horse, found him, and returned to dinner. Went to Mr Monro's Chapel in the evening, came to my son's, took supper and went to bed.

Monday 23 July. Waited on German, got his money and paid some debts for him. Gave Resolution a glass of aniseed, bought some things at my son's for German, Sugar, 25 lb. The weather looks dull, as if it would rain. Goes to bed and waits until morning.

Tuesday 24th July. Gets a cup of Coffee and some bread and meat, mount my horse and German mounts John's horse for my home. Unsaddle horses at Cooper's for two hours. I take dinner for /9 and gave Resolution two good glasses of water instead of brandy. He would like to have had a glass, for he said it would do him good, but he got none. German took two glasses of Wine, when we on saddles for home. Arrives safe; German is very lame and laid up.

Wednesday 25 July. Makes a pair of pumps for John Tharrat, 6/-.

Thursday 26 July. Takes them home, drinks a basin of Coffee and a piece of bread with Thomas Foss; rides to T. Ingram to buy some Indian corn, buys none. Bought a cheese 1/ 6, 3 lb. Rides off to Bathurst with a letter for my son George. Calls on Corp. McCarty, takes dinner with him, and coffee with Mr Lindsey. Buys at Thomas Hartley's 1/2 lb bluestone, 17t. Rides home; all is well.

Friday 27 July. Digged in the garden. Transplanted some pomegranates and figs. Greased my riems[125] and throat-straps. Let Mary go to Bathurst with Mrs McCarty.

Tuesday 31 July. Digging in the garden, put a pair of Boots on the trees, made a girth for my saddle. Rode to the fort at Bathurst, took tea with Corpl. McCarty and brought Mary home. Resolved not to give Resolution any more Spirits on account of having treated him for this 30 years and upwards. So I find that if I listen to him, in my Old days he will try to be my ruin, so no more for you, my old Chap.

Wednesday 1 August. At 10 AM. mounted John's horse for Graham Town. Arrive in town a little before 2PM. Delivered to John a pair of boots I had to stretch, and £3 Sterling I Gave to my Son George in part of payment of a bill of Dr Atherstone. Took from German's keg a Canteen of brandy for him, brought home my Wellington boots, mounted my horse for home. Treated Resolution with a glass of beer at Smith's beer shop, Graham's Town. Bought from Temblets 2/- Ginger bread, 2/- biscuits, rode for home. Called at Cooper's, drank 1 of Glass of beer, /6 : very dear. Mounted my horse and rode home, arrives safe at 25 minutes past 7 in the evening.

Thursday 2 August. Began my day's work by digging in the garden before breakfast. After breakfast went and gridded two chisels and my spade at Pike's. Received from Mrs Pike 4 1/2-, a debt due for mending Sarah's boot. Came home, went to digging in the garden all day. Wattled a little bit of the Hen house in the evening. Sarah went to Bathurst to buy some meat, 12t lb, 2/1; Soap, 2 1/2 lb, 1 / 8.

Saturday 4 August. Digging in the garden; planted some wheat in the garden. Cleaned my Clock. Resolution finds himself a great deal better now, then when I used to give him brandy. Therefore, I shall give him no more, as he is so well satisfied.

Sunday 5 August. At home all the day. Laid down on the bed for several hours, and took a good sleep, not having much Sleep the night before. Very uncomfortable in my mind for the loss of my amiable partner. The loss of a good Wife is great pain to the mind of the unfortunate husband who is the Sufferer.[126]

Monday 6 August. My birthday: I am 54 years of age. Ploughed part of back piece. Obliged to leave off ploughing, having a severe pain in my back. In the morning me and Henry dug a small piece in the garden. In the evening I made the Children some tammeletjie[127] as a treat on my birthday.

---

125. Leather thongs.
126. Sara Shone died on 26 December 1837 aged 44.
127. A traditional South African sweet.

Wednesday 8 August. Digging in the garden, ploughed a land in back piece. Went to Mr Davies to borrow his harrow. Sarah went to Bathurst, sold Mr Hartley 2 dozen of Eggs for 2 Shillings, bought 21lb of beef for 3/6. A shower of rain about 8 o'clock in the Evening. Very unhappy since the death of my beloved wife.

Thursday 9 August. Set out a bed of onions. Afterwards I went to James's Party to try to buy some Indian corn. I could get none. Called on George Brown, took dinner with him. Went to Bathurst, called at the two Canteens to try to buy some corn. Resolution had no desire at all for brandy. I think he sees the folly of drinking such stuff, and spending his money for nought. Likewise, I called on Corpl. McArther and took something to eat with him. Called on Mr Lindsey also, and then rode home.

Friday 10 August. This morning Thomas German started for Graham Town. Digging in the garden all the day. Borrowed from Mr Davies 22 3/4,lb of Rice.

Saturday 11 August. Rode over to Mr Pike's to get some barley and some rye, took breakfast. Inspanned six oxen and went to Joshua Davies to fetch his harrows, and some wood to make me a harrow. Came home and sowed part of back piece with barley and rye, and harrowed the whole piece. Dug a small piece in the garden and planted some horse radish. This evening my Spirits are very low when I think of my poor old woman, one of the best of wives. I shall never be happy

Sunday 12 August. Rose early this morn and prepared to get ready for Chapel, where I heard the Revd. Mr Bingham preach a sermon respecting the pureness of God and the beauty of holiness, and the righteousness of man before he is fit to enjoy that which is prepared for all them that love the Lord. His expressions on the subject were beautiful; they made me look at my own heart, which I found to be desperately wicked and self-righteous. At the same time I had an earnest desire to be saved, and often times prayed to the Lord to make me one of his Chosen people. And I believe that the Lord as often blessed me, but being possessed of many darling sins, which I could not part with on account of their worldly nature, Satan found means to deceive me.

When I take a retrospective view of my life, and behold the goodness of God towards me, a Vile sinner, for so many years, I am lost in wonder at the mercy and goodness of God to obstinate sinners, and which as caused me often times to say, 'Here is a proof that he desires not the death of any sinner, but rather that he should repent and live .' For when I look back to the year of 1800, when lived with an opulent merchant in the City of London, and who was a Christian called by the world a Methodist, this family loved me.

Being young I would not listen to them, yet the Lord did not forsake me, but followed me from one County to another. To the best of my recollection, think it was in the year 1807 or 1808 when I joined the people of God called Methodist, at a place Called by the name Givit[128]. In this place I found some comfort, but it did not continue long, for my poor old Father, being in the habit of allowing me some money every three or four months, for some years caused me to turn aside to enjoy the pleasure of sin, and sink deeper into the mire. Likewise, I will tell you the snares which Satan laid for me, and which answered his purpose well. He said, 'You see, those people who pretend to serve God are worse then you, for you are honest and not deceitful. But only look at them and you will see they are hypocrites, they are deceitful and unjust. As for your getting drunk now and then, it is nothing, they do the same privately and you do it publicity.'

Satan gained me to listen to him with attention, and as I was confident that there were many in the Society of this character, I thought I was better out of the Society then to remain with a people who pretended to serve God, and I was confident they were serving the Devil. I once spoke to a Minister on this subject; his answer was to me that it was a place for such characters, and I must not expect to find them perfect. His answer did not suit my mind, as I expected when people joined the Christian church they tried, with God's help, to forsake wilful sins and not to live in them as I have seen them do, and which as always been a Stumbling block to me, and made me forsake the society of such and take to the pleasures of Sin. For I have said, "If these people be saved, I am sure I shall too."

The next place that the Lord was pleased to visit me in Mercy was at a town in France called Sarrelibre, or Sarrelouis where resided a great many people called Methodist. The preacher was a sailor, a Quartermaster of one of his Majesty's ships of war. His name was Mr Biggs, and if there was ever a good Christian, Mr Biggs was one, for 'by the fruit ye shall know them,' as the scripture says. This kind-hearted man talked to me like a father many times, and I promised him many times to forsake sin, but I continued to follow the pleasures of sin. Yet the Lord, I believe, was so good to me as not to forsake me altogether, for my Conscience often upbraided for living in sin. When I knew that the Lord had commanded me to live holy, yet I was so bound in the snares of the devil as to continue to serve him for many years after this period, until my joining the Society called Methodist at Clumber, in Albany, South Africa, where I enjoyed, I believe, the love of God for a season. But Satan had not done with me.

This Society was full of very ignorant people, not given to drunkenness, for

---

128. Givet, in the Netherlands, upon the River Meuse, belonging to France

they were too selfish even to buy themselves the common necessaries of life. These people were backbiters, slanderers, Covetous, continually quarrelling among themselves, and picking holes in other people's coats, and so self-righteous that they did not allow any other sect to be entitled to go to heaven but themselves. All these defects Satan laid before me, which made me very uncomfortable in my mind, to see people professing to serve God, and at the same time faithful servants to the devil. I say these peoples was the cause of my falling away; and I have never had the resolution to meet with them again. Yet my Conscience has told me a thousand times since that I am wrong for taking notice of others, for 'What is that to thee? Follow thou me.'

I have a great desire at this present time to join in society with any people who are seeking of Christ faithfully and sincerely, having forsaken their sins and leading new lives. Of late years the Lord as been pleased to chastise and afflict me for my stubborn way, and it is good for me to be afflicted, I believe. For when I view his spared mercy towards me, am confident that he does not desire the death of any sinner, but rather that he should repent and live, as I am now a monument of his spared mercy, and it pleased him to take to himself one of my Children[129], which afflicted me very much. He also suffered the Xhosa to spoil all my substance and when he found that these warnings had no effect upon my stubborn heart, in his mercy towards me, desiring not the death of a sinner, he still spares me, But takes from me one of the best of Wives, a fond mother, a virtuous and faithful partner, beloved by all who knew her. She died the death of the righteous, having confidence in God, her Saviour. Again I say how merciful the Lord has been with me, to the present time. My whole desire is to be a true disciple of the Lord Jesus. May God grant me strength to serve him faithfully to my life's end. Amen.

Wednesday 15 August. Planted some Indian corn. Made a pair of boots for Mrs Hiscock's Child, received the money, 4/. Rec.d from Mary Low 4/ 6 for a pair Shoes and 2/ from Mrs Davies, the whole of my account with her. My son George arrived at our house this evening.

Thursday 16 August. Started on horse back for Graham Town. Off Saddled at Mr Curl's canteen for one hour. Paid sixpence for a bundle of forage for my horse. Started again for town. Mr Brown wished to treat Resolution with a Glass of the best brandy. I told him never to give him any, for if he did, he would want more, for he was never satisfied when ever he received a glass. Therefore, I never gave

---

129. Elizabeth Shone, aged 11, went out to herd cattle on 1 November 1832. She did not return. The next morning Thomas Shone and George Hodgkinson went to look for her and discovered her body in a "wolf-hole" She had been raped and murdered. A Xhosa herdsman of the Hulley Family was later hanged for the murder.

him any myself, or suffered others to treat him. I arrived in town safe, and bought from J. Phillips a bag of rice for 25 rix dollars. Paid in part one pound seven Shillings, leaving a debt of 10 / 6. Bought from Mr Pitt some kip leather for 10/6. Slept with J. Phillips at my Son George's.

Friday 17 August. Took breakfast and waited to see Mr Carney's wagon start for home with some things for me. Went to see Mr Moscrop of the Royal Artillery. Bought 3 penny buns and a pint of beer. Paid Mr Monro sixpence for a draught, having a severe pain in my bowels. Went in search of my horse to go home, but could not find him, but J. Phillips found him towards the evening. Very much fatigued. Staid all night and slept with John Phillips.

Saturday 18 August. Got breakfast and started for home very early. Met my son George on Manly's flat, rode on to Cooper's, off saddle and gave my horse a bundle of forage. Had a little talk with Tom Forse and John Tharratt. John Tharrat treated Resolution with a glass of beer. On saddle for home. Arrives at the same time as Mr Carney's wagon arrives, and gives the wagoner Enoch one shilling for his trouble. Lays down on the bed for an hour, goes in the field and helps the children to cut some oats. That finishes the day. Brought home four pair of Wellington boots to be stretched for Mr Phillips. Brought home for German some brandy, some sugar and Coffee, a paper of nails and some Shirts.

Sunday 19 August. I am very sorry to say that this Holy day as been taken up with too much of the world's business, in idle talk and other worldly things. But if the Lord be pleased to spare me to see a few more Sabbath days, I live in hopes I shall be able to give a better account of myself. For I declare to you that my living in a state of sin often makes me shudder. My trials since the death of my beloved partner has been great, which caused me to give way to drinking more than usual, knowing that, when I had lost her, I had lost the only faithful and true friend I ever had since I have been a man, and in whom all my comfort ever rested. It is true I have had many quarrels with that good woman when in a state of intoxication, and when sober I have often grieved and lamented to my self for ill—using so good and kind a Creature as my beloved Wife. For when I have asked her pardon for my bad conduct towards her, she as granted to me full pardon with that goodness of heart which as often made me cry to think how bad I have been to one of the best of wives, who was beloved by all who ever knew her.

As a Wife she was a faithful and true partner. As a Mother she was tender and affectionate, and loved her Children dearly. As an acquaintance, an agreeable companion, no tale-bearer or slanderer, but whenever she talked with such characters as these, her discourse was so lovely that they always went away ashamed of themselves. I am very unhappy, and always shall be, on account of losing such a woman as my wife, and if I was now fit to die, I would willingly depart to join with her, to sing praise to that great redeeming God. Yet I feel a desire to live on account of my poor children, That I may, with God's blessing, help to defend them from the insults and snares of this wicked world.

May the Lord enable me to teach them to walk in the way of his commandments, doing his will here on the earth, as the Angels, do it in heaven. May the Lord grant his Holy Spirit to enable us all to do it, for Jesus Christ sake, Amen.

Monday 20 August. This morning I cut out 2 pair Boots, closed them, and made one boot. The Children and Susan were reaping the oats in Lamas[130]. Sarah went to Bathurst for meat, Bought at Mr Hartley's 19lb of beef, 3/2. My mind is very uneasy on account of Sin, the enemy of man, likewise on account of my being in debt, and very little prospect at present of ever being able to pay all my debts. The Cursed Xhosa have been my ruin, and the Government at home have used us most rascally, on account of our case being laid before them by the enemies of the Colony. At the same time they would not listen to men who was capable of declaring the truth, and did declare the truth to them, but their words of truth respecting the Colony was as pearls among Swine, for they took no heed at all of what was said in favour of the poor ruined Settler.

Tuesday 21 August. My mind is still perplexed what to do.

Wednesday 22 August. My mind is still very uneasy on account of my children, which way I can provide for them the best. When a good mother is gone from her Children, and they are left to seek their own fortunes, hard is their lot, for the world is full of deceit and wickedness.

Figure 34: Back view of house in Beaufort St, 1835 - Frederick Timpson I'Ons

---

130. One of his fields.

Early Years of the Baptist Church

Rev. H.J Batts[131]

This introduction to the first years of the Baptist Church in South Africa was written for the centenary of the church. It provides insight into some of the characters involved in the early church.

A Mr. William Miller, a Settler of 1820, is regarded as the Founder of the Baptist Church in South Africa. In Professor Cory's Settlers' list there are two William Millers, one aged 29, with Mandy's party per ship *Nautilus*, and another with Gush's party, aged 42, per ship *Brilliant*, with whom was his wife Elizabeth and three children—Elizabeth aged 8, Mary Ann 6, and John 2. The William Miller of the Gush party on the ship Brilliant is he who is considered the Founder of the Baptist Church in this land. There was a John Miller with the Gush party, who was a younger brother of William.

Figure 35: William Miller, 1854 - Frederick Timpson I'Ons

All South Africans know that the great depression in England caused by the Napoleonic Wars led to much emigration from England to the Colonies, and those known as the Settlers of 1820 came out to South Africa in the hope of finding means of livelihood, and some opportunity for improvement and advantage at present denied them in the home country.

It would seem that the British Settlers to South Africa, when possible, were chosen of parties representing certain religious beliefs, presumably that there should be no disagreements on the voyage out in matters of faith, for in those days differences were sometimes very acute. The Gush party was Wesleyan, but as not a sufficient number of Wesleyan's volunteered for this particular party, the proper complement was made up by a number of Baptists, some seven or eight, who must have been peaceable folk, and evidently did not quarrel with their co-voyagers. In this party were the two Millers, William and John. The name of Jas. Temlett, who died in Grahamstown in 1862, during the

---

131. Extracted from Batts, HJ (Unknown). The story of 100 years: 1820-1920. Maskew Millar.

ministry of the Rev. Alexander Hay, appears in this list, whose descendants are with us to this day in the Alice and Queenstown districts. I find a number of other names of persons in different parties who have been associated with our Church life. I cannot say in every case whether they or only their descendants belonged to our Communion—such as Neat, Nelson, Kidwell, Wheeldon, Wilmot, Webber, Sterley, Rowles, South, Ralph, Hobson, Lord, and Shepperd. These are well-known names to many living today.

By a general understanding Mr. W. Miller is acclaimed the first pastor or leading brother among the Baptists of the 1820 Settlers, whose spiritual work began in Lower Albany, and if reports be true, they met for worship under a tree on the farm which now belongs to the honoured Senior Deacon of the Grahamstown Church, Mr. Stephen Smith. There these pioneers, like the Pilgrim Fathers of an earlier date, from the same stock, and with the same traditions, claimed their freedom to worship God according to the dictates of conscience, untrammelled by State restrictions or sacerdotal interference, and they set up their banner and reared their altar there long ago in the name of the Lord God arid Jesus Christ, His Sent One, and it is our joy to-day to honour their memory and to possess their heritage. They were sturdy men—men of faith and conviction, and the ground which has through the century brought forth abundantly was honoured by their prayers, and blest by their devotion.

The party in the ship *Brilliant*, Mr. Hockey tells us, were Wm. Shepperd (elected leader of the Baptists for the voyage) and family, James Temlett and family with William Miller, members of the York Street Baptist Church, London, Mr. and Mrs. Trotter, and Mr. and Mrs. Prior, members of Eagle Street Church. It is said that they had a meeting at once on arrival to express their thankfulness for the mercy of the safe deliverance, under a mimosa tree in front of William Miller's tent —(is this that which is on the farm of Mr. Stephen Smith ?)—(Miller was baptised in 1808 by the Rev. Edward Saunders, in the Edward Street Church, London)—and goes on to say: It was a strange way God had led them, but a right way, and they went forward in the name of the Lord God of Hosts, believing in the precious promises of the Gospel—that He. who had brought them hither would never leave nor forsake them.

> They held their joys in long suspense
> And thought of rest and home,
> Then wept with holy confidence
> Of brighter days to come.

They were removed in the first instance to Salem, where William Shepperd erected a small cottage, in which they held religious services, and formed themselves into a congregation, with William Miller as preacher. And here blessing came—the first person to be baptised by Mr. Miller was a Mrs. Rainer.

A short time after this W. Miller visited Grahamstown, and was invited by a few Baptist Brethren to conduct occasional services there, which he did, often walking the whole distance to do so. He preached in the house of a Mr. Paine, an old schoolmaster of some repute, from whom several men who became influential

Figure 36: The converted carpenter's shop

received their first rudiments of learning. The cause was said to prosper here, Mrs. Payne being added to the Church by public profession in baptism. After this the carpenter's shop was used, and W. Miller settled in town. Converts were immersed in a stream called Craggie Burn, which ran through the garden of Mr. Sellers whom many of us knew.

John Miller gave the ground on which the first chapel was built, and Brother William laid the foundation-stone and preached the sermon when the building was opened for worship on Sunday morning, from Psalm 132, verses 8 and 9. In the evening the Rev. W. Barker, of the L.M.S., preached.

A dispute arose, it would seem, over Mr. Miller's teaching, and it was determined to send for a minister to England, and with that in view the Rev. Mr. Dyer, of the B.M.S., was approached. This led to the appointment of the Rev. Mr.

Davies. It is thought that Miller was a hyper-Calvinist and intolerant.

The exact date when William Miller moved into Grahamstown from the country does not appear, but there were heavy floods in a season that was wild and unkindly, and he being a handicrafts man, opened a carpenter's shop, in which place services were held on Sunday, at the corner of Bathurst Street and Market Street, in the part of the town called Settlers' Hill—the dwelling-house is standing to this day. Mr. Cross suggests "that there might have been a division in the congregation, for there was a Mr. Duxbury who conducted services during Miller's time. He was a Settler, whose descendants are living now in different parts of South Africa." It is quite possible that they had a plurality of pastors, or Duxbury might have been one of the recognised preachers.

There is a reference in the pamphlet called "Methodism in Grahamstown" to a carpenter's shop on Settlers' Hill, where services were held. It adds: This was the only place of worship in the town for some years, so the Anglicans and Baptists were glad to have the use of it for their services, and a half-dozen services were generally held there on each Lord's day.

I am indebted to a relative of Mr. Duxbury for the following information, which reached me after the Assembly of 1920, which explains a great deal. I had not known of this gentleman before. It is written from Dordrecht, Cape Province, signed E. J. Duxbury, and dated September 18th, 1920.

He says:

> I was grieved to notice that at the Centenary meeting of the Baptist Conference (? Union) held in Grahamstown in April last, no mention was made of the pioneer work of the first Baptist preacher in South Africa of my grandfather, Mr.—afterwards the Rev. S. M. Duxbury, who came out with the British Settlers in 1820. My grandfather was in earlier life in business as a weaver in Bolton, Lanes., and consequent upon the commercial depression after the close of the Napoleonic Wars, he joined George Smith's party of Settlers as a Baptist preacher, and with his wife, son, infant son and daughter, sailed with other Settlers by the ship *Stentor*.
>
> This party was settled between the mouths of the Kowie and the Kleinmonde Rivers. My grandfather's labours were originally confined to the neighbourhood of Port Francis, as it then was, and Bathurst, but subsequent to the drought and rust period, and when the Settlers' capital was transferred from Bathurst to Grahamstown, he with his family removed to the latter place, where he continued

his Church work. Here both of his youngest children—Hannah and John—died. After labouring in the Baptist cause in Grahamstown till 1830, he proceeded with his wife to America, and accepted the call to the Haverstraw Baptist Church, New York.

His only surviving son, William, my father remained in South Africa, and did not accompany him to the U.S.A. The surviving grandchildren are Adv. W. S. Duxbury, M.A. (Oxon), Pretoria; Mr. A. J. Duxbury, 'Jakalsvlei,' Mowbray, C.P., and myself.

This is valuable information, as we had nothing definite concerning Duxbury beyond the fact that he was a Baptist preacher. However, Mr. E. J. Duxbury's statements are supported by the Rev. H. Dugmore, who refers to him in his volume, 'Reminiscences of an Albany Settler,'[132] and the Rev. Mr. Ayliff, in his diary, has a reference to a Wesleyan devotional service at either Bathurst or Fort Francis in 1823 or 1824, at which 'Mr. Duxbury, the Baptist preacher, was present.'

In a letter written by Duxbury from the U.S.A. later, recounting among other things his ordination in the church at Haverstraw, says:

'May the blood of the everlasting covenant make you perfect in every good work to do His will, working in you that which is well pleasing in His sight. To Him be glory My wife joins in kind respects to Mrs. Nelson, Mary Ann, and Edward. Salute my friends in Christ, Kidwell, all the surviving Fords (Mrs. John Geard, of whom more later, was a Ford), Mrs. Dixie and her husband, Mr. and Mrs. Overs, Mr. and Mrs. James, John Miller, and other of whom I may not think at the moment.'

There is no mention of William Miller in the letter. A descendant of Kidwell many years ago settled at Jamestown, near Aliwal North, and in the early days of our Baptist Union offered us land for Church purposes in Jamestown, but seeing no prospect of undertaking work there it was not accepted—this within my recollection. His name was often mentioned at our Executive meetings. A son of this Mr. Kidwell, a Primitive Methodist minister, has been prominent in the recent Settlers' Celebrations in the City of Grahamstown. Aliwal North and district is the only part of South Africa where a European Methodist Church exists which is not Wesleyan.

In considering the origin of the Church in Grahamstown, Mr. Hay thinks that some years elapsed before a Church was formed, as the Settlers were confined to their settlements. This may be so, but there is evidence that some of the Settlers, for

---

132. See page 20.

various reasons, did not remain long at their settlements, and Mr. Miller was likely one of them. It seems also fairly certain that the carpenter's shop already referred to, in which he carried on his business, was the place of assembly for worship not only for Baptists but for Anglicans as well, and it gives Miller a place of prominence in Baptist enterprise which seems to justify the impression that he was the Founder and Leader, though perhaps along with others, of the Baptist Church in South Africa. Incidentally, it may be said that several of us living to-day well remember Mrs. Miller, widow of John Miller, William's brother, and mother of the late Mrs. Thos. Grocott, a name that is still loved and cherished by us all.

Mrs. Miller lived for years after Mr. Cross became the minister of Grahamstown, and during Mr. Nuttall's ministry there. She was a very interesting old lady, who might have supplied much information which would be valuable at this present time. I knew her very well. Mr. W. Hay has copied the following from Miller's tombstone, which stands in the Baptist burying ground, Grahamstown, which is of upright slate:—

To the Memory of
— WILLIAM MILLER —
who departed this life 29th of November, 1856
aged 77 years and six months.
Deceased was one of the British Settlers of 1820,
and founder of the Baptist Church in South Africa.

On golden harps they praise His name,
His face they always view; Then let us followers be of them,
That we may praise Him too. Their faith and patience, love and zeal,

Should make their memory dear; And, Lord, do Thou the prayers fulfil
They offered for us here.

Also
ANN
the beloved wife of the above,
who departed this life 28th January 1857

Mr. Hay also furnishes from the old *Grahamstown Journal* the following advertisement, November 15th, 1832:—

The Baptist Chapel will be re-opened on Sunday, 18th inst., when three sermons will be preached —in the morning by the Rev. Jas.

Munro; afternoon, by Rev. W. Davies, Baptist Missionary from England; evening, 6.30, by Rev. Mr. Satchell. A collection will be made after each service to assist in liquidating the debts.

And later:

> November 22nd:—It affords us much pleasure to notice the arrival of the Rev. W. Davies, who has come out under the auspices of the Baptist Missionary Society, for the purpose of taking charge of the Baptist Church, which has been long formed here. It will be in the recollection of many of our readers that this gentleman suffered shipwreck in the 'Eclipse,' which struck on the island of Palmas in the beginning of February last, on which occasion he and his wife sustained much personal suffering, and also a severe bereavement in the loss of their only child. As this severe dispensation has caused much anxiety, we now cordially congratulate this body of our fellow Christians in the realisation of their long-cherished expectations. The Baptist Church was opened on Sunday last, on which occasion the pulpit was occupied by the respective ministers of the three dissenting congregations— (the English Church was Established in those days, hence the term 'dissenting'—Ed.)—and we trust that the cordial feeling this exhibits may never suffer the slightest interruption.

From this we learn two things, that a church had been long in existence, and the sad story of the shipwreck and loss the Davies' suffered on their outward voyage. According to Mr. Cross, there is a slight inaccuracy here. He says that on the occasion of the wreck Mrs. Davies gave birth to twins at Las Palmas. One died and was buried on the beach, the other was named Palma, and he was brought out with them. They had to return to England and await another ship, and finally about a year after arrived in Port Elizabeth, the date of which, November 1832, is furnished us by the *Grahamstown Journal*.

It would seem that the Brethren, on the death of Mr. Miller or before, entered into correspondence with the B.M. Society, who selected and sent out their new minister, whose voyage, in this instance, was so untoward, and whose sufferings were so great. The devotion and persistence of the Davies' after their great trials en route surely call for remark, and indicate something of their character.

Mrs. Davies died at Bathurst in 1837, and he in 1838. Mr. Cross adds: "Some of those baptised by Davies were in the Church in my time. There was a chapel then, now three cottages in St. Bart's Street, but in my day called Chapel Street, Setters'

Hill."

Mr. Hockey, who gives Davies' own account of the shipwreck, says he did not know Davies, but many of Davies' contemporaries he knew well. Davies' record must have been published somewhere, and to Mr. W. Hockey I am indebted for this long quotation. He says:

> Captain Davies—of the barque *Eclipse*, by which he journeyed—was found to be a gentleman attentive to our wants, as far as it was in his power. The first part of the voyage was pleasant, nothing to interfere with our comfort except one stormy night in the Bay of Biscay. It was about nine o'clock in the evening of that day—a day ever to be remembered. What we did not expect came upon us. How suitable Solomon's advice: 'Boast not thyself of the morrow, for thou knowest not what a day may bring forth.' Mrs. Davies had retired to rest, with her dear little boy, the Captain, Mr. Eager, and myself were sitting in the cabin, we had a fine breeze, all our sails were set, and under a full canvas we were cutting through the water at about eight knots an hour.
>
> The Captain appeared gloomy, and was evidently not without some apprehension of danger, he was not sure whether we had passed the Canary Islands or not. This led to a conversation on shipwrecks, which however shortly died away, and all was silence, nothing was heard, but the dull splashing of the waters, the creaking of our timbers, and the heavy measured footfall of the watch above us, made indistinct sometimes by the quick and hurried trampings of the sailors, as duty called them along the deck. There is something melancholy, dreary, something sublime in circumstances such as these fearing every moment that some evil was near at hand, yet hoping the while that our lonely barque would pursue the even tenor of its way, still blessed with the same tranquillity and safety which had hitherto been its portion.
>
> But, alas, how vain are the hopes of man in the time when we expected it not, came upon us the hour of danger and death. Instantaneously our skylight was opened, and the mate shouted with a loud voice, 'Land ahead, sir!' We at once perceived our full danger, the dark night, the strong wind, our barque carrying a full press of canvas, driving over the water at the rate of eight miles an hour with land ahead! In a moment we hurried on deck, it was pitchy dark, the

moon bad withdrawn her light, and the stars their brightness, heavy and portentous clouds were drifting over our beads, we could scarcely see the sails of our ill-fated barque. I went to the lea side of the ship to look for the land, in a moment or two I saw it indistinctly visible, like a dark thundercloud, like something that had a defined shape, blacker and darker than that which surrounded it perceiving our imminent danger that we were so near the shore, I went down to apprise Mrs. Davies of our real circumstances.

'What is the matter,' she said. 'There is no real danger, I hope.' I said, 'My dear, there is some danger, you had better dress for fear'; having put on a few things as quickly as possible, she appeared very calm and composed. I then took up my dear little boy from the bed, where he was sweetly and profoundly asleep, little thinking that I was going to assign him to the deep, and then went up to the deck to see how things were going.

As soon as I got up, I heard the Captain say, 'How is the helm, Jack?'; the man answered, 'Hard up, sir.' In a moment or two after the vessel grazed heavily on the surface of some rock, and in a moment the helmsman was knocked down, and the wheel flew in pieces about the deck. Then the Captain wrung his hands and exclaimed, 'O God! It is all over with us now.'

The vessel still went on for about four or five hundred yards, and then with a tremendous crash she finally ran aground. Previous to this the scene of confusion was truly distressing, everyone was overwhelmed with alarm, all were running, pulling, shouting, no one scarcely knowing what he said or did, the children were crying, and the women, as soon as the ship struck, screamed aloud with fear, thinking their last hour had come.

But to return to Mrs. Davies, having been advised by the steward, remained alone in the cabin, and when the vessel struck the second time she fully believed there was no hope of escape, but as she told me afterwards, she was not alarmed, she felt the solemnity of being unexpectedly called to appear before God, but she realised that her Father would be her Judge, and to Him she committed her soul with calmness and composure—'Blessed are all they who put their trust in Him.'

She was coming up the stairs from the cabin when the vessel

struck a second time, when she was thrown down with violence, but mercifully was not hurt, everything tumbled around her in wild confusion, all the lights were extinguished in a moment, and for some time she was in total darkness. Fancy then, my reader, without a coat, hat, or shoes, I was standing on the weather side of the quarter-deck, between the main and the mizzen mast, with my darling boy on my arm, just awake from his sweet and tranquil slumber.

Now the fearful crisis came, our labouring barque was among the breakers—I shudder as I write. I went again to the lea side. I saw them, I heard their hoarse and thundering roar as they fell in vast volumes on the shore, and boiled among the rocks with wild and fearful fury. I went again to the weather side, expecting the vessel to strike every moment, as it had already touched ground. I remember well, I put my hand on the companion and commended my soul to God, and I likewise prayed that our lives might be spared if possible.

We stood in the most painful and paralysing suspense, waiting the fatal moment, we felt that eternity was before us, and we were come to the gates of death. But we had not long to wait before the vessel finally struck, and fell on her beam ends. At the same moment an enormous sea broke over us, fell upon my head, threw me down, washed me among the spars, casks, boxes, and other lumber, where I found myself floating in deep water. Mercifully, however, I was not washed overboard, but oh! My son! My only son! Was carried away from my arms and perished in the waves—yes, little William is gone. Great God, how wonderful are Thy ways.

Here the narrative ceases in Mr. Hockey's manuscript, to which I am indebted. It would be interesting to know how they were rescued, and by what means, they returned to England. All this must surely appear in the place where Mr. Hockey found the interesting and sad story of the shipwreck, but which source I have, been unable to discover.

Mr. Hockey tells the story of Mrs. Davies' early death, and informs us that he never recovered from the blow, and died soon after. Hockey describes the last baptismal service conducted by him, as furnished by an eye-witness, who says that he stood looking calm and serene, his countenance lit up with holy joy as sixteen young believers were immersed in the water. The few now left that knew him bear testimony to his holy walk and conversation, and though young in years his work was done—he must rest from his labours.

Figure 37: Bathurst Street Church, 1843

Biographies of the Leaders[133]

Figure 38: William Kidson, 1849 - Frederick Timpson I'Ons

Of The fifty-six parties that were sent out under Government regulations, four only were numerically strong. These were Bailie's party, Willson's party, Sephton's or the Salem party, and Parker's or the Irish party. They severally exceeded 100 families in number. The first to arrive was Bailie's party, to whom was assigned the post of danger, namely, the fringe of the northern border of the Zunsveld, immediately next to the Fish River Bush, with an established pathway through the bush into Albany across the location upon which Bailie's party were settled. Of this dangerous situation the unfortunate settlers had no idea when they were deposited upon their grants of land, and there was nothing to strangers unacquainted with Xhosa and their predatory habits to lead them to suspect they might be called upon to defend their lives and property by force of arms. This fate they cruelly experienced when the Xhosa, after frequent incursions in small parties, had succeeded in despoiling the settlers of their cattle, finally broke out into open general irruption and laid the country waste, murdering the defenceless settlers, burning their habitations and plundering them of their cattle. A short account of the fortunes of the heads of these parties will suffice to exemplify to a certain extent that which befell many of those who had accompanied their leaders to Albany and exerted their best efforts to establish themselves in the land of their adoption.

Bailie's Party

John Bailie, son of Colonel Thomas Bailie, of Inishargy, County Down, Ireland, and Anne Hope, daughter of Archibald Hope, of Dumfries, Scotland, was born at Angola, Carnatic, 5th July 1788. In 1793 Colonel Bailie returned to England and John Bailie and his brother Thomas Manborary Bailie went to France and were

---

133. Editor's note: The two sections that follows details biographies of some of the settlers. It should be noted that we have corrected information in some places but the content has not been checked for accuracy. These biographies were taken from Campbell, Colin Turning (1897). *British South Africa*. John Haddon & Co.

educated at the Polytechnique. In 1803 John Bailie entered the Royal Navy, and during his service in the navy visited the Cape. In 1809, he retired from the navy and entered the Foreign Office. He married Amelia Crause, daughter of Mr. William Crause, of Pembury, Kent.

After Waterloo, he was secretary for foreign claims in France, his duties being in connection with indemnities to be paid to allied subjects for losses and damages in France during the war. In 1817, he returned to the Foreign Office in London and worked out his pet scheme of settling the Cape with British settlers. He led the first, or Bailie's, party in 1819 on board the *Chapman*, which arrived in Algoa Bay in 1820. Chase, Godlonton, Stringfellow, Major Hope and some of the Crause family were of this party.

He held a dormant commission as Lieutenant-Governor for the new Settlement, which he resigned very soon after landing, because "the Whigs were in," and settled with his sons Charles Theodore, Archibald Hope, Thomas Cockburn and John Amelius, on the two farms, the Hope and Harewood, at the mouth of the Fish river in Albany. He and his sons served, during all the wars and disturbances, the expedition against the Fetcani, etc., until the Xhosa war of 1835 broke out.

Charles Theodore, the eldest son, was appointed Lieutenant in the first provisional battalion, and met with his death at the hands of the Xhosa, June 26, 1835, at Intaba-Ka-Ndoba, near the abandoned Pirie mission station, the spot being to this day marked and known as Bailie's grave. He was, says Moodie, an officer of the most cautious, though enterprising character, bold and undaunted, discreet and judicious, possessing every qualification to render him one of the highest ornaments of his profession. He had more experience in this desultory warfare than almost any other officer, and had frequently distinguished himself in his reconnoitres with the enemy. Being at the moment compelled from the nature of the ground to separate from his party, the whole, with the exception of their gallant officer, fell pierced with innumerable wounds. He did not fire with his men on their making their final effort, but sprang into a small thicket near the spot, where with matchless heroism he met his fate. Three of the enemy rushed upon him, two of whom were shot dead by a discharge from both barrels of his gun; one of these was a chief, Tchalusay; but having no further means of defence, he was instantly overpowered and slain. The spot was subsequently visited by the father of this gallant and amiable young man, who collected the remains of the brave men who fell, and consigned them to one common grave on a spot which is now marked by a heap of stones.

The Rev. Mr. Chalmers, of the Glasgow mission, was present on the occasion, and offered up, with the little party who had assembled, a most impressive prayer. The large and expensive residence which the father erected on his farm was burned to the ground and the whole estate laid waste, and his son's young widow, who had been obliged to flee from it for her life, was left so destitute that the only property she had in the world beyond her personal attire was a Bible found in her dead husband's belt and forwarded to her.

In 1824-5 John Bailie made surveys of the coast from Port Elizabeth to East London, and was mainly instrumental in getting Government to land stores at Waterloo Bay, Peddie district. Indeed, to convince Government of the practicability of landing stores at East London during wartime, he chartered the first ship that entered the Buffalo River mouth and took it in at his own cost. For some years after the war of '35 Mr. Bailie and his son Thomas lived on his farm, the Hope, and in Graham's Town, and went trading across the Orange river. During one of their absences from their station the license expired, and Du Plooy, the Field Cornet, seized and sold everything. On his return, July 8, 1845, Mr Bailie, hearing what had happened, went with his son Thomas to demand restitution. Du Plooy refused to refund, and he and Bailie had words about it. Du Plooy seized his gun, his wife shrieking to him to shoot the Englishman. Bailie closed with him, and in the struggle that followed Du Plooy was shot. Mr. Bailie always declared the gun went off accidentally. He had no arms, and was a calm-tempered man, not likely to do anything revengefully. The report of the gun brought his son Thomas from outside the door where he was talking to some of Du Plooy's friends. On his entering the room, his father said to him, "Look to your pistols."

At the trial, the witnesses swore that Thomas Bailie had fired at Du Plooy and helped his father in the struggle. The Dutch were all most embittered against them, and having no sense of honour, or regard for truth, did their utmost to prove them guilty, while the Bailies had no counsel and only one witness out of ten whom they requested to be summoned in their defence. After Du Plooy was shot, Bailie went to Colesberg and gave himself up to the authorities. On the report of Du Plooy's friends his son Thomas was apprehended. The accused, owing to the influence exerted by friends and the Press, were removed to Uitenhage for trial. In spite of all efforts, the jury, who were in deliberation all night, found them guilty, but accompanied their verdict with a strong recommendation to mercy, and Chief Justice Wylde sentenced them to death, April 1846.

While awaiting this, a number of prisoners endeavoured to escape. Thomas Bailie helped the gaoler to recapture them, which stood him in good stead. The death sentence was commuted to imprisonment for life, and some months later, additional evidence was given by Du Plooy's widow, which showed that the act had been committed in self-defence, which had all along been maintained by the elder prisoner. In December 1847, they received a "free pardon," that being the legal manner of release from confinement. They remained for some time after this in Port Elizabeth, where Mr. Bailie was connected with the harbour works.

Thomas returned to the Free State, where he spent many years in hunting and trading. In 1848 Mr. Bailie went to Natal and established a trading station at Durban, in 1852, after having made surveys of the coast from Durban to East London in his yacht called the *Haidee*, he commenced a coast trade between Port Natal and the mouth of the St. John's River and the Umgasi River. When returning on Tuesday, 27th July 1852, from one of these trips, the *Haidee* observed a barque in distress between the Umtwalumi and Umzintu Rivers. This proved to be the *Hector*, 600 tons. Captain Brooks, from Batavia to Bremen, laden with rice and sugar. Mr. Bailie at once went on board the Hector with three of his men, leaving only Captain Sorrel and one man on board the *Haidee*, to render what assistance he could. On Wednesday, at 2 a.m., a breeze sprang up, and the *Haidee* had to stand-off from the Hector and come on to Port Natal. After doing all he could to save the ship, the boat left for the shore, having on board the first and second mates and two seamen. On nearing the shore the boat capsized in the surf and was rendered incapable of again returning to the wreck.

All managed to reach the land on spars except Mr. Bailie and Benjamin Hoar, a West Indian, about fifteen years of age, son of one of the owners of the vessel. Bailie had only the use of one hand, the other had been injured. Those on shore watched him climb into the rigging, cling there for hours, then, losing his hold, drop into the raging sea. Throughout he had evinced the greatest coolness, firmness, and presence of mind. He thus died at the age of sixty-three years, just when he had pioneered the way to a new opening of coasting commerce, and while in the act of rendering his generous assistance to fellow-creatures in distress.

Of Mr. Bailie's children,

> (1) Charles Theodore, as already mentioned, was killed by Xhosa in 1835, leaving one son, Henry John, who settled and still lives in the Queen's Town district;

> (2) Archibald Hope, died in Port Elizabeth in June 1850, from injuries received during the war of 1846-7, leaving a daughter, who married Mr. G. G. Wright, attorney-at-law, in practice at Graham's Town, and two sons, Archibald Hope, who settled in the Free State, and Alexander Cumming, who was entrusted with several responsible and delicate duties on the

northern border, which he discharged with much sagacity, namely, making a peace between the Bakwena and Bakhabla, who were at war; prevented a Boer attack on Khama, chief of the Bamangwato; arranged with Khama and Sicheli for their countries to be handed over, and submitted offers to the Administrator of Griqualand West; arranged with Lobengula to receive a British resident; made a route map from Kimberley to Buluwayo; and later (1881), at urgent request of Government, proceeded to Basutuland as a Magistrate, and after serving in that country till 1884, received a letter of thanks from the Cape Government and H.M. Commissioner, three months' pay, and promise of re-employment; now living in the Harrismith district;

(3) Thomas Cockburn, who died in 1876, leaving two sons, Charles Campbell (Major Bailie), who died in 1883, and John Crause, who has settled in the Transvaal;

(4) John Amelius took orders and died at Cape Town in 1883, after a long missionary career principally in Namaqualand and Damaraland.

The daughter, Isabella Bennett, married Mr. C. H. Huntley, Civil Commissioner and Resident Magistrate of Graham's Town.

Willson's Party

Willson's party arrived three months after Bailie's party, and they were located at some distance from Bailie's people, in a more central position, between the plain called Waai Plaats and the Kowie Bush, a situation, however, fraught with danger in case of Xhosa disturbances. Mr. Thomas Willson, the head of this party, hailed from London. At one time he had been in the office of H.R.H. the Duke of York, and when his offer was accepted to bring out a hundred families, was connected with the Chelsea waterworks. It is from thence he dated his circular explaining his plans and the position he would occupy towards those who came out under his protection, which shows he had given full consideration to the project and its responsibilities. His circular was as follows :—

He proposed,

> First, that ten gentlemen unite an equal proportion of funds and form themselves into a committee of management of their own immediate concerns, and that each provide or take out five able-bodied men for the purposes of tillage and other requisite employments, with a sufficient store of implements, seeds, and the several necessaries of life, so as to enable them to cultivate immediately after their location

a proportion of land equal at least to one acre per family, and to erect a sufficient number of cottages of the simplest and cheapest character for the whole of their party before the rainy season sets in, and that until such covering is obtained a provision of tents shall be made as a temporary resort. As this arrangement is merely designed for the above society, it is submitted only as a principle upon which other societies of the whole party may be formed upon a rational proceeding.

"Second, that duly considering the feelings of a party of British subjects leaving their native country to take the benefit of the advantages held out by Her Majesty's Government, it will be my first care to make the most liberal provision and distribution of the lands with which I am to be invested by a grant from the Crown, in order that such subjects, who so well understand the nature and value of rational liberty, may enjoy an undoubted right, and be enabled fairly to prosecute those objects of my improvement by agricultural pursuits and the formation of a well-organized state of society as may be consistent with my individual rights as Lord of the Manor, the general good, the order, harmony, and welfare of the Settlement, with the reservations, laws, and public views of Her Majesty's Government.

"Third, for the better regulation and management of so large a party, I propose one individual shall be selected as a director to represent such party, which will create a division of time and labour that is well calculated for the interests of individuals, and will be a ready and direct channel for communication for the redress of grievances, at the same time that it insures a mutual support and protection.

"Fourth, if any doubt should exist as to the purity of my intentions in confirming to individuals who may become entitled to a grant of land, such individuals may have a guarantee under my hand more particularly specifying my intention of making such grant by paying a stipulated sum towards the Fund of Indemnity in liquidation of the expenses incurred in the formation of this Settlement; and though at all times I shall be happy to assist others with my counsel or advice in maturing their several projects, it is not to be expected that I could devote my time and services in aid of individual interests or the maintenance of general order without adequate pecuniary support to enable me to dispense such important objects of utility.

"Fifth, that there shall be no abuse of liberty which at all times it will be my glory to maintain in a pure state, consistent with the laws of the Colony, by sound principles of justice, humanity, and moral decorum. I invite the cordial support of every director of each ten of this party to unite with me in the dispensation of those benefits which I propose to all who confide in me their personal welfare and property, to protect them as far as I may be invested with power and authority from acts of aggression, illegal or improper conduct. And in all cases of difference or matters of dispute, more particularly as to the division and partition of land, I recommend an immediate recourse to the decision of a disinterested person, whose judgement shall be final and conclusive, reserving to myself the powers of interposing in cases where such judgement is not effective to dispossess both parties from the lands in dispute, and to assign to them a portion of land in such other situation as may be deemed consistent with the peace and general welfare of the Settlement.

"Sixth, in consideration of the heavy responsibility, severe anxiety, and great burden of expense, which naturally occurs in organizing a Settlement that combines individual benefit with objects of national importance, it is an indispensable part of the system upon which the settlers who are to participate in the advantages of a grant of land, that they also participate in the due proportion of expense for indemnification of what has been incurred, or what may hereafter accrue, in carrying into effect objects of general interest, and what may be considered necessary or important on public grounds.

"Lastly, it is essential for the convenience and accommodation of the Settlement that a communication should be held with the mother country to facilitate a return of cash payments for the produce of the Colony. I have therefore opened an account with a London banker of the highest respectability, which will afford a safe and honourable medium for all money transactions, and I shall likewise open an account with the Government Bank at Cape Town to give more immediate effect to the views of the Colony; and I conclude by recommending the establishment of a savings bank at the Settlement, as soon as circumstances will admit, as a security for the returns of honest industry and a stimulus to the exercise of the natural powers and energies of the mind."

Willson and his party were, like the other settlers, dismayed at the general order prohibiting landing on their arrival in Simon's Bay. Several gentlemen among them, Lieut. Alexander Bisset, half-pay R.N., Mr. Walter Currie, purser, half-pay R.N., Thomas Randall, James Collis, Thomas Cock, and James and Benjamin Wilmott, who had each brought their own servants and dependants asked permission to land to attend to their private affairs; and Willson himself, on behalf of the rest on board, writes to the Colonial Secretary from the ship at Simon's Town, May 20:

> The several persons of my party who receive half pay or pensions expect me to answer them. The clergyman looks up to me with his large family, to satisfy his pressing wants, his hopes, his fears! Several of the respectable part of the settlers, who have the means to return to England at their own expense, prefer, and have proposed, to adopt that course. Will you permit them, and furnish me with your permission, to have them landed with their goods at Simon's Town for that purpose? I really think it would be advisable. The enclosed letter is from a very respectable gentleman, who, I am persuaded, from his feeble state, will never reach our destined station alive. May he be permitted to land. In fact the whole party, from disappointed hope in the unexpected distance which they will have to travel at their own expense, appear exasperated and dismayed. They desire everything from me which they conceive themselves entitled to, and I have nothing to expect from them but murmur and disaffection and revenge! Yet under all these difficulties and disadvantages, feeling that my honour is in a manner pledged to Government, I will never shrink from this my disastrous agreement as long as I meet with due support from the Executive.

He applied for a moderate grant of useful land in the neighbourhood of Wynberg in lieu of 10,000 acres near Bathurst, which, however, he was told could not be entertained. Willson was more reasonable than Parker, and ready to acknowledge the efforts of Government to make things as comfortable and hopeful to them as could be expected. Thus, on arriving at Algoa Bay, eight days after the foregoing letter, he writes to the Colonial Secretary, May 28:

> On my arrival here, I find the paternal care of the Colonial Government is conspicuous in every arrangement which has been made for our reception and welfare. I shall therefore feel it my duty,

and cannot fail to exert myself in carrying into effect the plans of his Excellency the Governor; and it will afford me the highest satisfaction to be able to report to our friends in England and to the Government at home the advantages and comforts which the settlers have derived from so excellent an appreciation of the local means, both as to victualling and transport, and the superior wisdom and humanity which is displayed in every branch of the service.

Government not only provided conveyance for them to their destination; without charge, but also supplied them with rations while en-route, and for some time after their location. They had nothing to complain of. Having seen his party to their destination, Willson does not seem to have been enamoured of his prospects, as so early as August 10 we find him writing to Government imploring to be sent back to England; and finally, December 11, 1820, he embarked at Port Elizabeth, not, however, without an appeal by Mr. James Collis to the authorities for his detention till the claims of his party were adjusted.

Parker's Party

The Irish party was another instance of the mixture of elements not easily contented. It comprised five smaller parties under Mr. William Scanlen, Mr. Robert Woodcock, Captain Thomas Butler, of the Dublin Militia, Captain Walter Synnot, and Mr. John Ingram, besides the party tinder Mr. William Parker, who had once been Mayor of Cork. They were conveyed in the two transports, the *East Indian* and the *Fanny*.

Quarrelling began soon after embarkation among those on board the first named vessel, which contained Parker, his wife, and six children. The day after arrival in Simon's Bay Parker brought charges against the Rev. Francis McCleland,

> . . .that immediately on embarking in the *East Indian* he grossly insulted the wife of Dr. Holditch, the surgeon; and on the night of Sunday, January 30, in Cork Harbour, he vilified the English, saying he would get sixteen Irish who would flog any thirty English. He was so violent and insulting that he was threatened to be horsewhipped by John George Newson, Esq., an alderman of the city of Cork and a magistrate of the county; also by Thomas Parsons Boland and Edward Newson, Esqs., and Lieutenant Wentworth, R.N.

His animosity to McCleland continued, as December 17, 1820, he memorialized Government against his appointment to Clanwilliam:

. . .hearing that he is to be located at Klein Vallei, Clanwilliam, he earnestly entreated not to permit said McCleland to be established, as he has by his unremitted and scandalous ill-behaviour made himself generally despised, and forfeited by a continual course of drunken, immoral, profane, and irreligious conduct all the respect and veneration to which his sacred functions would otherwise have entitled him.

With such a beginning at first start it is not surprising that others besides this excitable clergyman should be involved in disturbances whilst on the passage, and charges were preferred by Parker against two others as being insubordinate and ill-behaved, viz., Thomas Seton, late Captain Madras establishment, and Matthew Nelson, a lawyer.

As no cognizance could be taken in the colonial courts of what had passed at sea, each party was recommended to forget or stifle their animosities or wrongs and join heartily in the endeavours for which they had left their country, as without unanimity, they were told, success could not be anticipated.

Seton, applying for permission to land with his wife and Miss E. Coyle, her companion, mentions that E. Coyle was inserted on Parker's list as Mrs. Taylor to make up the number required, and to save a separate deposit for her and John Taylor. Other instances of a similar practice on the list are mentioned, viz., Cavenagh and Bridget, his supposed wife. Miss Coyle herself petitioned the Acting-Governor "that she should be given into the hands of the Church missionaries." Her petition recited that "she was the daughter of an old servant of Government, in the Ordnance department in Ireland, that she came out with the determination of attending to the religious and moral education of the female children of the settlers coming out in the ship with Mr. William Parker, under the idea and with the promise from the said William Parker that she should receive the same protection and treatment as his own children."

That promise of protection had, however, she alleged, been cruelly and unjustifiably violated by said Parker. Before proceeding to the frontier, Lieut. General Sir R. S. Donkin, Acting-Governor, decided not to confine the location of the emigrants from England to the Zunsveld, but to place parties in several eligible situations through-out the Colony. This is another instance of Sir R. Donkin's not obeying instructions. The immigrants were to occupy the Zunsveld and not other situations in the Colony, however eligible. He gave instructions for locating the settlers from Cork when they should arrive in that subdivision of the district of Tulbagh, on the west coast, called Clanwilliam.

This situation, the residence of a Deputy Landdrost, had been very favourably spoken of to his Excellency by a magistrate who had long resided there. Well watered, it had the Elephant's River running through it, which, at a distance of only twenty miles, becomes navigable to the sea, when it is supposed not to be obstructed by a bar, as the rivers of the Colony mostly are. Subsequently, to Sir R. Donkin's departure for the Frontier, the *East Indian* and the *Fanny* transports from Cork arrived in Simon's Bay. Parker came to Cape Town and saw Colonel Bird, the Colonial Secretary, and was informed of the destination of the settlers under his direction.

He appeared disappointed, and alleged that he had been assured he should be allowed a choice of situation, and that he had come out with the full persuasion that he should be settled on the Kuyua. He was informed that the lands there were private property, and that there was no alternative but to order the transports to Saldanha Bay, where the emigrants would be disembarked and where every preparation had been made for their subsistence and conveyance to their ulterior destination. Parker begged to go to the place of location by land, and to join his party on their arrival at Saldanha Bay.

Facilities were afforded him for this object, and letters of introduction to the authorities at Clanwilliam were given to him by the Colonial Secretary. Parker proceeded to Clanwilliam and sent the transports to Saldanha Bay, where the Landdrost of the Cape district, to whom had been entrusted all the arrangements for the transport and maintenance of the several parties, awaited him. The parties under Messrs. Ingram, Synnot, and Butler set out for their destination in the most orderly manner and in good spirits.

Parker, however, informed the Landdrost he might dismiss the wagons collected for his party, as he was determined not to proceed so far from the seashore. His views were commercial and not agricultural, and the situation and soil of Clanwilliam were not calculated for his purposes in any degree. The place assigned to Parker's party was the well-watered loan place, called Klein Vallei. But Parker had an idea that he could found a new city of Cork at Saldanha Bay. He drew up an elaborate statement of what was possible and what he could do in this new-found place, covering several pages of foolscap closely written, which he submitted to the Colonial Secretary. He lost no time in requisitioning for various articles, such as tents, ploughs, etc., for the use of his settlers to be forwarded him first opportunity, and then applied to have the Deputy Landdrost removed and himself placed in the magistrate's chair.

On examination of the neighbourhood of Saldanha Bay, he found all the water-springs were on the property of a Mr. Watney, which he requested Government to acquire by purchase at a cost of £5,000. With these strange demands, incidental aids and advantages for his new city of Cork, he contemplated the establishment of a fishery, and projected great commercial speculations without the remotest view to agricultural pursuits. He asked for the right to graze sheep on certain islands in the Bay, also for a certain portion of the seashore as a landing-place for the purposes of trade and building stores, which were granted to him.

When he was told that the transports could not be detained longer at Saldanha Bay and that his party would be located with the great mass of the settlers in the Zunsveld, Parker changed his mind, and begged to be furnished with the means of going to Clanwilliam, which, being supplied, the party set forward and took possession of the location assigned them, Parker, his family and servants remaining in Mr. Watney's house at Saldanha Bay. Some of the settlers sent to Klein Vallei found it unsuitable to marine pursuits to which they had been accustomed. Seventy-six heads of families from the *East Indian* and forty-five from the *Fanny* required, by the stipulations of Government, 1,200 or 1,300 acres, but the whole of the land fit for cultivation in the neighbourhood, including the Drostdy, only measured 1,162 acres.

It was represented that ten families in the neighbourhood of Klein Vallei might be a desirable object for the purpose of establishing a place for farmers from the more northern regions partaking of refreshments on their way to Cape Town and Saldanha Bay; but the poverty of the adjacent country totally precluded the possibility of establishing an inland trade. Mr. Seton and his family and servants petitioned to be allowed to move on to Clanwilliam or elsewhere on the banks of the Elephant's River. Most of those by the East Indian and the Fanny proceeded to Clanwilliam and its neighbourhood; but the prospects were not cheerful to any of them. Thus, Parker writes to Viscount Ennismore, July 15:

> A sad and dismal disappointment to me and my large family that I was not particularly mentioned by Earl Bathurst for Government employ. The land at present assigned to me would not support twenty families, instead of the seventy-six that I brought with me. But I do not despair. My substance, however, will be wasted by unprofitably supporting my people, who most keenly feel my vast disappointment.

Mr. Robert Woodcock also wrote, July 16:

> . . . that unless something be speedily done for them by Government they must be compelled to abandon the Settlement

altogether and seek from the Boers a subsistence in return for their menial services, thus being fated to rank in the Colony exactly levelled with the Khoi population. The party arrived in the Colony on April 30, and most arrived here (Klein Vallei) on June 10, and now, after a lapse of exactly eleven weeks, most of these settlers find themselves as unsettled as when they landed, without land, without implements, and generally without money.

Mr. Ingram also, who brought sixty-seven settlers under him from Cork, dating from Partridge Valley, Clanwilliam, July 17:

> I should but ill discharge my duty by those people who have come out under my protection were I not to make an immediate representation of their situation, in order that my silence on the subject may not be construed into a tacit acceptance of the lands which have been allotted to me. Out of 2,700 acres, the most that can be cultivated is about 24 acres. Relying on H.M. Government that we should receive our full quantity of arable land as promised me by Lord Bathurst in presence of my friend and relation. Sir Benjamin Bloomfield.

Yet one who describes the colony in 1822 gives a different version of the Clanwilliam settlement. "The growth of prosperity at Clanwilliam appears to have exceeded anything displayed by Albany. On that which has been underrated, time and experience frequently affix a just value, and in the history of the locations, no estates have, as yet, attained a celebrity in the Cape newspaper equal to those of Clanwilliam."

Which statement is supported by quoting the following advertisement:

> John Ingram offers for sale by private contract the whole of his estates adjoining the deputy Drostdy of Clanwilliam, consisting of about 5,000 morgens of corn and excellent pasture land, in such lots as may be agreed upon; also two pieces of land at the Klein Vallei, one consisting of 100 morgens, the other about 166 morgens; and an erf, let to J. H. Niewouldt, at the Taaybosch Kraal, at the yearly rent of 20 muids of wheat, payable on the 1st of January, every year, for ever. The whole of the above lands, if not disposed of by the 11th of June next, will be positively sold by public auction at Patryze Vallei on that and the following day, 11th and 12th June, when a sale will be held, without reserve, of all his farming stock and implements, consisting of about 100 draught oxen, European (Vaderland) cows,

horses, sheep, goats, ploughs, wagons, etc., etc.; also household furniture, carpenters' and smiths' tools, and a great variety of merchandise too numerous to insert. Terms: one-third of the purchase-money of the estates to be paid in cash within one month; the two-thirds may remain at interest for one or two years on mortgage of estate. Good farmers fare, lots of wine, and a fiddle.

And another advertisement:

To be let in a new town proposed to be built immediately opposite the Drostdy of Clanwilliam, several lots for building, containing two acres of highly fertile land. The subscriber will give to each person, to build a house, agreeable to a plan beforehand laid down by him, 100 Rs. worth of timber, and not to commence rent for three years, or any such other time as may be agreed upon. There is a constant supply of excellent water all the year, commanding every lot, and offers to industrious tradesmen the greatest prospect of success. A fair is proposed to be held on the lands every 1st of September, . . . Apply to John Hugnam, Bloomfield Lodge, October 4, 1821.

It may be inferred from the foregoing that the sale in June was not a success, and that the experiment detailed was tried in October following with similar result. Ingram and his party left this unsuitable locality and were located in Albany.

Captain Thomas Butler and eleven others were assigned Tyber's Kraal, which consisted of five or six acres of land, a part even of which small quantity the Field-cornet claimed. Neither this, he alleges, nor ten times as much, would produce sufficient to feed his people. "Can it be possible," he asks, "that my country, which I served faithfully for twenty-four years, has sent me into the desert to starve, to be laughed at by the wealthy Dutch, many of whom tried this place before and gave it up as good for nothing? It cost me £1,000 to bring me here and what I have, and what I have not, and what has been destroyed."

From these descriptions of the locality to which they had been sent, it can hardly be said they were 'eligible.' Subsequently, at their request the five parties were removed to the Zunsveld, and there located amongst the rest of the settlers. As for Mr. Parker, on Lord Charles Somerset's return to the Colony, he was received at Government House as an injured man, and his memorial, and particularly a letter to the king, were corrected by the Governor himself. But his days of favour were not of long duration; his presence was inconvenient in many ways, and Lord Charles Somerset determined to send him to England to enlighten the Colonial Office on the oppression and indefensible measures pursued towards him by Sir R.S. Donkin and Colonel Bird. This he did at an expense to the public treasury of £450.

It may here be added that besides the Irish parties who were sent to other parts of the Colony instead of Albany by Sir R. Donkin, those of Messrs. Charles and Valentine Griffith and Captain Duncan Campbell were located on the Zonder (Endless) End River, in the neighbourhood of the Moravian mission station, called Genadendal. They did not find the situation eligible, and remained there but a short time, finding the land not of a quality to afford.

Biographies of British Settlers

Atherstone, John

John Atherstone came with Mr. Edward Damant's party from Fakenham, Norfolk, in the ship *Ocean*. He was married, and brought with him his wife, son, and three daughters. He had been resident house-surgeon at Guy's Hospital, London, before coming to the country. In August 1820, he applied for and obtained the district surgeoncy of Uitenhage, vice Mr. Mann, resigned, where he practised for a year. In 1823, he went overland to Cape Town, where he had the chief practice for several years. In 1828, he accepted the district surgeoncy of Graham's Town, vacant by the resignation of Dr. Cowie, where he remained until his death, which occurred in 1853, the result of a cart accident, aged 62 years.

He acquired the farm Nantoo, the original camp of Colonel Graham before he fixed upon the present site of Graham's Town, which he called Table Farm, by which name it is now known, about nine miles distant, where he combined horse-breeding and farming with the practice of his profession. He was twice-married: first to Elizabeth, daughter of Castel Damant, Esq., of Fakenham, by whom he had two sons and five daughters; amongst whom:

- William Guybon (See below),
- Catherine, married to George Cumming, sheep farmer of Hilton, near Graham's Town;
- Eliza, who died young;
- Emily, who married John George Franklin, Esq., editor of the Frontier Times, Graham's Town;
- Caroline, married Henry Hutton, Esq., A.D.C. to the Commandant-General, Sir A. Stockenstrom, Bart., ob. 21st January 1896;
- John, married Anna Bowker, and
- Bliss; and

- Ann, who married George White, Esq., sheep farmer, Braak Kloof, near Graham's Town.

The second family consisted of:
- Edwin, a medical practitioner, married to Armeni Girdlestone;
- Walter Herschel, Acting Surgeon-Superintendent, Port Alfred Asylum;
- Charles, married to Emily Dickson; and;
- Fanny, married to Hilton Barber, Esq., a noted horse-breeder of the Cradock district.

Atherstone, William Guybon

William Guybon Atherstone married, in 1839, Catherine, daughter of Edwin Atherstone, the poet. The career of Dr. William Guybon Atherstone was brilliant and interesting. He was only five, years of age when his parents arrived in Albany; and after completing his studies under Canon Judge and Dr. Innes, with a view to the medical profession, abandoned that idea and took up survey work. In the Xhosa war of 1834-5, he was assistant staff-surgeon to Colonel, afterwards Sir, Harry Smith's division.

At the end of the war went home and studied in the Meath Hospital at Paris, and at Heidelberg, where he passed with honours. He returned to England, married, and brought his bride to the Colony, joined his father, and remained in practice till 1887. He is well known throughout South Africa as a scientist, particularly in geology. He was the first to pronounce the opinion that the stone found at Colesberg Kopje, now Kimberley, in 1867, was a veritable diamond weighing $21\frac{1}{4}$ carats, worth £500, which opinion was afterwards confirmed by Messrs. Hunt and Roskell, the crown jewellers in London, to whom it had been sent for inspection, and the stone was bought by Sir P. E. Wodehouse, the Governor of the Colony. In 1883, he was elected a member of the Legislative Council as a representative of the South-East Circle, and sat in Parliament till 1891. He is living in retirement at Graham's Town.

Attwell

Attwell, Richard, wife and four children, Edwin, Sarah, James and Brooke.

Attwell, William, and

Attwell, Richard L., Richard L. Attwell married a Miss Whiley, and removed to Cape Town, where he became the founder of the now celebrated Attwell Baking Company

All settlers of Mr. George Scott's party from Surrey, by the *Nautilus*. They occupied the location assigned to the party near the mouth of the Fish River, where they remained till driven away by the irruption of the Xhosa, 1834-35, when Mr. Richard Attwell came to Graham's Town, where he died in 1846, leaving three sons and one daughter.

- Sarah, who married the Hon. Mr. Godlonton.
- James Attwell married a niece of Mr. Robert Hart, of Glen Avon, Somerset East, and took to farming;
- Brooke Attwell, who was only 9 years of age when he arrived, followed the trade of a boot and shoemaker in Bathurst Street, Graham's Town, having married a Miss Booth, until he was appointed Market Master of the Graham's Town municipality, which office he held for the long period of twenty-five years. He died in Graham's Town at the advanced age of eighty-one years in 1892. His eldest son is Mr. Benjamin Booth Attwell, J.P., practising in Graham's Town as an Accountant and Financial Agent.

Figure 39: High Street, Grahamstown, 1856 - Charles Jay

Ayliff, Reverend John

Reverend John Ayliff, came to the Colony with the British settlers of 1820 by the *Belle Alliance* as one of Mr. Willson's party. In 1827, he was ordained a Wesleyan missionary, and appointed to Xhosaland. He was at Butterworth as missionary to Hintza, the paramount chief of Kaffraria, until the war of 1835 broke out, when, with his family, he had to fly for safety. His dwelling-house and all his property were destroyed. At the close of the war, upon the urgent representations of Mr. Ayliff to the Government, Sir Benjamin D'Urban released the Fingoes from Xhosa bondage, and at the desire of the Governor, Mr. Ayliff, led them out, escorted by Colonel, afterwards Sir Harry, Smith, and the missionary had the satisfaction of seeing the vast multitude of Fingoes, numbering 16,000 men, women, and children, with some 20,000 head of cattle, safely settled under British protection in the Peddie district.

An Ayliff Memorial Church has, during 1894, been erected by the Fingo tribe at Butterworth, to the memory of this old missionary, costing about; £1 700. During 1840 Mr. Ayliff established a mission called Haslope Hills, in the Tarka district, for the emancipated slaves, and laboured there many years. In 1854, at the request of Sir George Grey, then Governor of the Colony, Mr. Ayliff superintended the erection, and established, the Heald Town Native Industrial Institution for the training of Fingo boys and girls. Here he successfully laboured for six years and trained some of the first native ministers, when his health broke down. He shared with other early missionaries the toil and difficulty of translating the Scriptures into the Xhosa language, and published a very useful Xhosa vocabulary.

After forty years spent in benefiting the native tribes of South Africa, he visited England once more, and with her who had been the partner of his toils and labour received honour such as is rarely paid to a missionary from abroad. On returning to his much-loved work his health completely broke down, and he died at Fouresmith, Orange Free State, May 17, 1862, aged sixty-four years, leaving his widow, five sons and three daughters. A short history of the Fingo tribe by Mr. Ayliff, in manuscript, is in the Cape Town library.

- Hon John Ayliff, died at Natal in 1877. He was appointed in 1846 by Governor Sir P. Maitland to raise a body of natives for service in the field during the Xhosa war. He acted as Field-Adjutant to Major Sutton's division, was appointed Commandant of Native Levies in the field in the following year, and in 1849 was made interpreter to the High Commissioner of British Kaffraria. During General Cathcart's campaigns across the Kei and against Moshesh he acted as Secretary to the High Commissioner, and in the same capacity to Sir George Grey when he visited Natal in 1855. After holding the appointment of Auditor in Kaffraria for some years he was appointed Treasurer in Natal in 1862; and up to the time of his promotion to be Judge of the newly-constituted Native High Court, in 1876, he continued to discharge the duties of that office, often in conjunction with other officers, as, for instance, when the two somewhat incongruous posts of Postmaster-General and Colonial Treasurer were combined. For some years his health, never very robust, had been failing; yielding at last to necessity, he sought to try the effects of a voyage to Europe. A favourable opportunity presented itself, but the day broke to find he had passed away. The remains were carried by the steamer Danube that they might be interred with his friends in the old Colony.
- Reuben Ayliff, the second son, was employed during the Xhosa wars of 1846-47 and 1850-51; during the latter served as Captain Commandant of native lines. Leaving business about 1864 and settling in Graham's Town, became Mayor of the city, and was elected three times to that honourable position. For several years he was one of the representatives in the House of Assembly for the electoral division

of Uitenhage. After this he became interpreter of the Eastern Districts Court in the Dutch and Xhosa languages, and held the appointment for seventeen years. During the latter years of his life he has devoted much valuable time to the cause of temperance, and for a long, time has been a staunch Good Templar. Twice he has been chosen as a delegate to the R. W. Grand Lodge of America, which country he visited in that capacity. For several years successively he held the office in the Colony of G.W.C.T.

- William Ayliff, the third son, has been a successful farmer, and for a long time lived on his farm "Wardens," near to the town and in the district of Fort Beaufort, which electoral division he for many years represented in the House of Assembly. He became Secretary for Native Affairs during the ministry of Sir Gordon Sprigg from 1878 to 1881, and in that capacity rendered valuable service to the Colony. During the long Xhosa and Bantu wars, both as Captain of Native Levies as well as Secretary for Native Affairs, he rendered valuable service, and, especially in the latter capacity, was sometimes placed in trying and difficult circumstances. He married the step-daughter of the Hon. Mr. Godlonton, and during late years has resided in Graham's Town, identifying himself with most of its principal institutions.
- Jonathan Ayliff, the fourth son, became an Attorney of the Supreme Court, and practised in Graham's Town, and after the death of Mr. George Jarvis, to whom he had been articled, became one of the leading practitioners in the city. He married the eldest daughter of the Hon. Mr. George Wood. Mrs. Ayliff did not long survive her husband, but died about a year after his death. For many years he was one of the members of the House of Assembly, and was chosen to represent respectively the important constituencies of Queen's Town and Graham's Town. While in the House he was often chosen to sit on Parliamentary Commissions, and was specially selected as one of the members of the Commission on Native Laws and Customs, under the able presidency of His Honour Sir J. D. Berry. Sir Thomas Upington, then in the House of Assembly, being called upon to form a Cabinet, chose Mr. Ayliff to be the Colonial Secretary, an office he held till stricken down by a serious internal complaint which compelled him to give up a position he prized and colleagues he much valued. He died in London at the comparatively early age of fifty-seven years, leaving six children, three boys and three girls, and his valuable services became lost to his family and to the country he loved so well.
- James Ayliff, the fifth and youngest son, was very early in life appointed by the Governor of the Colony to the office of Superintendent of the Witteberg Native Reserve in 1850, and during the long Xhosa war of 1851-52 became Captain commanding the Witteberg Fingo lines, in which capacity he rendered valuable service. He subsequently was appointed Superintendent of the Crown Reserve at Middledrift, Keiskama Hoek, and afterwards, about 1870, was appointed Civil Commissioner and Resident Magistrate of the newly-formed division of Wodehouse, where, at Dordrecht, he performed the duties of the office with satisfaction to Government. In 1873, at the special request of the Native Affairs Department, he was removed to the Transkei, where, as British Resident with the Chief Kreli, he remained some years till the war with the Galeka commenced. During this Galeka and Gaika campaign in 1877 he became Commandant of the Fingo Levies, and after the close of the war he received the war medal. From the

Transkei he was removed to the Civil Commissionership of East London, where he remained some time, was transferred to the same office at Cradock, in which important division he continued some years, and was then promoted to the first-class Commissionership of Graaff Reinet, where he continued till his retirement on his well-earned pension. His present residence is at Uitenhage.

Besides the five sons above mentioned the Rev. Mr. Ayliff left three daughters, two of whom have not married; but the youngest, Elizabeth, married the Rev. C. F. Overton MA., a gifted clergyman of the Church of England, who, after some twenty years of a happy married life, died in Graham's Town. The three daughters, now all living in Graham's Town, are actively engaged in all good works of charity and benevolence.

Biggar, Alexander

Alexander Biggar, retired paymaster of H.M.'s 85th Regiment of Foot, head of a party from Hampshire, in the *Weymouth*. The location assigned to them was in the Kareiga Valley adjoining Major Fraser's farm, and not far from the Theopolis Mission Station. In 1834, he removed to Durban, Natal, where about thirty Englishmen resided, either permanently or in the intervals between hunting excursions. In 1833, he was appointed Landdrost by Mr. Landman, in the name of the 'Association of South African Emigrants.'

He was suffering under great depression of spirits, consequent on the loss of his sons and his entire property, and declined to perform the duties of that office. On the 23rd December 1838, he was killed in battle with the Zulus.

- Robert was in nominal command of a force from Port Natal against Dingaan, comprising twenty English traders and hunters, twenty Khoisan, about 1,500 blacks, fugitives from Zululand, and succeeded in capturing 3,000 to 7,000 head of cattle, with which they returned to Natal. Soon after this, in command of another expedition against the Zulus, he was killed in battle 17th April 1838.
- George, was murdered by the Zulus in the great massacre of the Boers by Dingaan, 17th February 1838.
- Margaret Graham Biggar, died unmarried at Graham's Town, 31st May 1890, at the advanced age of ninety years.
- Ann, married Charles Maynard, Esq., a merchant at Graham's Town.
- Mary, married Kuhr, a merchant at Port Elizabeth.
- Jane, married H. von Ronn, merchant at Port Elizabeth; and
- Helen, married N. P. Krohn, merchant at Graham's Town.

Bisset, Lieutenant Alexander

Lieut Alexander Bisset, on half-pay R.N., was one of Mr. Willson's party from London by the *Belle Alliance*. He brought his wife and three children, all of tender ages. He lived at Fairfax, near the Kowie, and died in 18 —[134], and was buried at Bathurst. Of the three children that came out with him, the eldest, Sarah Maria, married P. W. Lucas, Esq., cashier of the Eastern Province Bank; Alexander Charles took to farming, which he carried on with varied success, and is still living at East London; the third, John Jarvis, only two years of age when his parents arrived in Albany.

John Jarvis Bisset, only two years of age when his parents arrived in Albany, had a distinguished career. He obtained his commission as Ensign and Lieutenant in a battalion of native infantry (medal). He was Field-Adjutant to a division of troops proceeding to Colesberg in December 1842, to suppress a rebellion of the Boers. He served throughout the Xhosa war of 1846-7, at the commencement of which he was appointed Deputy Assistant Quartermaster-General. Was present at the battle of the Gwanga, and all the minor affairs with the Xhosa, and twice slightly wounded. He was repeatedly thanked in general orders by successive General officers, and finally received the brevet of Major for his services during the campaign. At the close of the war he was appointed Brigade-Major of British Kaffraria. On the breaking out of the war, in 1850, he was severely wounded in the first engagement with the enemy at the Boomah Pass in the Amatola Mountains (medal). Was also present in the operations subsequent to June, 1852, C.B. 1867, K.C.M.G. 1877.

Boardman, Reverend William

Reverend William Boardman, a clergyman of the Church of England, who came out as chaplain to Mr. Willson's party by the *Belle Alliance*. Of his antecedents nothing is known; but in one of his letters to the Colonial Secretary soon after arrival Mr. Willson describes him as "a most worthy and respectable clergyman of the Church of England." He was stationed at Bathurst, and there officiated, as well as at Graham's Town and at Cuylerville. He also kept a school at Bathurst, where he finally died, in 1825, aged forty-nine years. He brought with him his wife and six children— three boys and three girls—and two unmarried sisters. A son of his was a farmer at Spion Kop, district of Albert, where he died somewhere about 1860. One of the sisters married Major John Crause, who was farming near Graaff Reinet, but had no family.

---

134. 12 July 1848 according to www.1820settlers.com.

Booth, Benjamin

Benjamin Booth, was one of Mr. Sephton's party who came by the *Aurora*, and were located on the Assegai River, about sixteen miles from Graham's Town. The village of Salem was founded by this party. He brought a wife and three daughters, all of tender years. He left Salem, and resided at Green Fountain, near the Kowie, a farm now occupied by the family of the late Mr. Richard Walker. He was unsuccessful at farming, and, crops failing, he removed to Graham's Town, where he carried on a general business. Afterwards he retired and lived at Bathurst, where he resided during the war of 1846-7. He died at Graham's Town, April 28, 1862, his wife having pre-deceased him in June 1847. He left one son and six daughters, of whom only the son and two youngest daughters are now living. His son, Mr. B. Booth, the present representative of the family, is living at Port Elizabeth, being Superintendent of Natives.

Bowker, Miles

Miles Bowker, head of a party from Wiltshire, who came in the *Weymouth*. He was of gentle birth, a scholar, and a good botanist. His first residence was at Olive burn, near the coast, and subsequently at Tharfield, on the Lynedoch or Kleinemond River. He was appointed, with Captain Duncan Campbell, Heemeraad[135] of Albany for many years, but resigned office, preferring the cultivation of his farms to politics. He died early in the year 1839, in the seventy-fifth year of his age, and was buried at Tharfield. He brought with him from England eight sons and two daughters. His youngest son was born at Oliveburn, making nine sons in all. Their names are well known in the Frontier districts and Colony. They all followed in their father's footsteps as farmers and agriculturists, and all took an active share in the numerous Xhosa engagements, giving their services for the benefit of their country,

- William Monkhouse Bowker, J. P., M.L.A., Commandant of Burghers, Eastern District, served in the Fikani Expedition in 1828, was Commandant of the Bathurst Corp of Guides during the war of 1835-36, served in the Kei patrol under Sir Benjamin D'Urban, and through the war of 1846-47. He was the first to raise the Somerset Volunteers in the war of 1851-52, and go to the rescue of families in the Winterberg, and was in command of burghers at the battle of Balfour and taking of Fort Armstrong.
- Miles Brabbin Bowker, served throughout the wars of 1835-36, 1846-47, and 1851-52.

---

135. Councillor / Representative.

- John Mitford Bowker, J. P., Commandant of Burghers, served on the Fikani commando in 1828, in the war of 1835-36, and was wounded. He was Commandant under Sir A. Stockenstrom during the war of 1846-47. He died in 1847.
- Thomas Holden Bowker, J. P., M.L.A., served on the Fikani expedition in 1828, served as an officer in the Graham's Town Native Infantry in the war of 1835-36, and served through that of 1846-47, commanding old Kaffir Drift post until close of the war. After Resident Magistrate of Kat River, defended Whittlesea during the greater part of the war of 1851-52. He drew up a plan for the defence of the Frontier, which he submitted to His Excellency Sir George Cathcart, Governor, and was partly carried out in the formation of the district of Queen's Town, which town he founded, preventing Xhosa incursions for many years. He was further engaged in the greater part of the action taken along the upper Kei border against Kreli, and was in 1872 appointed member and Secretary of the Land Commission on the Diamond Fields. He was many years in Parliament, representing the electoral districts of Albany, Victoria East, and Queen's Town.
- Bertram Egerton Bowker, J. P., a farmer, lived on the eastern Frontier of the Colony since 1820. In 1827 he was commandeered by Captain John Crause against marauding Xhosa; in 1828 commandeered under Major Dundas to put down marauding Zulus under Matawani their leader, served eight weeks, together with commando and Tambookie army, retook 50,000 head of cattle; in 1834 commandeered on Christmas Day, remaining in active service until peace was proclaimed, after which had charge of 6,014 head of Government cattle; in 1846 had command of a camp with fifteen English and Dutch families, patrolling the neighbourhood till the end of the war; in 1851 again had charge of a large camp), doing good service in constantly patrolling; in 1873, when the police were dead beaten at the Ibeka, volunteered for active service, when Kreli's house and kraal were burnt and his tribe driven over the Umtata. On returning from the Transkei was put in command of East London district. Was on active service when Tainton and Brown were murdered; caught two of the murderers, who were hanged. The Government offered a reward of £200 for the capture of the leader; caught the leader, who died in gaol, but never received the reward. During the last skirmish with the rebels had two men killed, one wounded, and two horses shot. In 1876 was returned as a member of the Legislative Council for East London.
- Robert Mitford Bowker, J.P., M.L.A. and M.L.C., served with the Corps of Guides during the war of 1835-36; was at the taking of Murray's Kranz and other engagements until close of the war. Served in the Zuurberg and other points during the war of 1846-47. Volunteered for the rescue of Winterberg families in 1851, was at Balfour and taking of Fort Armstrong, carried out a wounded comrade under close fire. Elected member of the House of Assembly for division of Somerset East in 1854, and served in Parliament for over thirty-six years.
- Septimus Bourchier Bowker, J. P., served throughout the wars of 1835-36, 1846-47, and 1851-52.
- Octavius Bowker, served during war of 1835-36, and during that of 1846-47 in the Zuurberg. In 1851 accompanied his brother, W. M. Bowker, and was at the battle of Balfour and taking of Fort Armstrong. Served with the Free State forces during

the Basutu war, and engaged in various affairs up to annexation of Basutuland in 1868.
- James Henry Bowker, J.P., F.L.S., F.Z.S.,F.R.G.S.,F.S.S., gold medalist, served in the war of 1846-47 and in that of 1851-52, was at the suppression of the Kat River rebellion and capture of Fort Armstrong (medal and clasp) in 1846-47. Inspector of the Frontier Armed and Mounted Police, 1855; served in the Transkei Expedition, 1858, and remained in Transkei until withdrawal in 1865. Associated with Sir Walter Currie in locating Fingoes in Transkei; served in expedition to Basutuland, 1868, and appointed High Commissioner's Agent for that territory; engaged also in settling the boundaries and formation of the different districts. Commandant Frontier Armed and Mounted Police, 1870. Commanded expedition to the Diamond Fields for annexation to the Cape Colony; appointed one of the three commissioners, and for some time Chief Commissioner of the Diamond Fields; commanded expedition for annexation of Tembuland, carried it out, and also selected site for present town of Umtata; planned expedition which led to the suppression of Langalalibela outbreak and capture of that chief, thanked by Secretary of State. Reappointed Governor's Agent, Basutuland; retired in 1878 with the honorary rank of Colonel; appointed one of the Commissioners for Natal, Indian and Colonial extradition; was twice thanked by Secretary of State for service done; is a Justice of the Peace for the Cape Colony, Natal, and under William IV, to 24th degree of south latitude; also under Victoria, ditto.

Bradfield, John

John Bradfield, a settler by the *Albury*, in the Nottingham party, of which Dr. Thomas Carlton was the head. He brought a wife and four children with him, and was accompanied by Edward Bradfield, John Bradfield, and John Bradfield, jnr. The location assigned to the Nottingham party was near Bathurst, through which the Torrens, formerly the Brak, River flows, to which the name of Clumber was given in honour of their patron, the Duke of Newcastle. There are at this day many of the name of Bradfield living at Clumber, engaged in agriculture. One of this family emigrated to Dordrecht, in the Wodehouse division, carrying on trading and farming there, is well known as a successful and enterprising colonist, who represents the electoral circle of the Eastern Province, —the Hon. John Linden Bradfield, M.H.L., Dordrecht.

Butler, Captain Thomas

Captain Thomas Butler, of the Dublin Militia, was head of one of the Irish parties. Arrived in the Colony per the *Fanny*, and was first located by the Acting-Governor Donkin in the Clanwilliam district. But as that part of the Colony did not suit him, he was removed to Albany. He suffered like the other settlers from failure of crops, the exceptional flood of 1823, and finally from the Xhosa irruption of

1834-5. Subsequently, he acquired a farm on the main road from Port Elizabeth to Graham's Town, adjoining that of Mr. Pullen. He brought his wife, two sons, and a daughter, the eldest a boy eleven years of age, and the youngest a girl one year old.

Figure 40: A camp of 1820 Settlers - Frederick Timpson I'Ons

Caldecott, Dr Charles

Doctor Charles Caldecott, came as surgeon in charge of the emigrants by the *Brilliant*. He brought his family with him, and settled at Port Elizabeth. Pringle, who came out in the same ship, describes him as 'a little dogmatic, Anabaptist surgeon,' who used to preach on board ship. He died, soon after arrival, from drinking cold water when overheated, having walked to Bethelsdorp Mission Station, nine miles from Port Elizabeth, which produced acute indigestion, followed by inflammation of the bowels.

- Charles Henry Caldecott (Third son), married Martha, the eldest daughter of William Wright, Esq., merchant of Graham's Town. He was driven from the farm Prospect, district of Toroka, by the irruption of the Xhosa in 1846, and came to Cradock, where he established himself in business. In 1857, he retired from business and removed to Graham's Town. He took an active part in all the political, social, and municipal movements for the improvement and development of the town and districts. He was twice returned to Parliament as member of the House of Assembly for the electoral division of Cradock, in 1857, and again in 1859, but resigned his seat in the latter year. In 1865, he was returned as a member of the Legislative Council. He was also Mayor of Graham's Town in 1860. He died at Kimberley in July 1879, his wife having predeceased him, leaving seven sons and six daughters; viz.,

- Rev. William Shaw Caldecott, Wesleyan Minister at Tsomo, Transkei, married to a daughter of Mr. J. B. Hillier;
- Charles Henry, married Elizabeth Booth, daughter of Mr. J. Williams;
- Harry Stratford, attorney of the Supreme Court, married Joanna, daughter of Mr. J. J. Sauer, of Aliwal North, in practice at Johannesburg;
- Robert Torkington, died by drowning in the river Severn, near Wick St. Lawrence, Somersetshire, 27th July 1868;
- Frederick Horatio, died at Cradock, 27th August 1856;
- Alfred Edward, Attorney of the Supreme Court, married Ella, daughter of Commissary-General Sir William Drake, died at Salisbury, Mashonaland, where he held the appointment of Crown Solicitor, 5th July 1894;
- Frederick Reginald, married Fanny, daughter of Mr. Warren, of Bleak House, Kei Road.

The daughters were:
- Emily, who married Mr. Selby Coryndon, an attorney of the Supreme Court, who predeceased her, and died at Kimberley, 5th July 1889;
- Charlotte Isabella, died at Cradock, 27th October 1850;
- Jessie Lucretia Baldwyn, died at Port Elizabeth, 11th January 1852;
- Rosa Wright, married 14th October 1872, John E. A. Dick-Lauder, Esq., second son of Sir John Dick-Lauder, Bart., of Grange and Fountain Hall, Scotland;
- Alice Annie Martha, died 25th July 1863; and
- Maud Isabella who died at Queen's Town, 8th June 1881.

Campbell, Dr Ambrose George

Doctor Ambrose George Campbell, fourth son of General Campbell, was a passenger by the *Dowson*, which brought twelve others sent out by the General. He had lately been admitted to practice his profession, and for a short time set up in Pimlico, at that time a suburb of London. He gave up his prospects there, married, and came to the country as one of his father's party. He fixed his residence at Graham's Town and there practised his profession, acquiring an extensive practice over the enormous districts of Uitenhage and Somerset as well as Albany. His quick perception and prompt decision made him eminently successful in the treatment of his cases, while his skill in operations was marked in several cases of delicacy and difficulty.

During the time that Graham's Town was a garrison town his house was noted for his hospitality, which was extended with generous liberality as well to travellers and others passing through the town. After a residence of forty years he made a voyage to England, and after a short stay there, finding the climate unsuited to him, he returned to the Colony, and shortly after died at Port Elizabeth, 12th December 1884, at the age of eighty-five years. The doctor was twice-married, first to Rose, daughter of Thomas Ainswick, Esq., merchant, of London, having by her one son

—Lionel Donald Williams Campbell, now at Johannesburg, —and two daughters ; the eldest, Janet Isabella Suffield Campbell, married Herbert Penderell Longlander, Esq., MA., Oxon, now at Maritzburg, Natal; the youngest, Ambrosina Georgina van der Dupen Campbell, who married William Henry Daniell, Esq., of Sidbury. His second wife was Johanna Sophia van der Reit, daughter of F. van der Reit, Esq., C.C. and R.M. of Uitenhage, by whom he had one son, who died in infancy.

Campbell, Captain Duncan

Captain Duncan Campbell, a half-pay officer of the Royal Marines, who came out in the Weymouth at the head of a party consisting of thirteen men, eight women, and eight children from Hampshire. After an unsuccessful attempt at farming on the Endless River (Zonder End) with Southdown sheep that he brought with him, he was removed to Albany. He was not long in coming into prominence, being appointed Heemsraad, with Mr. Miles Bowker, another settler, under Major Jones, whom the Acting-Governor, Sir Rubane Shaw Donkin, had made Provisional Landdrost of Albany. This appointment he held for a short time only, neither he nor his colleague being able to concur in the arbitrary acts of the Governor, Lord Charles Somerset. When, however, changes were made in the condition and style of the appointments previously prevailing under the Dutch system of Government, Captain Campbell was appointed Civil Commissioner and Resident Magistrate of Albany in 1828.

During the administration of Sir Benjamin D'Urban, then Governor of the Colony, he was in 1833 appointed Commissioner-General of the Eastern province, a more important office, in succession to Captain Andries Stockenstrom, who was retired on pension. When that, however, was abolished, he resumed his duties as Civil Commissioner, and in 1836 was required to perform the duties of Resident Magistrate of Albany as well.

There was a good deal of feeling, even at this early date, in the history of the Eastern Frontier, on the benevolent policy of Sir Benjamin D'Urban, the causes of the war of '34-35, and the treatment of the Xhosa by the colonists, which was greatly accentuated by the Rev Dr. Philip and his party in Cape Town, who did all they could to calumniate the settlers, charging them with perpetrating atrocities on the Xhosa. This strongly-marked party feeling led to the appointment of Captain Andries Stockenstrom as Lieutenant-Governor of the Eastern Province, with whom Captain Campbell came into unpleasant collision, and figured as defendant in an action at law instituted against him by Stockenstrom for "maliciously and unlawfully causing and procuring him to be falsely charged with having deliberately fired at and killed a Xhosa child 'during' the operations of a Commando under Captain Fraser in 1813, which was carefully inquired into by the Supreme Court before Wylde, C. J., and Menzies and Burton, J. J., in 1838, with the result that the shooting, of the Xhosa was held proved, but that the deed was a lawful military act, which established Captain Campbell's plea of justification fully and satisfactorily.

Stockenstrom pursued his hostility against Captain Campbell in a further accusation of neglect of duty in allowing the land books of Somerset to fall into arrears, which was the immediate cause of his retirement, his health giving way. Whether Captain Campbell was entitled to a retiring allowance rested on the accuracy of Stockenstrom's charges. Campbell retorted by taking up a newspaper scandal and accusing Stockenstrom of corruption in having received a free grant of the farm Maastrom, consisting of 5,000 morgens of the best land in the old ceded territory. The charge and counter-charge came before the Secretary of State, and was referred to the Governor of the Colony, Sir George Napier, who completely exonerated Captain Campbell, and he was allowed a pension of £200 a year.

Stockenstrom was able to show that he had obtained the farm from Sir Rufane Shaw Donkin in a perfectly honourable manner, at a time when land was being given away by the Government to any official who applied for it. Captain Campbell is described by Sir Rufane Donkin as "a man full of energy and expectation, a gentleman of considerable acquirements, with a strong tincture of the military character."

He was a married man thirty-nine years of age when he arrived in the country, but left no issue to inherit his honourable name. He resided on his farm on the race-course flat above Graham's Town, which he called Thorn Park. A valued correspondent writes:

> "Captain Campbell always lived on his farm, three miles from Graham's Town, on the Fish River side of the town. In my girlhood I used to stay with Mrs. Campbell, frequently for months together. She was a bright and cheerful woman; the old Captain was quiet and thoughtful, and a great politician. Major White, of Table Farm, would frequently ride over and dine with the Captain, talk politics for hours, often till one o'clock in the morning. Then Major White would jump on his horse and ride home in the dark. Captain Campbell was one of the first sheep farmers in the Eastern Province, and perhaps the first man who ever made it pay. He had a good overseer, and took great interest in sheep farming."

Campbell, Major-General Charles

Major-General Charles Campbell, brought out a party of settlers by the *Salisbury* in December 1820, having previously sent out two other parties, who arrived before him. He was the youngest son of Colonel Charles Campbell, of Barbrick, Argyllshire, Scotland, and had seen active service at home and abroad, his last command being that of Commander of the Forces at Newfoundland. He obtained a grant of land near the Kasonga river, close to the Theopolis Mission Station, which he called Barville Park. He was thrown from his horse whilst riding from Graham's Town to Barville Park, and sustained internal injuries which resulted in his death, May 9, 1822, aged fifty years. He lies buried in the military ground adjoining the Drostdy at Graham's Town, where also his infant daughter Catherine was interred, June 4, 1829, aged eight years and four months.

The sons who came to the country with their father and mother were:

- John, who obtained a clerkship in the office of the Protector of Slaves at Graaff Reinet, and by diligence and care rose to various positions of trust and importance, in all of which he earned distinction and the approval of his superiors. In 1847, he obtained leave of absence and visited England, where he married a Miss West. His last appointment was that of Resident Magistrate of Cape Town, from which he was retired on full pay in 1884, after upwards of sixty years' faithful service. He died at Cape Town, August 26, 1888, at the advanced age of eighty-two years, leaving a widow, three sons, all in responsible positions in the public service, and four daughters.
- Frederick, who served as a Volunteer and afterwards as a Provisional Ensign in the Cape Mounted Riflemen throughout the Xhosa campaign of 1835 (medal). In 1844, he proceeded in command of a troop to Port Natal and was engaged against the revolted Zulu chief, Tolo. In September 1848, he commanded three squadrons at Bloemfontein, and advanced to Winburg for the suppression of the Boer rebellion. Served throughout the Xhosa war of 1851-3, including the operations in the Amatolas, passage of and operations across the Kei in December 1852, and other desultory operations. Commanded a squadron with the force under Sir George Cathcart against the Baralong chief, Moshesh, in December 1852, and January 1853, which service concluded the war. He received a serious injury whilst actively engaged against the enemy at Buffalo Post, 27th February 1852, by the dislocation of the right ankle and fracture of the bone of the leg. He retired from the army October 26, 1858, and resided at King William's Town, where he died, December 26, 1884, at the age of seventy-four years. He married late in life, and left three sons.
- William, who returned to the Colony after completing his education in England, and was for some years manager of the Port Elizabeth Bank, and later a General Agent at Alexandria. He married Miss Jessie Malet Lucas, and died at Graham's Town, 19th December, 1879, at the age of sixty-six years, s.p.
- Edward Andrews, also completed his education and returned to the Colony. He owned a farm on the Bushman's River, near Sidbury, and was a flock-

master. He married Priscilla, daughter of Lieutenant R. Daniell, R.N., of Sidbury Park, and soon after sold his farm and removed to Graham's Town, where he died of consumption, 26th June 1857, in his fortieth year, leaving a widow and two daughters, the eldest of whom married Charles A. Dickson, Esq., merchant at Cape Town.

Campbell, Dr. Peter

Dr Peter Campbell, was one of the Salem party under Mr. Hezekiah Sephton by the *Aurora*. He brought his wife, two infant daughters, and a female servant with him. He was of Scottish descent, but born at Omagh, County Tyrone, Ireland. He studied medicine, and took his diplomas from the Royal College of Surgeons, Dublin, December 14, 1809. He practised his profession in Great Marlborough Street, London, as a surgeon, apothecary and accoucheur[136], up to the time of his embarkation for the Colony.

He settled in Graham's Town, lived in Bathurst Street, and continued in practice till his death, 31st July 1837. He was a Freemason, and owing to his exertions the first lodge on the Frontier was built in Graham's Town, viz., the Albany Lodge 389, in January 1828. He was elected Senior Warden, and in 1831 Worshipful Master thereof. In 1832-33, on his retiring, was presented with a past-master's jewel; and in August 1837, the Lodge went into mourning for Dr. Campbell.

Dr. Campbell was twice-married. First in England to Miss Sarah Sanderson, of Cutland, Cumberland, a cousin of Captain Cook, the navigator. By her he had two daughters:

- Margaret Ann, the eldest, born December 1817, married Thomas Bailie, had three children, two sons and one daughter, is still living in Potchefstroom with her second son, John Crause Bailie. The daughter and eldest son are both dead.
- Sarah Lucy Cecilia, born July 2nd, 1819, never married, and is still living at Alice.

These were the two children who came in the *Aurora*. Their mother died 21st July 1825, after the birth of twins—a boy and a girl—who died in infancy. On the 28th July 1826, the doctor married Mary Anne Gumming, the eldest daughter of Thomas Gumming an officer, who had served with his regiment —the Rifle Brigade—through the Peninsular War, and had come to Africa to join the Royal African Corps, which, on arrival, he found was disbanded. Of this marriage only two children lived, viz.,

- Alexander Gumming Campbell, born July 9, 1827, who married a Miss Martha Nel, now dead, has a family of five sons and four daughters, and is living in Tembuland; and

---

136. A male midwife.

- Rosina Jane, born 17th May 1834, married Mr. Richard Harris Blakeway, the youngest son of John Blakeway, formerly in the 21st Light Dragoons, and later Adjutant in the Gape Mounted Rifles; had four sons and three daughters. In 1870 Richard Harris Blakeway was murdered by a Xhosa at Gounbie, and in 1880 his eldest son, William John Blakeway, was killed in action against the Tembus.

Damant, Edward

Edward Damant, head of a party from Norfolk, by the *Ocean*. The Damant family originally came from Ghent and Antwerp after the revocation of the Edict of Nantes. Doctor John Atherstone had married a sister of Commissary General John Damant, who married Miss Korsten, of Cradock Place, near Port Elizabeth, and it was this circumstance which led to the Damants and Atherstones coming to settle in the Colony. Lieutenant Edward Damant, above named, formerly of the 38th Regiment of Foot, came from Fakenham, Norfolk, and brought his wife and two daughters with him. He had been in Sir Thomas Willshire's company at the storming of Badajos, and led the company over the walls, coming out with only four men. He died at Table Farm, near Graham's Town, at an advanced age, his elder brother, John, who was one of the party, having died there in 1846. The only son of Mr. Edward Damant is Mr. Hugh Damant, who has long resided at Kimberley, and has a large family.

Carlisle, John

John Carlisle, head of a party bearing his name from Staffordshire, arriving by the *Chapman*. He was a young man and unmarried. He was a terrible sufferer by the Xhosa irruptions, his house and buildings being destroyed by fire, his stock swept off, and his crops un-reaped. He lived at his farm called Belmont, in the Kowie Valley, about four miles beyond Graham's Town. He married Catherine, the eldest daughter of Thomas Phillipps, Esq., and dying left three sons.
- Robert, a farmer, who married a Miss Botha;
- Sydney, an attorney of the Supreme Court, who married a daughter General Sir John Bissit, died s. p.; and
- Edmond, a farmer, who married a daughter of Dr. Eddie, of the C.M.R.

Carlisle, Frederick

Frederick Carlisle, brother of the foregoing, and one of the same party. He lived in Graham's Town after being driven from his location by the Xhosa, and was for many years Deputy-Sheriff of Albany, Bathurst, and Victoria East. He married a daughter of Mr. Frederick Phillipps ; died and left two sons, the younger of whom, William Montagu, survives, and who served in Basutuland and Transkei, 1872 to 1884, as clerk to the Resident Magistrates, and also as lieutenant in the Mafeking native contingent during the Basutu rebellion, and is now in the public service at Kimberley.

Cawood, David

David Cawood, was one of Mr. Hazelhurst's party, whose location was on the north-east of the Nottingham party. He was accompanied by six sons—James, William, John, Joshua, Samuel and Joseph—and three daughters. The Cawood's were descended from a Yorkshire family, many of whom, according to the chronicles of Cawood and Cawood Castle, held important positions and offices as far back as 1201. David Cawood and his family settled on the farm known as "Cawood's Post," in Albany, but no long time elapsed before the sons, young and enterprising, moved off, the war of 1835, scattering many others also who never returned to their locations, finding more satisfactory openings for their energy elsewhere.

Previous to this period the young Cawood's went through Xhosaland to Natal— no ordinary feat in those days— on a hunting and trading expedition. They penetrated as far as Dingaan's Kraal, and were received and entertained by that chief for ten days. Although well treated while at the kraal, after they had left, Dingaan sent an impi after them with orders to kill them and take their property. Providentially the party took the route along the coast, whereas the impi took the inland road and so missed them.

James, the eldest son, was the senior partner in the firm of Cawood Brothers, consisting of William, Samuel and Joseph, who for many years carried on a large mercantile business in Graham's Town with several country branches, and they were army contractors for some years. They took a prominent part in public matters as Municipal Commissioners, etc., James, Joshua, Samuel and Joseph having been returned to the Legislative Council and House of Assembly respectively, where they ably represented Eastern Province interests.

William Cawood, served in Southey's Corps of Guides, when the forces entered Xhosaland and brought the Fingo tribe out of slavery. He was present at the death of Hintza, the great paramount chief of those times. These men have left a name for courage, enterprise and honesty, second to none, and their descendants are to be found throughout the Cape Colony, Natal and neighbouring States, possibly more numerous than any of the immigrants of 1820. The Rev. H. H. Dugmore, in his Jubilee lecture delivered at Graham's Town in 1870, gives the united generations then living as 356, the original family comprising nine, of whom Mrs. Stuart and Mrs. Gradwell are the only survivors.[137]

Cawood, Samuel

Another colleague of Mr. Godlonton's in political strife, and a co-operator with him in various local undertakings, was Samuel Cawood, who came with his parents with Mr. Hazelhurst's party in the transport, John being then thirteen years of age.

Godlonton, Wood and Cawood have always been bracketed together as Fathers of the Settlement. At one time the firm of Cawood Brothers, of which Samuel was a member, were contractors to the Imperial forces, and in a large way of business. Samuel Cawood owned landed property in Lower Albany, and was unceasing in his efforts to induce farm owners and others to cultivate cotton on their lands, the seeds for which he procured with some difficulty and expense, and distributed gratuitously. He was in consequence familiarly called 'King Cotton.' He was one of the most active promoters of the meeting at Graham's Town of such of the settlers as survived with their direct descendants to celebrate the Jubilee of their arrival and landing in Algoa Bay in 1820. And as the result of that gathering of the settlers and the interest that the proceedings evoked in the history of the Settlement, he was mainly instrumental in raising a permanent monument in the shape of the "Settlers' Memorial Tower,"

Mr. Godlonton laying the foundation stone amidst much enthusiasm. Six or seven years later the Town Council of Graham's Town determined to build a Town Hall, when it was suggested that this Memorial Tower should form part of it. When the tower was up to its first floor, it was determined to convert the upper bell-turret into a clock chamber. The corner foundation stone of this Town Hall was laid with much ceremony by his Excellency Sir Bartle Frere, then Governor of the Colony, during the mayoralty of Mr. T. M. Parker. The old memorial foundation stone was subsequently removed and re-laid by Mr. Godlonton as the foundation stone of one of the buttresses of the present tower, which is 120 feet high. A clock with illuminated dials has been put into the Settlers' Memorial Tower.

The Town Hall was publicly opened by Samuel Cawood, Acting-Mayor, 7th May 1882, when the tower was completed, which is as much a memento of himself as of those whose advent it is intended to honour and commemorate. In 1855, he

---

137. See page 20

was returned to Parliament and continued to represent his constituency for seven consecutive years. Then came a break of nine years in his useful Parliamentary career, until, in 1869, at the General Election, he was returned to a seat in the Legislative Council, which he occupied until 1873. In 1872, he entertained at a banquet at Graham's Town the then Governor, Sir Henry Barkly, and 200 of the leading citizens whom he had invited to meet his Excellency. In 1880, he was elected Mayor of Graham's Town. He died at his residence Waybank House, Graham's Town, 15th June 1887, aged 79 years. The descendants of the Cawood family are of the most numerous of the British Settlers, and are to be found in almost every part of the Frontier districts as well as in the neighbouring States.

Chase, John Centlivres

John Centlivres Chase formed one of Mr. Bailie's party, arriving by the *Chapman*. He was a married man; his daughter Louisa, an infant child, died in the Bay of Biscay on the passage out. Bailie's party was located at the mouth of the Fish River, and the place was called Cuylerville. Mr. Chase was not cut out for agriculture, and his wife dying at the Kowie, in 1830, leaving four children, he removed to Cape Town, where he practised as a Notary Public, and there married for the second time a daughter of Mr. Korston (of Cradock Place, at one time a Lieutenant in the Dutch Navy) and widow of Commissary General Damant, by whom she had two sons.

About 1835 or 36 he returned to the Frontier and continued to practise as a Notary till Sir Henry Young was Lieutenant-Governor (1847) at Graham's Town, where he acted as Secretary to Government till Sir Henry left, when he was appointed C.C. and R.M. to the newly-formed division of Albert. He founded Aliwal-North, designed and presented its seal, and from there was promoted to Uitenhage as CC. and R.L, where he remained till he retired on pension, 1855.

In 1864, he was elected Member of the House of Assembly for Port Elizabeth, but resigned his seat. At the General Election in 1869 he was elected as a Member of the Legislative Council. He was regarded as an authority on statistics relating to the Colony; author of a continuation of Wilmot's History of the Colony and other volumes descriptive of the Eastern Province; also published Green's Journey to Natal in 1829, with a map of the country traversed by Green and his companion. Dr. Cowie.

Mr. Chase was twice-married. By his first wife he had two sons—Henry and Frederick —and two daughters. His second wife was a daughter of Mr. Korston, of

Cradock Place, near Port Elizabeth (at one time a Lieutenant in the Dutch Navy), and widow of Commissary-General Damant, by whom he had two sons and four daughters. Both sons by the first wife are dead; the sons by the second wife survive, viz. , L C. Chase, auctioneer at Rouxville, O.F.S.; and Frederick Korston Chase, H.M.'s Customs, Port Elizabeth. Mr. Chase died at his residence, Cradock Place, about five miles from Port Elizabeth, his death being hastened by his being thrown from his carriage some time before, December 15, 1876, aged seventy years. The head of the family is Mr. Harry Chase, Attorney-at-Law, Uitenhage.

Collett, James

James Collett, was one of the settlers brought out by General Campbell, who arrived with others in the brig *Salisbury*. He was a man fairly well-educated, intelligent, and cautious. He made his way into the Cradock district, where he commenced sheep farming. After a few years he acquired by purchase the farm Green Fountain, about three miles beyond the town of Cradock, and married a daughter of Mr. Joseph Trollip, a settler of Hyman's party, who had also removed to Cradock to pursue sheep farming. This union of families has been fruitful to a degree, the names of Collett and Trollip being found all over that large district. In 1834, James Collett was returned as a member of the House of Assembly for the electoral division of Cradock, but forfeited his seat, preferring his pastoral pursuits to the toil of a long and tedious journey to Cape Town, and the distractions of a parliamentary session.

Cock, William

Mr. William Cock, the head of Cock's party, who, with several other small parties, came out by the *Weymouth* transport, was located on the banks of the Kowie, near its mouth. He was a young man, twenty-six years of age, married, and had three children when he landed. His first impressions were inseparably associated with an inlet which engaged his attention to his dying day, and for which he never faltered in predicting for it full importance. Blighted harvests, flooded rivers, and Xhosa depredations were only the more prominent difficulties the pioneers were called upon to contend with, and which, to a large extent, caused a break up of the locations and the dispersion of the settlers.

Among the latter was Mr. Cock. Intuitively a man of business, a printer by trade, and constitutionally active and pushing, he was soon found at Graham's Town, then in its infancy, elbowing his way and joining others in laying those commercial foundations upon which subsequent generations have securely built.

At one time he was a contractor to Government for supplying the Mauritius with salted beef and other provisions, compelling him to go over to that Island and to St. Helena; anon in partnership with the wealthy Cape Town firm of Heideman, Hodgson & Co.; and again establishing a successful wholesale business in Graham's Town in connection with the same firm.

Amid all this bustle of life and clash of commercial competition, while his energy was conspicuous, his integrity was equally so. After a few years of successful enterprise the partnership with which he stood connected was dissolved by mutual consent, Mr. Cock retiring from it with a moderate competency. Here again, it is remarked in the obituary notice of him published at the time of his death, that the attraction which drew him to the Kowie was remarkable. In the course of the firm's previous business transactions a good deal of land had been either taken over or purchased; and among these were several farms at the mouth of the Kowie. These assets were, at his own desire, allotted to him, and he then gave practical effect to the idea he had always cherished of forming the Kowie estuary into a commercial harbour.

A brief visit to his beautiful native country of Cornwall did not dissipate these sanguine hopes. He shortly returned to the Cape, and in conjunction with Messrs. Hayton succeeded in establishing another mercantile business in Graham's Town. After a few years he retired from this, and then concentrated his whole attention on the improvement of the harbour. This was only done at the expense of immense personal labour and an almost ruinous outlay of capital. It may be said that for a time he stood alone in this project, and it is impossible to overestimate the pluck which enabled him to sustain the weight of responsibility resting upon him, and that too coupled with discouragement of the most depressing character.

It was during this period of his career that he was nominated by the Governor of the Colony, Sir Henry Pottinger, a member of the Legislative Council, thus opening up to him a new phase of colonial life. As a member of the Legislature no one ever displayed more sturdy independence or approved himself a more ardent lover of his country. It was impossible to be associated with him without feeling assured of the firmness of his political principles or of his readiness to stand up and do battle for the rights and welfare of his fellow colonists. It was at this time, during his membership in the old Legislative Council, that he succeeded, in conjunction with his only colleague from the Eastern Province, Mr. Godlonton, in getting the Bill for the improvement of the Kowie passed into law. This was conceded grudgingly, and then only on condition that half the £50,000 required for the work should be raised by the people themselves, impoverished as they were by the innumerable difficulties which at the time surrounded them. This Act was a great step in advance, which however only excited him to more incessant exertions and more vigilant oversight. The issue may be anticipated.

He wore himself out in the service of his country and in a most laudable attempt to carry to perfect completion a grand idea; and though he eventually broke down, he was permitted to see, to a large extent, the fruition of his most sanguine hopes. He died at Graham's Town, February 9, 1876, aged eighty-three years.

He left three sons and five daughters. The sons were all engaged in agricultural pursuits, but also took an active part in the wars of 1835 and 1846. When the war of 1835 broke out, the boys were at school on Sir Richard Southey's farm, and had a narrow escape, Sir Richard's brother-in-law, John Shaw, being killed by the Xhosa.

- William Frederick Cock, married Miss Lucy Netherton, and died in 1884, leaving three sons.
- Cornelius Cock, the second son, did a great deal of active service, particularly in the war of 1846; was engaged in a big fight at Kowie West defending his father's cattle, some six hundred head, which were swept off; again at Wolfs Craig, under General Somerset. Was Captain in Meurant's levy under Colonel Armstrong, and subsequently in charge of the Commissariat from Waterloo Bay to the Kei under General Somerset's division. In the war of 1851 served under Sir Walter Currie, clearing the Blackwater's point on the Fish River, and in the Amatolas under Colonel Percival and Colonel Eyre. Was personally thanked for his services by Sir George Cathcart, and at the request of the Magistrate of the district made a J.P., which honour he has held for forty-four years. He was twice-married, first to Miss Letitia Smith, by whom he had three sons and two daughters. She died in 1860, and in 1870 he married Miss Edith Jaffray, by whom he has six sons and one daughter. He is now living at Lessendram, district of Peddie.
- The third son, Nathaniel Cock, also did good service during the wars, particularly at the surprise of Hans Bunder, a notorious Khoisan, and his party, when he captured sixteen guns in one batch. He married Miss Mary Bacher, and had a family—three daughters, all married—who now live in Bechuanaland. He died at Johannesburg, February 14, 1895, aged sixty-five years.

Currie, Sir Walter

Sir Walter Currie's father, Lieutenant Walter Currie, a purser in the Royal Navy on half pay, came with Mr. Willson's party in the *Belle Alliance*, and lived on the location assigned to Mr. Willson's party, south of Manley's Flat, otherwise called Beaufort Vale, near Bathurst. Subsequently, he acquired a farm near that, which he called Langholm. Here young Currie was brought up from infancy, being only one year old when his parents arrived in Albany. In the war of '34-35 he took the field as a volunteer in the corps of Guides, under the command of Captains W. Bowker and R. Southey.

After the war Walter Currie returned to his farm, declining a commission in the Army offered him by Sir Benjamin D'Urban, and on his father's death removed to the little Fish River, near Somerset, where he had a sheep farm. During the war of '46 he did good service, scouring the country and driving the Xhosa from their strongholds. In 1850, he disarmed the disaffected Khoisan at Theopolis, and made prisoners of the ringleaders and took command of several wagon trains between Graham's Town and Cradock. In 1852, when Governor Sir George Cathcart arrived and found the Eastern Districts in a still insecure state, he was appointed Commandant of the Albany District in the new corps, which was styled the Frontier Armed Mounted Police, in which corps he distinguished himself by his valour and daring, to which Sir George Cathcart gave expression in garrison orders, 12th January 1853.

On Sir George Grey's arrival, realizing the importance of a constant patrolling police force on the Frontier, arrangements were made to organize the force permanently, and Currie was appointed to continue at its head and superintend its management as General Commandant. Under this new force Currie distinguished himself in the expedition against Queesha and Vadanna in the Queen's Town district, and the after expulsion of the paramount chief Kreli from beyond the Bashee. These services were brought to the notice of Her Majesty the Queen by special despatches from Governor Sir George Grey, and Currie received the honour of knighthood, and also to mark His Royal Highness Prince Alfred's appreciation of his services during the long and interesting tour which that member of the Royal Family made in 1860.

Sir Walter Currie's routing and dislodging of rebellious Khoisan and Korannas, who had established themselves on the islands of the Orange River near its mouth, and were a source of annoyance and damage to the colonists in that part by their predatory and lawless habits, was a service in which daring and hardship were equally combined, but which brought his active career to a termination. The fatigues of that campaign and the successive drenching in reaching the islands and getting back to land, brought on an attack of acute rheumatism which rendered him a cripple till his death, which occurred at his residence, Oatlands, near Graham's Town, July 7, 1872. He left no descendant to bear his honoured name.

Dyason

Isaac, wife and four children;

Joseph, wife and two children;

George, wife and two children;

Robert, wife and three children;

came with sixteen others as Dyason's party by the *Zoroaster*, and were located between Mr. Willson's party and the Nottingham party. Mr. Joseph Dyason had been a Quartermaster in the Royal Navy, and six years master in the Mercantile Navy. He was employed by Government to survey the mouth of the Kowie River, to determine whether it was navigable.

Mr. George Dyason became Resident Magistrate at Bathurst, and finally Civil Commissioner and Resident Magistrate at Graaff Reinet. A survivor of the family writes:

> I can just remember living on our farm, Rokeby Park, joining Mr. Currie's, between Graham's Town and Bathurst. The old chief Pato lived near, and when he came to see my father would say, 'Kill sheep,' for his councillors. He himself used to drive with my father sometimes. He always wore, I have heard, a black tailcoat and a bell-topper. Another circumstance I have heard my father speak of was, when they lived at Lushington Valley, how the elephants rubbed themselves against the corner of the house, which was made of wattle and daub, and how terrified the inmates were to go out. There some vines were planted—the very first; also the first merino sheep my father got from England.

> During one of the wars, I don't remember which, my father was magistrate at Bathurst; my mother would not leave him and go to Graham's Town with all of us, so we were for three months barricaded in the church, each family having a pew. We had the vestry, being the principal people, and the Ayliff's had the inside of the communion rails. We used to have stumped mealies with them one night, and the next they would come and have what we had. Provisions were becoming scarce, when, luckily, a schooner put into the Kowie, and my father paid £5 for a bag of fine flour. There was no kind of communication with Graham's Town until the 73rd Regiment came to our help from Mauritius.

A very dear brother, George, was killed by Xhosa on his way from the Fish River farms with wool for Graham's Town merchants, 15th June 1851. The bodies of three Xhosa were found near his body who he had shot. Commandant Currie, who went to the rescue, found the rebels had cut the bales of wool off the wagons to make a kind of scherm[138]. The Khoi drivers and leaders had run away. Another of the family, William Dyason, was shot by Xhosa while on duty under Commandant McTaggart in the islands of the Orange River, 10th April 1879. From Bathurst my father was sent to Graaff Reinet as Civil Commissioner and Resident Magistrate. We had a party of soldiers sent from Graham's Town to protect us through the Kowie Bush, as we had to go in ox-wagons to Port Elizabeth, and so to Graaff Reinet.

Mr. George Dyason was retired from the service in 1855, after having served thirty-five years. He died at his residence at Port Elizabeth, August 7, 1862, aged seventy-one years. Field-Adjutant Dyason was killed in an engagement with the Korannas, on the Orange River, April 1879. The Dyason family is represented by Durban Dyason, Esq., attorney-at-law, Port Elizabeth.

Forbes, Alexander

Alexander Forbes, one of the settlers in Mr. Parker's party, from Cork, Ireland, by the *East Indian*. He was an industrious shoemaker, was, on the breaking out of the war of 1834-5, attacked in open day by Xhosa at his dwelling on Waai Plaats, despatched by numerous assegai wounds, his dwelling fired and reduced to ashes. His wife, with a family of seven young children, fortunately escaped.

Garcia, Maurice

Maurice Garcia, was one of the settlers introduced by General Campbell, who arrived in the brig *Dowson*, after a protracted voyage of nearly six months. He brought letters of recommendation to the Governor of the Colony, who advised him to purchase the site on which Port Elizabeth has been built; but he obtained from a friend an unfavourable report of the appearance of the place, describing the shores around the port as nothing but bare sand hills. He therefore did not proceed to the Frontier, but succeeded in obtaining a Government appointment at George as Clerk of the Peace, with leave to practise as an Attorney of the Supreme Court. He was

---

138. Screen

well qualified for the position, as he was a gentleman who had received a liberal education in England and France. He studied Dutch in the Colony, and was duly admitted a sworn translator of the Supreme Court. He held the office of Clerk of the Peace until 1861, when it was abolished. He then accepted the magistracy of Richmond, and eventually that of Riversdale, where he died in 1884. He left two sons in the Civil Service, Arthur Garcia, Esq., C.C. and R.M. of Uitenhage, Paymaster-General and Inspector-General of the Colonial Forces during the wars of 1878-81, and at one time Private Secretary to the late General Gordon; and Egbert Garcia, C.C. and R.M. of Queen's Town.

Glass, Thomas

Thomas Glass, was one of Mr. George Southey's party which came out in the *Kennersly Castle*. He was married, and brought his wife and six children, four sons and two daughters, two more sons and one daughter being born to him in this country. He took to farming, and acquired a property near Graham's Town, which he called Coldstream, where he successfully pursued his operations till his death in 1849, at the age of sixty-five years.

Of his six sons, John and James became carpenters and builders at Graham's Town, John eventually migrating to the district of Peddie, where he died about 1871. James went to the Diamond Fields soon after they were discovered, and attracted a large population in 1872, and followed his trade at Kimberley until his death, which occurred in 1874. Both John and James left a numerous family. Thomas and Benjamin (who was born in Albany) were both masons. Thomas met with his death by a fall from a scaffold to a house he was building; Benjamin is still alive, and at present on the farm Coldstream. Daniel and William followed in their father's footsteps and became farmers. Daniel acquired land near Driver's Bush, a little beyond Graham's Town, and farmed it till he met his death about 1874, a young cow having gored him, from which he died in a few hours. William went into the Victoria East (Alice) district and acquired farms there. He too, met with an untimely death. While placing a tarpaulin over a load of grain on his wagon, he fell over and broke his neck. A son of James Glass served in the Zulu war, and was present at the battle of Ulundi; and a son of Benjamin's who was a member of the Yeomanry Corps was killed during the Basutu war.

Godlonton, Robert

A settler whose name will remain familiar even to a succeeding generation, and whose fame will not die out, was Mr. Robert Godlonton, one of Mr. Bailie's party in the ship *Chapman*. He was born in London in 1794, and having to fight his way in the world, was, at an early age, apprenticed to the trade of a printer in one of the largest London offices. Thomas Stringfellow, who became Civil Commissioner and Resident Magistrate of Fort Beaufort, was employed by the same establishment, and the two friends, then married, attached themselves to Mr. Bailie's party and came to Albany with the settlers of 1820.

On his first arrival he shared the hardships of the pioneer settler's life on a location. That they were not trivial, may be gathered from the fact, often mentioned by Mr. Godlonton, of the walks with a companion or two from the Fish River mouth over the roughest hills and bush paths into Graham's Town, to get a few loaves of contractor's bread, then considered an epicurean luxury, with which they would walk back again to share it with their families and friends. The hardships and uncertainty of location life, as soon as Government rations were no longer forthcoming, caused him to remove to Graham's Town. After a short time he accepted employment in the Landdrost's office at Graham's Town and the revenue department of the Eastern Province, under Captain Duncan Campbell, whose confidence he fully obtained.

One of the chief responsibilities of his office was the collection of taxes, the "Opgaaf" as it was then called, a duty attended both with difficulty and serious responsibility, involving as it did the collection of taxes based upon the pastoral wealth of the farmers, collected from the rural population by visitation from farm to farm. On these expeditions his only safe was his wagon-box, and his honesty the only security the Government could obtain.

Whilst in office, he had offers of promotion in the service, but declined these offers, preferring to embrace one far more congenial to a man of literary tastes. He was a man of intelligence, with a strong determination, and resolute in maintaining the rights and liberties of the people, strongly opposed to the tyranny and oppression of Lord Charles Somerset's rule. This made him a chosen leader, and he was among the foremost to oppose that Governor in his attempts to suppress the popular voice.

In the same ship with himself, and of the same party, was Dr. Edward Roberts, who brought a printing press to be used by Godlonton under his control, in conjunction with Stringfellow and Mollett, who were also fellow emigrants in the same vessel, of the same party, and of the same trade. It was contemplated producing a newspaper as a means of communication between the settlers and other inhabitants and friends at home. The project, however, came to nothing, as on arrival of the vessel and the discovery of this "infectious machine,"

Sir Rufane Shaw Donkin, the Acting-Governor, confiscated it, paying its cost to Dr. Roberts. Mr. Noble, in his Past and Present (p.44), says Godlonton and Stringfellow had been engaged in the King's printing office, Schackelwell, and that Mr. Rutt, the manager, anxious to give them a fair start, had given them a complete plant for a printing establishment, upon the understanding that if they were successful, he should be paid for it ; if not, no demand would be made for it. Stringfellow was allowed to go ashore, and by negotiation with the Government printer the amount of the invoice was paid and remitted by Dr. Roberts to Mr. Rutt in England. This press and material were, some years after, sent to Graaff Reinet to be used for printing Government notices and similar innocuous matter. By a strange irony of fate, this identical press was, after a considerable interval, purchased by Mr. Godlonton, by whom it was preserved in 'cotton and lavender' as one of the curiosities of the past.

It is impossible to do justice to the character of this remarkable man in a short memoir, or to refer in detail to all the political movements which he directed and successfully accomplished. There was no more strenuous and unflinching champion of the rights and liberties of the subject, no more valiant defender of the character of the immigrants against the unjust and uncharitable aspersions that were levelled at them, and the calumnies that were circulated against the settlers at the seat of Government and in England.

It was not till December 1831, that the Graham's Town Journal was launched by Mr. L. H. Meurant, to which Mr. Godlonton was one of the principal contributors. It was in order to share an interest in the venture, of which he subsequently became the sole proprietor, that he relinquished his position in the Civil Service. He conducted the Journal with marked ability for a long period of years, and which was popularly termed the "Settlers' Bible." He published several pamphlets of great service at the time, notably his *Narrative of the Irruption* of the Xhosa in 1834-5, and his Case of the Colonists in reference to the Invasions of the Xhosa in 1835 and 1846.

The influence thus gained led to his being chosen as one of the two elective members, Mr. Cock being the other, to represent the Eastern Province under the first form of constitutional government that was granted to the country. Upon the Colony having its constitution developed by an increase of elective representatives, he was at once returned. He lived to see the fruits of his incessant labours in the cause of political freedom and progress, the eventual concession of responsible government, though he and his colleagues did all they could to delay the introduction of that step, holding that the Colony was not sufficiently advanced to take upon itself self government, and that the Eastern Province would be ruled by the Cape Town party, who were hostile to the settlers and to Frontier development.

In 1858 he, with his family, revisited his native land after an absence of thirty-eight years, spending three years renewing old associations and friendships. On his return to the Colony he retired from the prominent position he had so long occupied in public life and from editorial duties, but in his retirement enjoyed a vigorous old age and the unaffected respect and attachment of his fellow citizens and of colonists at large. He died at his residence, Beaufort House, Graham's Town, May 30, 1884, at the advanced age of ninety-one years. A marble monument was subsequently erected over his grave in the Wesleyan Cemetery bearing the inscription:

> Robert Godlonton,
> Born in London, 24th September, 1794,
> Died at Graham's Town, 30th May, 1884.
> A British Settler of 1820. The recognised Father of the Press in the Eastern Province of the Colony, and for many years a valued member of the Legislative Council of the Cape of Good Hope.
> "Mark the perfect man, and behold the upright, for the end of that man is peace." Psalm xxxvii. 37.

Gray, William

William Gray, one of Mr. Bailie's party from London, who came in the ship Chapman. He was then nineteen years of age. He was first in the employ of Mr. Ford, surveyor and farmer, grandfather of the Fords now living near to Highlands railway station, on the Graham's Town and Port Elizabeth line. Afterwards he became the senior partner of the firm of Gray & Harper, farmers and contractors for oat-hay, etc., who also had a business as jewellers, etc., in Howard's party, Kowie Valley, about seven or eight miles from Graham's Town. He was a grantee of a small farm between Graham's Town and Bathurst, which, however, he never occupied. He also possessed property near the Fish River mouth. He married Elizabeth, daughter of Mr. George Marsden, one of Mr. Dixon's party of settlers. Eventually he bought the farm Walsingham, near Southwell, from Captain Crause, who gave the name to the farm.

Here he carried on agriculture extensively, being with the Dells and other settlers in that neighbourhood, a contractor for the supply of oat-hay to the Commissariat for the military garrison at Graham's Town. He was Field Cornet of the ward Southwell during the sudden defection of the Khoisan of the Theopolis mission station nearby in 1848. His house, stacks of forage, wheat, etc., etc., were burnt down and stock all taken in the two successive Xhosa wars of 1835 and 1846. He was Commandant of the Levies which went from Graham's Town to attack the rebel Khoisan of Theopolis, when he lost his life, being shot dead by one of the rebels on the 2nd June, 1850, in a dense bush called the Gorah, where the villains had formed a camp. A memorial window was erected in the church of Southwell to his memory by the inhabitants of Southwell, and the Government granted to his widow a Captain's pension for life.

He left three sons; viz., (1) George Gray, now a wealthy sheep farmer in the Komgha district; (2) William Marsden Gray, farmer in Lower Albany; and (3) James Wakelyn Gray, farmer and scab inspector near Lady Frere, district of Queen's Town; also several daughters, one of whom married the Rev. William Henry Turpin, missionary of the English Church in charge of St. Philip's Church and Mission Schools in the Xhosa location, Graham's Town, related to the Baronets Coningham and Plunket of Ireland, from the latter of whom the present Archbishop of Dublin is descended.

Greathead, James

James Greathead, head of a small party from Worcestershire by the *Kennersly Castle*. His location was about halfway between Graham's Town and the coast, with Messrs. Erith, Southey, Phillipps, and Scanlen for neighbours. He was a surveyor by profession, and built a house at Bathurst, where he resided. He died of sunstroke about 1830, leaving a widow and one child, a son ten years of age.

After some years the widow married Mr. William Smith, a land surveyor, and died in Graham's Town in 1843. The son, James Henry, was actively engaged in mercantile pursuits, and became senior partner of a large firm in Graham's Town. He married Julia, daughter of Mr. William Wright, by whom he had twelve children, all except one, who died in England, surviving him. He died in 1864.

The sons are:
- William Wright, formerly living at Aliwal North, superintending the working of a mill on his late father's estate, subsequently a successful farmer in the Orange Free State, married Miss Emilie Halse.

- James Henry, an engineer of repute in connection with the subterranean works under the River Thames, in England, now a member of the Council of Civil Engineers, married. Blanche Coryndon;
- Herbert Harding, a farmer in the district of Fort Beaufort, married Miss E. V. Halse;
- D. C. R. Greathead, merchant and miller at Aliwal North, Mayor of that town for some years, married Miss E. Burnet;
- John Baldwin, M.B. Edin., M.R.CS. Lond., living in Graham's Town, enjoying an extensive practice, married (i) Esther Louisa Merriman, (ii.) Miss E. Bubb.
- Walter Horatio, Civil Engineer and Surveyor, who surveyed most of Griqualand West, now living in England, or working there, unmarried;
- Octavius Ernest, for some time in the Mounted Police at Aliwal North, and fought in Basutuland, married Miss Philips, subsequently retired and went to Johannesburg, where he was killed by the falling of a building (Roode Porte);
- George Alfred, surveyor practising in the Transvaal, formerly in the Colonial Civil Service, unmarried.

The daughters are Rosa, unmarried; and Julia Emily, married Hon. C. T. Smith, a judge of the Supreme Court of the Colony.

Griffith, Charles

Charles Griffith, a retired First Lieutenant of the Royal Marines, was head of a party from Cardiganshire, Wales, arrived in the *Stentor*, and landed at Cape Town, 19th April 1820. He was accompanied by two brothers and three sisters.

The brother were Valentine Griffith, also a retired officer of the Royal Marines, and John Griffith, a doctor. The Acting-Governor of the Colony, Sir R. S. Donkin, fearing to pour too many settlers into Albany all at once, located Mr. Griffith at the Endless River[139] in the district of Caledon, where he first started sheep-farming. After spending some time on a farm at Groen Kloof, and finding the locality unsuited to his purpose, he was removed, at his own request, to Graham's Town, where he held the appointment of Barrack Master at Fort England until after the war of 1835, when he again turned sheep-farmer, and lived near Graham's Town at Burnt Kraal, being with Lieutenant Daniell of Sidbury, the first to introduce the merino breed of sheep. Here he remained till 1843, when he gave up sheep-farming and moved to Cape Town and Port Elizabeth, where he resided till 1849, when he was appointed Clerk of the Peace at Cradock, which appointment he held until his death in 1855. In or about 1826, Mr. Griffith married at Cape Town the widow of Lieutenant James Fitchat, also of the Royal Marines, and by her had four children, namely,

---

139. Zonderend river

- Anna Elizabeth, who married the Rev. E. P. Green, MA., rector of Queen's Town, and now vicar of St. Simon Zelotes, Bethnal Green, London, E.
- Charles Duncan Griffith, who married Dorothea Mounsey Gilfillan, fourth daughter of William Gilfillan, Esq., Civil Commissioner and Resident Magistrate of Cradock.
- John Valentine Griffith, who went to Tasmania, in 1851 married and settled there. And
- Mary, who married Colonel E. C. Saunders, of Her Majesty Commissariat Department.

The brothers: Valentine Griffith only remained a short time in the Colony, and then went to and settled in Tasmania, where he died leaving a family; John Griffith, the doctor, lived a few years in Cape Town, where he died.

The three sisters lived and died in Cape Town. The son of the above, Charles Duncan Griffith, distinguished himself in the Xhosa irruptions, notably in the capture of the chief Vandauna during the war of 1846-47, for which service he received the distinction of C. M.G. (1887). He held various appointments in the public service, the duties of which he performed with uniform care and credit, which led to his being selected for the delicate and onerous position of Chief Magistrate and Governor's Agent in Basutuland, which responsible office he held till that territory was taken over by the Imperial authorities in 1883, when he was retired on pension. He represented the native constituency of Tembuland in the House of Assembly from the date of its creation as an electoral division of the Colony in 1891 to 1894. He lives at East London.

Hartley

Hartley, Benjamin, with wife and two daughters, belonged to Mr. Hazelhurst's party from Lancashire.

Hartley, John, with wife and eight children belonged to the Nottingham party under Dr. Calton by the *Albury*.

Hartley, William, one of Mr. Wainwright's party from Yorkshire by the transport *John*, was forty years of age when he arrived, and not married.

The name of Hartley is to be found scattered over the Colony and beyond it, some engaged in commercial, others in agricultural pursuits. The original settlers did not remain long on the locations assigned to them. The parents soon opened a small business in Bathurst, while the young men started on a life of adventure as hunters and traders on the Xhosa border, which latter was forbidden without special permit from the authorities.

At that time the Kowie Bush and the Fish River Bush teemed with large game, such as elephants, buffaloes, seacows[140], etc., and parties of young men left the more peaceful and safer pursuits of agricultural and pastoral life for the rougher and more dangerous but profitable and exhilarating life of hunting and trading. The war of 1835 put a stop to this to a very great extent.

Some years before this event the eldest brother, William Hartley, had found his way into and established a home in the country beyond the Fish River boundary then known as the Tarka, where he settled down to a farming life combined with shop-keeping among the Boers in that part. He was fairly successful, and was appointed Field Comet, and generally acted as Government Agent among the Boers and the Tambookies on the border. When the Boers decided on the 'Great Trek' across the Orange and Vaal Rivers, he declined the offer of a command of some of their party, and shortly after removed to Graham's Town, where he settled until after the war of 1850, when the Tambookies having been driven across the Black Kei, their country, now known as the Queen's Town district, was allotted to farmers, and opened business in the new township.

Whilst residing in Graham's Town, he was for some years one of the Municipal Commissioners and took his share of the public duties of a citizen, as he did wherever he resided. He finally followed his children, who had, most of them, settled at the Diamond Fields, and died at Kimberley at the ripe age of ninety years. Some of his children are settled in the Transvaal, the eldest son living, however, is Mr. C. H. Hartley, who edited and published the Independent newspaper at Kimberley for about sixteen years, and was the first to start a daily paper on the Diamond Fields, the second or third daily newspaper in South Africa.

Thomas Hartley, the next brother, established himself at Bathurst, where he carried on the business of farmer and storekeeper. In the dearth of medical men, he made himself very useful in the surrounding neighbourhood as an unprofessional doctor in simple cases, having studied sufficiently to be able, in cases of emergency, to advise and prescribe until a medical man could be brought from Graham's Town. He also died at a ripe old age. He left a large family, the young men of which removed to Kaffraria on the settlement of that country, and are still farming in the neighbourhood of King William's Town.

Jeremiah Hartley went into the Wesleyan ministry and laboured as a missionary among the Basutus, Baralongs, etc., in Bechuanaland and Basutuland. He established the important mission station of Thaba 'Nchu, where the chief Moroko finally settled with his tribe. One of the results of his work was shown in the steadfast loyalty to the white man of that chief and his people during all the native

---

140. Hippopotamus

disturbances which affected the country. This devoted missionary died at his post, among his people, and his grave may be found in the cemetery on the old station. His eldest son was for some years Town Clerk of Cradock, and died at that place while still in office in 1893.

Of John Hartley nothing is known beyond that he settled in Graham's Town and died about thirty years ago.

Henry Hartley, the youngest, early left civilization behind him and was one of the very few white men who ventured into the dominions of that cruel, bloodthirsty despot Moselikatze, chief of the Matabeles. When that country was more of a terra incognita to the civilized world than the 'dark' continent is to-day, this adventurous member of the Hartley family hunted elephants and rhinoceros in the far north, bordering on the regions of the Zambesi. Hairy almost as a lion himself physically, he was a terror to the king of beasts, and for about forty years hunted and traded in that country at the proper season of the year. He made a home for himself on one of the slopes of the Magaliesberg, which he called Thorndale, where hunters and travellers were always sure of a hearty welcome and entertainment. He gained the confidence of the cruel tyrant of the Matabeles sufficiently to get permission to hunt in his country, but the guides supplied by the chief had strict instructions not to allow any search for precious minerals, the presence of which in the country was firmly believed in by Mr. Hartley. He died at Magaliesberg somewhere about 1875, having been severely mauled by a rhinoceros about twelve months previously, when he had two or three ribs broken, which no doubt hastened his death. One of his sons died in Matabeleland, having overstayed a few days the proper season in the elephant country.

Baines, the traveller, built a tomb and engraved a few lines to keep the memory green of his favourite son Willie, Jewell, a fellow traveller, taking a photo of the little heap of bushes which, under a tree marked J. W. H. 29(5)70, were all that marked the early grave of the gallant boy. 'Hartley Hill' was named after Henry Hartley by Baines the traveller as an acknowledgement to him who had first shown him the locality of the Simbo gold reefs (Gold Regions of South-East Africa, p. 29), 1,157 miles from Pieter Maritzburg). The Hartley family bore their part in the Xhosa wars, most of the sons having been on the different commands as volunteers. One of the sisters, Mary, lost a husband murdered by Xhosa, the other sisters married and settled with their families in and about the neighbourhood of Graham's Town and Bathurst.

Haw, Simon

Simon Haw, a settler of Mr. Dalgairn's party from London, who came in the *Northampton*. He was married, with a wife and one child. He resided in Graham's Town, where he carried on the business of a money lender to his brother settlers. He died about 1860, at the age of seventy-seven years, leaving a numerous family. His eldest son, Charles, had an honourable career in the public service in various capacities, was Civil Commissioner and Resident Magistrate of Victoria East. A son died prematurely at Cradock. The third son, William, was a hardware merchant at Graham's Town, who married a daughter of Mr. George Slater, M.L. A., farmer, at Quagga's Flats; and Edward, who practised for many years as a general law agent at Graham's Town and who survives.

Hobson, David

David Hobson, was one of Mr. William Smith's party by the *Northampton*. He was quite a young man, being twenty-two years of age, and was accompanied by his brother Carey Hobson, aged fourteen years. The brothers began sheep farming in Albany, on the farms Salem and Cotlesbrook, but lost everything during the three successive Xhosa wars, in which they took an active part, being noted as dead shots. During the war of 1835 David accepted service in the Commissariat department. In 1842 the brothers left Albany for the Karroo—Carey first, David following, bringing with them a few merino sheep, up to that time unknown in the Graaff Reinet district, the Boers there farming only with the Cape sheep and common goats.

They settled down in the neighbourhood of Lot's Kloof, being then the only English farmers in that large district. By dint of undaunted perseverance they became the owners of many square miles of land, and were fairly prosperous. David married Mary Anne Robinson, and had four sons and five daughters. He died at his farm Wellfound, aged seventy-three years. Carey married Susan Bonin —two sons and two daughters. He died at Graham's Town. At the present day the descendants are numerous, and among the influential inhabitants of the Graaff Reinet. The oldest of the name alive is Mr. D. E. Hobson, who has been a member of the Licensing Court and Divisional Council of Joannesville from Reinet and Uitenhage, and after him his son, Samuel Bonin Hobson, and after his death Jonathan Hobson.

Holditch, Dr. Robert

Dr Robert Holditch, was one of Mr. Scanlan's party from Ireland by the East Indian. He, with others of the Irish party, was sent to Clanwilliam, where he was appointed Provisional Medical Officer to the Deputy Drostdy of Clanwilliam, which appointment, however, he resigned 31st December 1820. He subsequently met his death by drowning, as per letter of the Landdrost, of Stellenbosch, dated 25th December 1822.

Hoole, James

James Hoole, one of Mr. Bailie's party from London by the *Chapman*. He brought his wife and three children, the eldest of whom was only eight years of age. Nothing is known about the parent, but the two sons were prominent figures in the wars of 1835 and 1846. They were both engaged in mercantile pursuits, and James Cotterell Hoole was one of those elected in 1866 to represent the Eastern Districts in the Legislative Council, and took his seat till 1869, when the Council and House of Assembly-were dissolved. In 1870, he was re-elected, and sat till the Responsible Government Bill was passed in 1872. The other brother, Abel Hoole, was a trader at Whittlesea. Of the family the only members now living are Mrs. Dick and Mrs. George Wood, jnr.; also Mr. Benjamin Hoole and Mr. T. T. Hoole, son of Mr. James Hoole, jnr., and two Miss Powells, daughters of the late Mrs. James Powell, sister of Mrs. George Wood, jnr.

Hudson, Hougham

Hougham Hudson was the successor of Captain Campbell in office as Civil Commissioner and Resident Magistrate of Albany, "a man of Kent," from Canterbury, who came with Mr. Dyason's party in the *Zoroaster*, as a young man twenty-six years of age, with a wife and one child. He found farming in the Zuurveld unsuited to his tastes and habits, and obtained permission to leave the location, and removed to Graaff-Reinet in 1821. A clerkship in the Landdrost's office happening to be vacant, he availed himself of the opening, and was appointed thereto. By dint of industry, zeal and integrity he was successively promoted to the office of District Clerk and Magistrate at Port Elizabeth.

He was much esteemed by Sir Benjamin D'Urban, Governor of the Colony, and at the close of the war of '34-35, when the settlers were permitted to return to their homes for the purpose of getting in crops of grain, an arrangement was made whereby a little assistance was given to those who were utterly ruined. Of the money lent by Lord Charles Somerset to the sufferers by the flood of 1822, a portion had been repaid. Sir Benjamin D'Urban appointed Mr. Hudson a Commissioner to lend this fund again, which amounted to £6,792, in small sums to the most distressed of the settlers. This fund was augmented by £9,019, received for captured cattle sold by auction, and these amounts were distributed in proportion to losses sustained.

After this Mr. Hudson was appointed Agent-General of the New Province of Queen Adelaide, stationed at Graham's Town, where he was also to perform the duties of Resident Magistrate, which office he ceased to hold in 1836, when he was appointed Secretary to the Lieutenant-Governor (Stockenstrom) of the Eastern Districts; and finally, on the retirement of Captain Campbell, became Civil Commissioner and Resident Magistrate of Albany. In all these positions of trust and importance Mr. Hudson proved himself an active, faithful public servant, discharging his duty effectively, and to the entire satisfaction of his superiors.

He was retired from the office of Civil Commissioner and Resident Magistrate of Albany owing to ill-health, 1st October 1852, and placed on the pension list. In a letter addressed to him by His Excellency Sir George Cathcart, Governor of the Colony, dated 18th September 1852, this sentence occurs: "I sincerely regret the cause which has induced you to resign an office which you have so long and so ably filled in most difficult times. But it must be satisfactory to you to know that though you are unable to perform service as Civil Commissioner of Albany you contribute to the public service in another generation of your family a Civil Commissioner for the district of Somerset (his eldest son), than whom no officer in that capacity carries on his duties more entirely to my satisfaction.

Mr. Hudson had altogether twelve children—nine boys and three girls. His first child was born at Bathurst and died in Graaff Reinet. He died at his son's residence, Hougham Park, Coega, near Port Elizabeth, 5th July 1860, aged sixty-seven years, leaving the following children:

- Hougham, who became Civil Commissioner and Resident Magistrate of Graaff Reinet, was retired on pension January 1890, and is living at Graaff Reinet. He was twice-married, first to Helen Maria Currie, sister of Sir Walter Currie, by whom he had six children, two of whom survive; second, to Fanny Carlisle, widow of Joseph Currie, by whom he has one son. Dr. Hudson, the present district surgeon at Graaff Reinet.
- Andries, who died at his farm, 1893;
- Charles, who served in the Crimea, and attained the rank of colonel in the army, died in England.

- Mary, who married Matthew Woodfield, Assistant Colonial Engineer, and died in England;
- George, who married a daughter of Mr. Wm. Smith, of Port Elizabeth, and at one time was British Resident at Pretoria, South African Republic, and afterwards head of the detective department at Kimberley, retired on pension January 1895, and now living in England; and
- John, who married Dora, daughter of W. Gilffilan, Esq., Civil Commissioner of Cradock; at the time of his death, in 1893, was Civil Commissioner and Resident Magistrate of Oudtshoorn.

Huntley, Charles Hugh

Charles Hugh Huntley, son of Captain Huntley an Officer of the Royal Officers Corps who fell at the attack on Grahams' Town in 1819. He was born soon after the battle in one of the few houses that existed in the embryo of town. He became identified with the Settlers by his marriage with Miss Bailie, only daughter of the head of the party, one of the first to land at Algoa Bay by the *Chapman*.

At the age of 19 he entered the Public Service and served in the Lieutenant-General's office in 1845. He took his share of the war of 1846-7, and was Captain of Graham's Town Volunteers in 1860, commanding the escort to HRH. Prince Alfred when he visited Graham's Town in that year. He filled various offices of importance up to 1869, when he was appointed Civil Commissioner and Resident Magistrate of Graham's Town, which City he did much to improve by tree-planting along the streets and other useful works.

He was finally retired on pension after forty-six years of active service. In 1887, he received the distinction of CMG. He died in England, August 16, 1889. His wife, by whom he had a large family—six sons and four daughters — predeceased him.

- Hougham Charles Huntley, obtained a commission in the army, in the 10th North Lincolnshire regiment, September 8, 1863, and is now Lieutenant-Colonel in command of that regiment, stationed at Singapore.
- Henry, died at Aliwal North, November 1867;
- Hugh Campbell Huntley, took to farming, and is known as an intelligent sheep and ostrich farmer, at Highlands, near Graham's Town;
- Charles Huntley, was in the public service, and was Acting Civil Commissioner and Resident Magistrate at King William's Town at the time of his death, in December, l886, at Graham's Town;
- Gordon Merriman Huntley, entered the public service in 1878, and was appointed accountant to the Administrator of British Bechuanaland in 1885, which appointment he still holds;
- Douglas Huntley, is employed in the gold mines, Johannesburg.

The daughters:
- Jessie, married Mr. Frederick Holland, a merchant in Graham's Town, and died 3rd January, 1874;
- Agnes, married Benjamin Herbert Holland, Esq., Registrar of Deeds at Cape Town;
- Amy D'Esterre, married the Hon. Arthur Gilliebrand Hubbard, who died 7th March 1896; and
- May, married Owen Dunell, Esq., merchant at Port Elizabeth.

Figure 41: Mr. Quinn - Unknown Artist   *Figure 42: Mrs. Quinn - Unknown Artist*

Jarvis, George

George Jarvis, one of Mr. Willson's party by *La Belle Alliance*, a young man twenty-one years of age when he arrived. He was a prominent figure in Graham's Town, where he practised as an attorney of the Circuit Court, taking a leading share in the various plans for the improvement of the town and the prosperity of the district. He acquired a farm, which he called Orange Grove, a few miles out of Graham's Town, beyond Howitzon's Poort, which was a pleasant place of resort for himself and his friends. He married a Dutch settler's daughter, by whom he had two children—a son, Frederick, who died at an early age of consumption ; and a daughter, who married Major Charles Hurland Bell, of the Cape Mounted Riflemen, two of whose sons hold important positions under Government in Basutuland.

Keeton, Benjamin

Benjamin Keeton, came as a lad with the Nottingham party, by the *Albury*, being then nineteen years of age. He early took to trading and hunting, which was a great attraction to the young men of the Settlement, and in which pursuit he was successful. He married Miss Ford, a settler's daughter, and, having acquired the farm Lombard's Post, not far from the Kowie. He took to farming. He renamed the place Southwell, after his native town in Nottinghamshire. Besides growing oat-hay to supply the troops in garrison at Graham's Town, cattle rearing and horse breeding on a small scale, he cultivated the orange tree, which of late years formed a feature on the estate, a very large quantity of this delicious fruit finding a ready sale at Graham's Town and elsewhere. He was a liberal donor to the English Church, granting to the Bishop of Graham's Town a site for a school and dwelling for a mission station, and subsequently a further grant on which to erect a church for the use of himself, family, and neighbours. He died at a good age, about 1870, leaving two sons, both known as intelligent agriculturists in that part of the Albany district —the eldest, W. Parry Keeton, who lives at Paarde Kraal, and Bucher Keeton, who lives at Southwell.

Lucas, Philip

Philip Lucas, one of the settlers introduced by General Campbell, arriving, with others sent out by the General, in the brig *Dowson*. The vessel had a protracted voyage of nearly six months' duration. She had on board a detachment of the 54th Regiment, commanded by Major Cuyler, and among her other passengers Frank Power, the comedian. Mr. Lucas brought his wife, two sons, and one daughter. General Campbell's premature death no doubt affected his prospects. He carried on farming in an amateur fashion at Eland's Kloof, Reedfontein and in Howitzson's Poort, but not with success. He was very fond of flowers, and whilst at Reedfontein, in the bush in front of the house, had splendid walks cut out, and a maze in which the children could easily lose themselves for a time.

His latter days were spent in Graham's Town, where he died October 11, 1855, aged seventy-one years. His eldest son, Philip William Lucas, was first a clerk in Mr. Antonio Chiappini's office in Cape Town, and shortly afterwards entered the business of Mr. Heugh, at Uitenhage. He came to Graham's Town in 1823 or 1824 as Mr. Heugh's confidential clerk, and afterwards became a partner in the mercantile establishment of Heugh and Fleming, at that time the principal establishment on the Frontier. He did not like business, and was glad to accept the agency of the Cape of Good Hope Bank at Graham's Town, which he resigned on being appointed cashier of the Eastern Province Bank, which was established in 1839 at Graham's Town, and which he held till the dissolution of the Bank in 1872.

He married a daughter of Commander Bissit, R.N., of Fairfax, Kowie, and died at Graham's Town June 25, 1892, aged ninety-one years, leaving one son, William Tyndal Lucas, who served during the war of 1851-3 as a Volunteer under Mr. Dodds Pringle, and had his horse shot under him in action. Joined the original Frontier Armed Mounted Police as Lieutenant, and was wounded 8th January, 1853. Mr. Lucas's other son, Frederick, married Miss Lamont, daughter of Lieutenant Lament, of the 2nd Queen's, and was for many years Secretary of the Eastern Province Trust Company at Graham's Town. He died at East London in 1873, leaving a large family, who unfortunately have been unsuccessful in life. The daughter married John Philip Camm, Esq., an officer in the Commissariat Department stationed at Graham's Town.

Mahoney, Thomas

Thomas Mahoney, head of a party who came from London by the *Northampton*. He was a married man with a daughter and a son. He was located on the frontier line of the Zuurveld, with the Fish River Bush just behind him, a situation of great danger in case of an outbreak of the Xhosa. The Komst River bordered the southern extremity of his location, and at the point of his boundary in that direction were the "Clay Pits," a place famous among the Xhosa tribes, where they were accustomed to procuring the red clay, with which, at certain seasons, they anointed their bodies.

The peril of the situation was cruelly experienced by Mr. Mahoney on the irruption of the Xhosa in 1834-5; he and his son, and his son-in-law, Henderson, a merchant at Graham's Town, who was on a visit at the time, were found murdered by the roadside about a mile from their house. Mrs. Mahoney and two grandchildren (having two other grandchildren in Graham's Town with their mother) were in the bush all night, and had walked some twenty miles over a rough and difficult road on their way to Graham's Town, where they were rescued from a cruel death by a search party that had been sent out to the assistance of Mr. Mahoney. Their daughter, Jessie, married Mr. Middleton, a merchant at Port Elizabeth, and later left the Colony. Her mother married Mr. Joseph Smith, a merchant at Port Elizabeth, of the firm of W. & J. Smith, was again left a widow, and afterwards died at sea.

Mandy, John

John Mandy[141], head of a small party who came with others by the *Nautilus*. He came from Foot's Cray, Kent, was a married man with two sons, John Wilkinson and Stephen Day, aged respectively six and five years. On the voyage another son was born to him named William. The location assigned to him was at the mouth of the Fish River, near Shaw Park, next to that of Mr. Rowles. From this he was driven by the irruption of the Xhosa in 1835, and took refuge in Graham's Town, where he resided till his death. May 25, 1848, aged sixty-one years, his wife having predeceased him, 15th February 1823, aged thirty-five years.

The sons established themselves in business in Graham's Town, where they took a leading part in promoting the prosperity of the town and district. Stephen Day carried on a large wholesale and retail wine and spirit business at the corner of Bathurst Street and High Street. He was a bank director and a member of the Graham's Town municipality. His brother John Wilkinson was in the business, and he died at Graham's Town 23rd June 1853, at the age of thirty-nine years. Stephen Day retired from business and went to reside in England, where he died 4th June 1869, aged fifty-four years.

William settled on the farm, Lushington Valley, near Bathurst, which afterwards became his own. Experience gained in former Xhosa wars secured him the post of Commandant of Burghers in the war of 1850-53, in which he and his followers did good service to Lower Albany. After the war of 1850 the late Sir Walter Currie organized his famous Frontier Armed Mounted Police Corps, and selected William Mandy as one of the first to take command of one of its troops, which trust he refused. Sir Walter knowing what he was made of, insisted upon his joining, which he eventually did, and served for several years as sub-inspector at Cawood's Post and Waai Plaats. But the wear and tear of active service proved too much for his health. He retired to his farm against the wishes of his friends in arms, who offered him several good appointments, and died there 20th January 1887, aged sixty-seven years.

Mandy, Joseph

Joseph, a younger brother of the above John Mandy, by trade a coach-maker, was also a passenger by the *Nautilus*, and then unmarried. He settled in the Orange Free State district of Harrismith, but little is known of him. His son Francis Mandy was a very successful farmer in that district, and he died in August 1892.

---

141. See page 63

Maynard

Maynard, James Mortimer,—

Maynard, Joshua,—

They were two brothers who came with Mr. Sephton's party by the *Aurora*. They did not long remain with the Salem party, but obtained leave to remove to Cape Town, where they settled and worked as sawyers. From this humble beginning, by patient industry they soon acquired wealth, and by lending small sums of money at high interest to needy men both laid the foundations of their fortunes.

James, the elder brother, was by far the most shrewd, and the fortune he amassed was immense. He purchased land, had miles of forests at Wynberg and Newlands, and held mortgages on properties in Cape Town, it is said, to the extent of £300,000. He held a large number of shares in the Wynberg railway, had a good deal to do with its construction, and was a director. He sat in Parliament as one of the members for Cape Town at the opening of Parliament by Lieutenant-Governor Darling in 1854 and for several successive years, but did not offer himself for re-election. He died September 9, 1874, having two or three years previously been seized with a serious fit, aged seventy-four years. He was a very liberal donor to the Wesleyan Society, of which he was a member, as well as to other charitable institutions. He left his enormous wealth to his nephew, Mr. William Maynard Farmer, merchant at Port Elizabeth.

McCleland, Rev Francis

Reverend Francis McCleland, BA, TCD, came out with the Irish party of which Mr. William Parker was the head. He was then a young married man, and was approved as a properly ordained minister of the United Church of England and Ireland, and as such Earl Bathurst directed that he should be employed, and a salary provided for him by the local Government. He was at first sent by the Acting-Governor, Sir R. S. Donkin, with other immigrants, and located at Jan van Dissel's Vley, district of Clanwilliam, where he remained for about two years. Being thrown almost entirely amongst the Dutch, he acquired the language sufficiently to preach in it, but the pronunciation he never really mastered. "I remember," says his daughter, "being much amused by an old Boer remarking, with more candour than politeness, that he spoke it very 'kromme' (crooked).

That situation was quite unsuited to the newcomers, and they were finally removed to Albany. Mr. McCleland officiated as Colonial Chaplain at Graham's Town until appointed to the chaplaincy at Port Elizabeth, which he held for over thirty years, where he built St. Mary's Church, and died July 10, 1853. His income for all the years of his pastorate was only £200 per annum, with a trifle for house rent, and some glebe land from which it was expected that he might make something considerable; but it was rarely tenanted, being barren, worthless ground, and the only addition to his income from that source was a dozen white-handled knives, two pieces of Boer chintz, and an occasional brace of wildfowl.

He was allowed to take pupils, and he had a very successful school for boys for some years, most of them well-known names on the Frontier—Chatunds, Pullens, Watsons, Hugh, etc., etc. I can remember but few of the names of the party who came out with my father, but I know there were the Scanlans, one of whose descendants is Sir Thomas, Frans, and Francis, the latter being Collector of Customs for many years in Port Elizabeth, where he died.

He had two sons and five daughters. Frank, the eldest son, married in England, and as dead; George, the other, is supposed to be living somewhere in the Uitenhage district. The eldest daughter, Elizabeth, married Mr. Higgins, a merchant at Port Elizabeth, and is dead; Anna, the third daughter, married Mr. H. M. Scrivener, attorney of the Supreme Court, in practice at Port Elizabeth, and is also dead; Adelaide, the fourth, daughter, married Mr. W. Fleming, merchant, of Port Elizabeth, and is living in England; Margaret, the second daughter, and Georgina, the youngest, are unmarried, and living at Wynberg, near Cape Town.

Mills, Daniel

Daniel Mills, head of a small party from London by the transport *Sir George Osborne*. He was sixty years of age when he arrived, and brought his wife and six children—Martha, Harriet, Daniel, Maria, James, and Catherine. His location was on the Kasouga River, on which there was an abandoned house which had been occupied by the Boer who had previously lived there. He was quite unsuited to farming, his tastes being literary. He soon found farming in Albany beyond his powers, and obtained permission to remove with his family to Graaff Reinet.

Here his daughters, two accomplished young ladies, set up an academy, and he having nothing to do, and being fond of books, was glad to accept the post of Librarian to the Public Library just then formed. His income was miserably small, and as he saw better prospects in Cape Town, he proceeded thither with his family.

Moodie

There were three of that name identified with the eastern part of the Colony, viz.,

(1) Benjamin Moodie, who, in June 1817, brought out about 200 Scotch families, and who subsequently obtained a grant of land on the Beka River from the Acting-Governor of the Colony, Sir R. S. Donkin, which grant was cancelled by Lord Charles Somerset, as not being Crown land within the Colony, and who, in consequence, left the Colony and settled in Upper Canada, where he died in 1835.

(2) Lieutenant J. W. D. Moodie, 21st Fusiliers, who arrived in 1819, and after a residence and struggle of ten years abandoned the Colony. And;

(3) Lieutenant Donald Moodie, R.N., who followed his brothers, and arrived about the time of the British settlers. He was appointed by Lord Charles Somerset Provisional Magistrate at Port Frances (now called Port Alfred), in 1823. After the breaking up of that establishment he was appointed Clerk of the Peace and Protector of Slaves in 1834, which appointment he held till 1836, when he was entrusted with the task of compiling the records regarding intercourse between the Colonists and the various native tribes of South Africa. On 13th November 1845, he was appointed Secretary to the Government of Natal. He was afterwards Speaker of the first Legislative Council, and died at Maritzburg, August 27, 1861.[142]

Moorcroft, James

James Moorcroft, one of Mr. George Scott's party from Surrey by the *Nautilus*. He was a married man with wife and two children when he arrived. He devoted himself to agricultural pursuits, and after being driven off his location in Lower Albany by the wars of 1834-35 and 1846-47 he removed to the Winter Mountain, beyond Fort Beaufort, where he continued to carry on farming till his death. His son, Mr. Sidney Moorcroft, is a noted horse breeder in the Queen's Town district.

Oates, John

John Oates, was one of Mr. Sephton's party, arriving by the *Aurora*. He was a

---

142. His wife is Sophia Pigot (See Page 72).and had 13 children — Sophia Eliza; Catherine Jemima; William James Dunbar, George Pigot, Donald Hugh Menzies, Charlotte Mary, Benjamin Charles, Richard James Frederick, John Bell, Duncan Campbell Francis, Frederick Walter Octavius, Caroline Maria Mackenzie, Edith Jessie Georgina and Alfred Harding West. (Rainer, 1974)

married man with wife and two small children—a girl aged three years and a boy aged one year. He was located with the Salem party on the Assegai River, where, with others, he carried on farming under difficulties. After being ruined by the three successive Xhosa wars, he removed to Graham's Town, where he carried on a baking business in High Street for many years. The daughter, Mary Ann, married — Dugmore, one of Mr. Gardner's party of settlers; the son was also married, and had a family of seven sons and one daughter. They all migrated from Albany to Griqualand West in 1870, where the old man died on his farm, adjoining Kimberley, in 1870. The grandsons are spread over the country in various directions, one of them being a Wesleyan minister at Cala, Transkei.

Painter, Samuel

Samuel Painter, one of Sephton's party who came in the *Aurora*. He had a wife and four children. His eldest son, Richard Joseph Painter, settled in the Fort Beaufort district, where he acquired property and influence. He was elected member of the House of Assembly for that division in 1854. He is described by 'Limner' in his Pen and Ink Sketches in Parliament, like a man who had borne the heat and burden of the day, and the scenes of blood and devastation that he had interpreted as having a powerful impression on his mind. He was re-elected for the same constituency in 1859, but resigned his seat. Again, in 1864, he was elected to represent the electoral division of Port Elizabeth, but resigned that seat also. In 1866, when the members of both Houses were augmented by annexation of British Kaffraria by the Act 3 of 1865, he was returned as a member of the Legislative Council, but at the General Election in 1869 did not offer himself for re-election.

Palmer, George

George Palmer, one of the Nottingham party by the *Albury*. He was driven from his farm at Waai Plaats by the war of 1835, and then took up his residence in Graham's Town, occupying the premises at the corner of Somerset Street and African Street. He was a great horse breeder and patron of the turf. Towards the end of his days he contracted to convey the mails between Graham's Town and Cradock, which service he carried on for some years. His eldest son, Mr. James Palmer, is a farmer at Cypherfontein, a little above Graham's Town, and the younger, who used to ride the race-horse "Clear the Way" at the turf meetings, is farming at Waai Plaats.

Phillipps, Thomas

Thomas Phillipps head of a party from Pembrokeshire, Wales; arrived by the *Kennersley Castle*. He was a man of opulence, had been a banker at Haverford-West, and was in middle life. He brought his wife, seven children, and three female servants. His location was towards the coast, with Mr. Greathead and Mr. Southey as immediate neighbours. Here he applied himself to the cultivation of the land, and the erection of his dwelling-house, Mr. George Thompson, who travelled through the Settlement in January 1821, and again in May 1823, gives a pleasing description of the progress made by the settlers, their cheerful homes and their anticipations of prosperity. He gives a vignette of Mr. Phillipps's house, 'Glendour,' at p. 146 vol. ii., and refers to him as one of the leading inhabitants in industry and enterprise. All prospects of future happiness were ruthlessly destroyed by the irruption of the Xhosa in 1835, when his house was consumed by fire, his crops destroyed, and his cattle and other properties carried off. He was all at once entirely ruined, and thankful that he and his family escaped with their lives to Graham's Town. Adversity followed him through the rest of his life.

- Edward removed to Natal, and there settled.
- Catherine married Mr. John Carlisle, and left issue;
- Charlotte, married Mr. Temple Nourse, and left two sons and two daughters;
- Sophie, the third daughter, was the only one who survived her father, and died at Graham's Town, 1892, at the age of eighty-four years.
- Frederick, the second son, married Miss Mary Ann Currie, and was killed by lightning on his farm near Bedford, leaving one son, Edward, and a daughter, who married Mr. Frederick Carlisle. This son Edward left two daughters only, so there is no male representative of the family. Singularly, Edward, walking behind his cart up the Katberg was struck by lightning, and about the same time his sister, travelling by wagon, had a narrow escape, six or eight of the oxen being killed and the wagon also struck.
- John, the youngest son, died in Cradock in 1852. [143]

Mr. Phillipps was a staunch Freemason, and, by his efforts and those of Dr. Peter Campbell and others, obtained a charter from the Grand Lodge of England, granted by HRH the Duke of Sussex, KG., 3rd January 1828, as the Albany Lodge, No. 817, then 584 in 1832, and in closing up the numbers in 1863 was renumbered 389. The first officers for this Lodge, the oldest but one in all South Africa, the British at Cape Town being the premier, for 1828-29 were—Bro. Thomas Phillips, W.M; Bro. R. M. Whitnal, LW ; Bro. Peter Campbell, SW.; Bro. W. E. Smith, Treasurer; Bro. G. F. Stokes, Secretary. Bro. Phillipps was re-elected W.M., 1829-30.

---

143. The seventh is Emma according to 1820settlers.com

Pigot, George

George Pigot, head of a party from Berkshire by the transport Northampton. He was located with Dr. Dalgairns on a grant of land in the Kowie River Valley, about fifteen miles from Graham's Town. It is presumed he was a widower, as he was there forty-five years of age, and a daughter aged seventeen years accompanied him.[144] He was once a cavalry officer, and he brought with him; £5,000 to lay out in improvements among the settlers, besides having several hundred pounds a year of income. He spent a large sum of money in building a fine house and enclosing his cultivated lands—sinking; £3,000—which he called Pigot Park, by which name the estate is still known.

He was actively engaged with Captain Duncan Campbell, Mr. Phillipps, and others of the most influential among the settlers, in measures against the reversal of Sir R. Donkin's plans, which Lord Charles Somerset did not approve of. He was a great sufferer by the war of 1834-5[145]. He died June 20, 1830, and was buried at Graham's Town, leaving his daughter, Catherine Mary Pigot, executrix of his will, and bequeathing the Pigot Park property in trust in such a way that the executrix was obliged to obtain an Ordinance of the Legislature to enable her to sell and dispose of the landed property and to invest the proceeds thereof in the names of trustees for the purposes provided by his will (Ord. 12 of 1848). Except for this property the name would have died out in Albany.[146] Pigot Park is now owned by Mr. William Wicks.

Pote, Robert

Robert Pote, was one of Mr. Scanlan's party who were included in Mr. Parker's, or the Irish, party, as they were called. He was the eldest son of Edward Ephraim Pote, who was in the East India Company's service and became Governor of Patna twice, and then returned to England after having amassed a large fortune. Robert was educated at Eton to become eventually a priest in the Roman Catholic Church, and on his marrying a Miss Grant, of Edinburgh, where his children were born, his father 'cut him off with a shilling,' which led to his embarking on board the vessel *East Indiaman* on his way to India to join his brothers, where he was induced by this party of settlers to change his mind and remain at the Cape, which he did, and

---

144. As well as his other daughter and second wife. See 72.

145. He had died in 1830 so it is not certain what the original author's meaning was.

146. Some information in this paragraph is in contrast with that in Rainer (1974). His Daughter Sophia married Donald Moodie and had a large family.

regretted it ever afterwards, as he was quite unfit for the rough life of the settlers, having been brought up in luxury.

He was, with other settlers, brought out by Mr. Parker, sent to join Van Dissel's Vley, district of Clanwilliam, but that locality was altogether unsuited to them, and Mr. Pote removed to the Frontier, where he joined Norman's party on the Assegai River, which he left before the war of 1835 broke out, and brought his family into Graham's Town; so they escaped all the troubles and trials which the other settlers had to endure. Here he opened a school. The work was distasteful to him, although doing well, and his wife's health failing, they were ordered to Port Elizabeth, where he died in 1826.

His son, Charles Pote, was then sixteen years of age, and left with the burden of a large family of seven children to look after besides his mother, who died in Cape Town in 1856. He had the management of Messrs. Thomson & Watson's business in Port Elizabeth and Graham's Town, and was obliged to live for a certain portion of the year in each place. He struggled on, gaining the confidence of his employers, and, working industriously, he was enabled to marry a Miss Wathall in 1837, when he had comfortable means and was fairly wealthy, which wealth he afterwards lost through his brother's folly. He finally settled at Graham's Town, where he carried on a large business as auctioneer and appraiser. He became a member of the House of Assembly for the electoral division of Graham's Town in 1854, but resigned his seat. At the general election in 1859 he was returned as a member of the Legislative Council for the term of ten years, and re-elected for a similar period in 1864. He carried on a very extensive auctioneering business in Graham's Town, in which his strict integrity was conspicuous, and took an active part in all political, social and municipal movements for the advancement of the town and country. He was also a zealous Freemason, and elected W.M. of the Albany Lodge 389, 1847 to 1849, and for six years afterwards.

Misfortune followed him towards the close of his life, his ruin being caused by a man whom he had trusted too implicitly, and he died at his residence, Oakville, Graham's Town, October 4, 1882, aged seventy-two years, his wife having predeceased him in 1876, leaving five sons and seven daughters.

Robert Pote, the second son, took to farming and was fairly successful. He and his wife died at their farm, Hopewell, district of Somerset East, in June and July 1894.

Peter, the third and youngest son, succeeded to his brother Charles's auctioneering business in Graham's Town, and resided in that city. He was twice-married : (1) Miss Wathall, by whom he had two daughters and one son; (2) Miss

Yelling, by whom he had eight children, two boys and six girls. He died at Graham's Town, July 1895, aged seventy years.

Pringle, Thomas

Thomas Pringle, head of a small party from Scotland, who were located on the Baboon's River[147], beyond Albany, after successively planting his little band of relatives and followers in this remote corner of the Frontier, he removed to Cape Town, where he intended to devote himself to literature. He was appointed librarian to the Public Library, Cape Town, and with the assistance of his friend and fellow-countryman, James Fairbairn, whom he induced to come to the Colony and join him, projected and commenced the publication of a newspaper, which, however, owing to the narrow-minded fears of the Governor, Lord Charles Somerset, that it might become an engine of evil, was suppressed. After years of appeal to the authorities in England, and by his personal influence and that of his friends, he succeeded in overcoming all obstacles to the publication and left it in the hands of his colleague, Fairbairn, to become a power in the land in the direction of public thought and liberty of speech and action.

He returned to Scotland and then died, December 5, 1834. He wrote an account of the settlement of the British immigrants, and a volume of poems, which are prized for their simplicity and description of African scenery.

Pullen, Thomas

Thomas Pullen, came out with Mr. Thomas Owen's party by the *Nautilus*. He brought his wife, twelve children, and a female servant. Two daughters and one son were born to him after his arrival. Owen's party were located near the mouth of the Fish River, between the locations of Mr. Charles Crause and Mr. Thomas Rowles. The family remained in Port Elizabeth, the father and three sons only going on to the location. They got back to Port Elizabeth before the war of 1835 broke out.

- Thomas, the eldest son died;
- Edward, served in the expedition against the Fitcani in 1828, afterwards married widow Plackett and took to farming, near Uitenhage;
- Tendall, the third son, married a Miss Maritz, and also took to farming. T
- William Turner, served with the auxiliary forces in the three Xhosa wars of 1835, 1845 and 1850, is still alive, living near Pretoria with his sons, aged eight-three years and nine months.
- Charles, died young;

---

147. Baviaans River. See Page 78

- John Arthur, engaged in farming, married Miss Raymond, and died at his residence, Cuton Park, near Port Elizabeth, in 1892.

The nine daughters married severally:
- Dorothy, John Anthony Chaband, attorney-at-law. Port Elizabeth;
- Adelaide, Captain Walton, who died and left a son farming near Sandflats;
- Augusta, Mr. William Metelerkamp, of Zuurbron, division of Humansdorp, and died October, 1894, aged ninety-one years;
- Julia, Mr. Joseph Butler, farmer, of the Kei Road division of Komgha;
- Ellen, Mr. Sievwright, farmer, near King William's Town;
- Harriet died young;
- Lavinia, Mr. Leonard Bean, farmer, Uitenhage district ;
- Octavia, Mr. John Smith, also a farmer, near East London; and
- Emily, Mr. Dewes, farmer, near Addo Bush, division of Alexandria.

All the sons and daughters are remarkable for large families, and the descendants of Mr. Thomas Pullen are to be found in most parts of the Frontier districts and in the Transvaal.

Roberts, Dr Edward

Doctor Edward Roberts, one of Mr. Bailie's party of settlers from London, which arrived in the *Chapman*. There were two surgeons and a physician among these settlers, viz. Dr. Roberts and Dr. Walker of the former, and Dr. O'Flynn the latter, the party numbering one hundred and one families. Soon after arrival at Cuylerville, at the mouth of the Fish River, where Mr. Bailie's location was fixed, these gentlemen found there was no scope for the pursuit of their profession. They accordingly obtained permission to remove from Albany—two to the Western Province, the other, Dr. O'Flynn, being appointed provisional medical officer at Uitenhage. Dr. Roberts married Louisa, the eldest daughter of Mr. Simon Biddulph, who was a fellow passenger in the same vessel, and settled at Cape Town, where he practised successfully his profession until his death in 1830. He left a family of four sons, one of whom is Alfred Biddulph Roberts, Esq., Landdrost of Fauresmith, O.F.S.; another, Richard Miles Roberts, Esq., J. P., secretary to the Mining Boards at Du Toits Pan and Bultfontein.

Surmon, William Henry

William Henry Surmon, came in the *Nautilus* with Mr. Thomas Knowles's party. He was a married man, with one child, a boy a year old, also named William Henry. He settled in Albany, and worked at his trade as a master carpenter in Graham's Town. He died in 1836, leaving five sons, namely, William Henry, James, John, Thomas, and Henry, and four daughters.

- William Henry was also a master carpenter in Graham's Town, and followed his trade till appointed Inspector Frontier Armed Mounted Police. He was wounded in the Xhosa war of 1852, died of Bright's disease in 1866. He was married, and left five sons: William Henry, James Edward, George Thomas, Edward, and Walter, and four daughters.
- James worked at his trade of a carpenter in Graham's Town till he joined the Frontier Armed Mounted Police, in which force he rose to the rank of Inspector, afterwards Captain, when the name of the corps was changed to C.M.R. He was shot at the head of his troop in first attack on Morosi's mountain, April 1879. He married, but his wife predeceased him, leaving two daughters, who were granted a pension of £50 each by the Cape Government.
- John, also a carpenter, now farming on the Fish River, near Graham's Town, married, and has four sons, all farmers.
- Thomas, a carpenter, working at his trade in Johannesburg, has two sons, who are working with him.
- Henry, who at Johannesburg has several sons and daughters.

The grandson of the original William Henry Surmon is the present Assistant Commissioner at Gaberone, Bechuanaland Protectorate, who was educated at St. Andrew's College, Graham's Town, has had various service in Basutuland as Magistrate, Assistant Commissioner, Captain in the Basutu Contingent, in the Morosi Campaign, and as Commandant of Mohali's Hoek Contingent in the Basutu War of 1880-81. He was present at the relief of Mohali's Hoek and Mafeteng, and took part in most of the fights during the war, and was mentioned in dispatches. He is married, and has four sons and three daughters.

Scanlen, William

William Scanlen, head of a subsidiary party that came out with Mr. William Parker, of Cork, Ireland, in the *East Indian*. Mr. Scanlen came from Longford, and brought with him a wife and five children. His location was between the Assegai and Nazaar Rivers, adjoining that of Captain Butler, also one of the Irish party. Mr. Scanlen was a man of mature age, not fitted to endure the rough life and usage of the first Settlement, and he removed to Graham's Town before the outbreak of the Xhosa in 1835, where he died about 1854 at the age of eighty-four years.

One of the descendants of his son Charles recalls:

> In my earlier years, I have often heard him[148] tell the events of that Christmas (1834). Late in the afternoon of that day he saw from his front door a neighbour named Forbes running with a gun towards some horses in the valley separating their houses. He went in the direction of Forbes to see what was amiss, and when about a couple

---

148. Charles

of hundred yards off, saw some Xhosa rush from the corn in the valley and stab Forbes to death. He turned to reach his own house, and was under the shelter of a stone wall round a bend for some distance. Reaching his house, my mother handed him at the door the only weapon at hand, a musket with a defective lock. During the previous week he had visited Graham's Town and left for repair his double-barrelled fowling piece. The Xhosa halted about a hundred yards or so from the house upon his pointing the musket at them; and while they were apparently deliberating upon the course of attack, a horseman appeared at a distance upon the brow of the hill. The Xhosa rushed off after this man, whose fate I do not remember. While they were in pursuit, a fog came over the rise between the house and the party of Xhosa. Taking advantage of this, my father concealed in a cattle kraal a writing desk containing papers, the only thing he saved. My father and mother, carrying myself, fled to a kloof in the opposite direction to that in which the body of Xhosa had gone, and they had not been there long before the lurid glare in the sky indicated that their house and the house of Forbes were in flames. They remained in the bush that night, and the next morning my father, under cover of the bush, got on to the highest ground he could reach to look out. He descried a party of horsemen approaching from the direction of Bathurst, and from the glint of the guns in the sunlight concluded that they were friends. Using his shirt as a flag, he attracted their attention, and when they galloped up found that upon the news of the inroad reaching Bathurst the previous night, the party had been sent out to bury the dead! Under care of this escort they reached Bathurst, and subsequently went on to Graham's Town."

Of his four sons:
- William died about 1839 at Port Elizabeth, leaving one son, now in the Transvaal, and a daughter;
- John died about 1834;
- Charles lived on the farm Waay Plaats, near the Fish River. He joined the Corps of Guides got up under the auspices of Colonel, afterwards Sir, Henry Smith, and proceeded to the front under Captain Southey, now Sir Richard Southey, and served during the war, being near the spot where Eno, the Xhosa chief, was shot, but not actually witnessing the event. After the war of 1835 he went to Cradock, and carried on a mercantile business there for some years. He served as a volunteer during the war of 1846, and was present at the attacks on Farmerfield during that year. In 1850, he was out with the Cradock Volunteers, was present when

Thackwray shot a native chief during the attack on Shiloh, and in one of those skirmishes a bullet struck his watch in his pocket. That watch, with the dent caused by the bullet, is still in possession of his son. Sir Thomas C. Scanlen. His mercantile business suffered by this war, and after that he carried on a general agency business. On the granting of the present constitution he declined a requisition to go to Parliament, Mr. J. Collett and Mr. W. T. Gilfillan being the elected (1854). Subsequently, he was elected a member of the House of Assembly, and represented Cradock until his health failed in 1869. He died in 1870, at the age of sixty-four.

- The youngest son of the original William Scanlen, Thomas Ross Scanlen, was wounded in an action near Fort Broner, and died of his wounds in 1851 at Graham's Town, aged thirty-six years.
- The only daughter, Hannah, was married to Mr. Samuel Roberts, who had a boot and shoe warehouse in Church Square, Graham's Town. Both are dead. Their eldest son, Mr. Samuel Henry Roberts, is the Native Location Inspector, who did good service in that capacity in Albany, and is now stationed at Queen's Town.

Thus, the only descendant of this family is the son of Mr. Charles Scanlen, born in July 1834, near Cawood's Post, Fish River, who became an attorney of the Supreme Court of the Colony, and by industry and natural talent raised himself to the distinguished position of Premier of the third Ministry under responsible government in 1881, representing the constituency of Cradock in the House of Assembly from 1870 to the present time. In May 1881, he was created a K.C.M.G., and is now Solicitor-General to the British South Africa Company at Salisbury in Mashonaland.

Shaw, Rev William

Reverend William Shaw, missionary of the Wesleyan Society, came out with the Sephton party by the *Aurora*, who were located on the Assegai River, where they founded the village of Salem. He was General Superintendent of Wesleyan Missions in South East Africa, and returned to England in 1856. He was elected President of the Wesleyan Conference in 1865. He died in London after a long career of usefulness, aged seventy-three years, 4th December 1872, leaving two sons and two daughters.

- Rev. W. Shaw, MA., Vicar of Zealand Conyers, Cornforth, Lancashire, England, who died in 1890;
- Matthew Ben Shaw, who discovered the falls on the Tsitsa River in 1843, served during the Xhosa war of 1846-47, and was appointed by Governor Sir Harry Smith to act as "mediator between all tribes to whom a British Resident is not nominated." He was also entrusted with various duties of primary importance connected with the Xhosa, representing the government as British Resident under High Commissioner in Xhosa-land. His present appointment is that of Magistrate of the Territory of Port St. John's, Pondoland.

- The eldest daughter married Henry Blaine, Esq., merchant at Graham's Town;
- the other daughter married the Rev. William Impey, Oatlands, Graham's Town.

Shepstone, John

John Shepstone, one of Mr. Holder's party of settlers from Gloucestershire, who came in the *Kennersley Castle*. He was a married man and had one son three years of age on arrival.

The family is known chiefly through the distinguished services of this son, Theophilus Shepstone, who early became identified with the history of the settlers. Shortly after the beginning of the war of 1835 he acted as guide to a party of volunteers from Port Elizabeth to Wesleyville, to rescue white people, to the number of one hundred, who had taken refuge at that Wesleyan Mission Station in Tatsu's country. After serving as interpreter during the war, he was appointed clerk to Mr. Hougham Hudson, who had been created Agent-General of the new province of Adelaide, stationed at Graham's Town. In December 1836, he acted as interpreter for Lieutenant-Governor Stockenstrom, when that officer concluded treaties with the Xhosa and Fingo chiefs. In November 1838, he was attached to the military force sent by General Napier to occupy Port Natal as interpreter. In February 1839, he succeeded Mr. J. M. Bowker as Diplomatic Agent with the Fingoes, and was stationed at Fort Peddie, and marched in 1843 with a Fingo contingent to support Lieutenant-Colonel Somerset in an attack against Sandilli, and in the same year assisted in an unsuccessful expedition against a Xhosa chief. Tola. In November 1844, he was sent to Butterworth to obtain Kreli's signature to a treaty concluded with that chief by Sir P. Maitland in October previous; and after to Pondoland, to obtain Faku's signature to that treaty, acknowledging him paramount chief over the whole country between the Umtata and Umzimkulu Rivers; and 13th November 1845, when Mr. Martin West was appointed Lieutenant-Governor of Natal, he was appointed Agent for Natives.

By his wise management the Colony of Natal escaped the horrors of an invasion. Up to 1879 the Zulus were always peaceably disposed towards the colonists, and previous to the war which broke out in that year, Theophilus Shepstone was entrusted with the crowning of Cetewayo as King of Zululand. He was deputed by the Imperial Government to annex the Transvaal in 1877, when the attempt at autonomous existence as a Boer Republic proved a miserable failure. This delicate business he accomplished without even the semblance of resistance. Unfortunately, he was not retained as Administrator of the Transvaal territory, or possibly the after occurrences ending in the retrocession of that country to the

Boers would have been avoided. For his distinguished and long service he was made a K.C.M.G. He died in Natal in 1893.

Southey, George

George Southey, head of a party from Somersetshire by the *Kennersley Castle*. He was a married man, and besides his wife brought four sons, two daughters and two servants. His location was the east corner of Mr. Willson's, along the edge of the plains of Mount Donkin, or the Roundhill, a striking landmark showing where the Zuurberg range gradually sinks into the plain near the coast. A signal station, now disused, was formerly erected there. Richard[149], the second son, was, for five years, clerk in the firm of Heugh & Co. He left this situation to join his brothers who purchased the farm on the Kap River, about halfway between Graham's Town and the mouth of the Fish River. They had nearly completed the erection of commodious and extensive farm premises when the war of 1835 broke out. The Xhosa drove off 800 head of their cattle, and waylaid and murdered a young man named John Shaw, a near relative, who had quitted Graham's Town to their assistance.

The sons, William, Richard and George, did good service during that war, as members of the Corps of Guides. Richard, as Captain under Mr. William Bowker, as Commandant of the Bathurst Corps of Guides, assisting the military operations by their intimate knowledge of the country and of the Xhosa language and character. It was George Southey who helped to track the chief Hintza, and pursued him through the defiles of the Fish River bush, when Colonel, afterwards Sir Harry, Smith was engaged in his capture, and who, at a critical moment, when that Xhosa chief had already thrown his assegai[150] at Colonel Smith, and would certainly have killed him, shot him dead.

After the war, the brothers removed to Graaff Reinet, where they engaged in farming and trade. On his return to the Colony as Governor, Sir Harry Smith remembered Richard Southey, and employed him in various capacities. William Southey, the elder brother, acquired influence among the Boers of the Graaff Reinet district, and was returned as a member of the Legislative Council in 1855, and after the dissolution of both Houses was re-elected in 1859, but declared disqualified.

---

149. See the next entry.
150. Spear

Southey, Richard

Another of the settlers who rose to distinction, and whose career has been one of exceptional brilliance and usefulness, is Sir Richard Southey, who came with his parents as a lad, eleven years of age. Southey's party, of which his father, Mr. George Southey, was the head, came from Somersetshire. They were located between Manley's Flat and Bathurst, with Holder's and Great-head's parties for immediate neighbours. Like other of the sons of the settlers growing up in the district, he acquired the language and became familiar with the habits and customs of the [Xhosa], and acquainted with the numerous by-paths through which those marauders penetrated into the Settlement and robbed the settlers of their cattle.

During the war of 1835 he with his brother George and other young sons of the settlers, formed a Corps of Guides to direct the military forces under Colonel, afterwards Sir Harry, Smith, to reach the Xhosa and fight them in their stronghold, the Fish River Bush. In this capacity he did good service, which led to his employment under Sir Benjamin D'Urban's Government as Magistrate in the New Province of Adelaide, subsequently abandoned.

He then returned to Graaff-Reinet, where he resided for ten years. On the return to the Colony of Sir Harry Smith as Governor in 1847, he was appointed Secretary to the High Commissioner and accompanied him through the Colony, the Orange Free State, and Natal, and was present at the battle of Boomplaatz in August 1848. Mr. Southey was left as President of the War Tribute Commission, formed for the purpose of levying fines upon persons who had been engaged against the Colony, both as a punishment and to pay expenses. Within six months he collected and paid into the treasury £9.000. In 1849, he was appointed Civil Commissioner and Resident Magistrate of the large district of Swellendam, which, even in those days, contained many disaffected persons, whom, however, he managed to conciliate and reduce to obedience to law and order. In 1852, he acted as Colonial Secretary during the absence on leave of Mr. Montagu, till his return in 1854, when he returned to Swellendam.

In 1855 Mr. Southey was appointed Secretary to the Lieutenant Governor General Jackson, who was also Commander of the Forces on the Frontier, and resided at Graham's Town. In 1859, he was appointed Auditor-General, but had to give up that appointment to Mr. E. M. Cole who had been nominated by the Home Government. But soon after he again acted as Colonial Secretary during the absence on leave of Mr. (now Sir) Rawson W. Rawson. Finally, in July 1873, Letters Patent were issued appointing him first Lieutenant-Governor, of the

Province of Griqualand West, which difficult and responsible position he held till 1875, when the Imperial Government decided to withdraw local Government, and eventually annexed the province to the Cape Colony. In 1891 his long and meritorious services were acknowledged by the distinction of knighthood. Sir Richard Southey is still alive and well, living at Wynberg, near Cape Town.[151]

Slater, Charles

Charles Slater, a brother of Thomas, came in the same ship. He carried on business in Beaufort Street, Graham's Town, as a tallow and soap maker. He was an estimable person and much respected. He represented Albany in the House of Assembly previous to the introduction of responsible government in 1856, 1859, and 1870.

Slater, Thomas

Thomas Slater, one of Mr. Sephton's party, the Aurora, a married man with wife and six children. His eldest son George was a well-known farmer and post contractor when he lived at Quagga's Flat, on the main road between Graham's Town and Port Elizabeth. He was member for Albany in the House of Assembly in 1866 and 1869. He had several daughters, one of whom married Mr. William Haw, hardware merchant, Graham's Town; another, Mr. Thomas C. Strut, a farmer near Sidbury. A son, John, was an agriculturist on the Bushman's River.

Smith

There were many of this name among the settlers. Two of the parties were headed by persons of this patronymic —Mr. George Smith's party from Manchester, and Mr. William Smith's party from London. The former had been an officer in the 95th Rifle Brigade, and his location was along the coast between the Lynedoch and Kowie Rivers; Mr. William Smith's was on the northern border of the Settlement on the road to Trompetter's Drift, adjoining Mr. William Clark's, an exposed situation in close proximity to the Fish River Bush. Both were driven from their locations by the irruption of the Xhosa in 1835, escaping with their lives.

To distinguish one Smith from another, they were known by epithets indicating their personal appearance. Thus, there was "long-armed" Smith, "short-armed" Smith, "punche" Smith, "boatswain" Smith, etc., etc., otherwise it would have been

---

151. Died 22 July 1901 according to www.1820settlers.com

difficult to identify the particular individual intended.

Mr. William Smith, head of the party from London, married the widow of Mr. James Greathead, and practised in Graham's Town as a land surveyor, where he died leaving a family. His son, Mr. William Benstead Smith, served in the Imperial Commissariat Department during the wars of 1846-47 and 1850-53. During the latter war he was in charge of the transport, and received the Xhosa war medal. He was for many years Secretary to the Kowie Harbour Improvement Board, and, finally. Registrar of Mines on the Diamond Fields, where he died in 1892. A daughter married Mr. Skeleton Wimble, a merchant, at Graaff Reinet.

Another of the name, Mr. John Hancorn Smith, one of Mr. Willson's party of settlers who arrived by the *Belle Alliance*, devoted himself to agriculture, and owned one of the largest and most beautiful farms in Lower Albany. Owing to the successive Xhosa wars, he became greatly impoverished, and having a family of ten children, all small, to support, the outlook after the last war was more hopeless, and it was a struggle for existence to the last. Latterly, he lived at Assegai Bush, a farm about sixteen miles from Graham's Town, on the main road to Port Elizabeth, where he died in 1857, aged seventy-nine years, leaving a wife and ten children. He married a Miss Stringfellow, and she died at Kimberley in 1862, aged eighty-six years. His three sons:

- John Hancorn was killed by lightning in 1874,
- Thomas W. died at Kimberley in 1872, and
- William, who had explored the interior far beyond the Zambesi, was attacked by the prevailing fever, carried in a palanquin by natives 200 miles trying to reach the coast, but died three days beyond Senna in 1885. He was buried at Senna, the particulars being sent to his wife with his diary by the British Consul at that place.

Five of the daughters married:

- Captain Nicolson, of the 27th Regiment, late of H.M.'s Cape Mounted Riflemen;
- Colonel Lyons, Royal Artillery;
- (3) Sir Drummond M. Dunbar, Bart.;
- (4) George Harding, Esq.;
- (5) the Rev. C. F. Taberer, missionary of the English Church in charge of the important Xhosa Industrial Establishment at Keiskama Stock, near King William's Town; and
- (6) Mary, who remains unmarried.

Stanton, William

William Stanton, one of Mr. Willson's party by the *Belle Alliance*, with wife and four children—William, Sarah, Catherine, and Robert. He was driven from the location by the war of 1834-5, came to Graham's Town and settled there, pursuing the occupation of a wagon builder. He was for many years Field Cornet of Graham's Town. Died in 1855, at the patriarchal age of seventy-two years.

- William, only thirteen years of age when the family arrived, was returned as member of the House of Assembly for the electoral division of Fort Beaufort, in 1859, but was declared disqualified. He was, however, elected for the constituency of Victoria East in 1869. He lived at the drift of the Kat River, on the north side of the town of Fort Beaufort, where he carried on the business of a soap boiler and trader.
- Robert, who was only three years of age on coming to the country, lived in Graham's Town, where he carried on the wagon-making business, which has made the name famous in that speciality. He died in Graham's Town, December 11, 1894, at the advanced age of seventy-seven years and ten months. The sons, descendants of the foregoing, are numerous, and for the most part engaged in the same line of business.

Stringfellow, Thomas

Thomas Stringfellow, one of Mr. Bailie's party by the *Chapman*. He was a married man with wife and three daughters. He was a printer by trade, and not fitted for agricultural occupation. He had a long and honoured career in the public service, his last appointment being that of Civil Commissioner and Resident Magistrate of Fort Beaufort, where he died in 1860.

Stubbs, John

John Stubbs, one of Dr. William Clarke's party from London by the *Northampton*. He brought a wife and six children. He was killed by the Xhosa at the Clay Pits, near Graham's Town, on the outbreak of the war of 1834-5. His second son, Thomas[152], was a well-known figure in Graham's Town during the war of 1846-7, being in command of an irregular force called 'Stubbs's Rangers,' which did good service in scouring the surroundings of the city and clearing it of small parties of marauders. He carried on the business of a saddler and harness maker, and was the first to commence the running of a passenger cart to and from Port Elizabeth, in 1848, at first as often as the conveyance was full, afterwards regularly once a week. His brother, William Stubbs, was a trader at Whittlesea, and did also good service during the war of 1846-7.

Temlett, James

James Temlett, one of Mr. Erith's party from Surrey, which came in the

---

152. See page 131

Brilliant. He was a young man just married, his eldest son being born in the Bay of Biscay, taking the name of the ship. He engaged in mercantile pursuits, and lived in Graham's Town, on Market Square, where he carried on his business of a general dealer. His eldest son, James Brilliant Temlett, lived at Alice, where he kept a general store; his second son, John Temlett, carried on his father's business; and one daughter married Thomas Aylesbury, who kept the roadside house of accommodation on the road to the Kowie. The family were all Baptists, and strong supporters of that sect. The name has died out, neither son having any issue. Mr. Temlett died at Graham's Town, 16th November 1862, aged sixty-five years.

Trollip

Trollip, Joseph, with wife and six children, —

Trollip, William, with wife and infant child, —

Trollip, John, young married man, and

Trollip, Stephen, also a young married man,

They were all of Mr. Hyman's party from Wiltshire, who came by the transport *Weymouth*. Hyman's party were located between Bathurst and the mouth of the Lynedoch River. The war of 1835 dispersed the unfortunate settlers, and the Trollips migrated into the Cradock district, where they are now numerous, and flourish as sheep farmers. The descendants of the original settlers of this name are, next to the Cawood family, the most numerous of all the others. The senior representative of the name is Mr. Joseph Trollip, sheep farmer, of Mount Pleasant, Dagga Boer's Nek, district of Cradock.

Wedderburn, Christopher

Christopher Wedderburn, with wife, two sons and three daughters, were among the settlers brought out by Mr. George Smith, late of 95th Rifle Brigade. They came from Manchester, and sailed from Liverpool in the transport *Stentor*. The voyage occupied three months, and they arrived in Algoa Bay in April 1820. From there they proceeded by ox-wagon to Green Fountain, Albany, where they were located. Christopher and his son William received grants of land in the location assigned to Mr. Smith, about three miles from Port Alfred, near Rubane's River.

Christopher became a successful farmer until the cruel Xhosa war of 1835, when the Xhosa carried off all his cattle and destroyed all the homesteads. He, with the other settlers, sought refuge in Graham's Town, as all lower Albany was overrun by the savages, who murdered all the white inhabitants they caught. For eight months the settlers were driven from their homes, when peace was again restored.

In 1845, they bought a farm near Salem, on the Assegai River, where George and his father carried on farming, and, with a good market in Graham's Town, being noted for their excellent cheese, butter and oat-hay, obtained good prices and did well. Another drawback was experienced when the war of 1846 broke out. This time the farmers banded themselves together, and by sheer pluck defeated the Xhosa at the Kariega River, who had stolen all the cattle from the encampment. After several hours' fighting all the cattle were recaptured and the Xhosa gave the Salemites a wide berth, George Wedderburn being conspicuous with others for his bravery.

Peace was again restored until Christmas day, 1850, when, with the help of rebellious Khoisan, the Xhosa again invaded the Colony, murdering right and left, George Wedderburn being among the fallen. He lingered some months, and died of his wounds, leaving a widow and five small children to battle with the world.

The father and mother passed away previous to this war, only William and Esther remaining of the original stock. William early left the location and started business in Graham's Town as a tailor, married Martha Patrick, also a settler, had thirteen children, four of whom survive. He had six sons, and died October 27, 1894, aged sixty-five years, John and Christopher being his two male representatives. John is well known in Graham's Town as a successful wagon builder, whose vehicles are in demand all over the Eastern districts, on the Diamond Fields, Bechuanaland, and the Interior. The first white lady who penetrated to the Zambesi was conveyed in a wagon built by John Wedderburn.

White, Thomas Charles

Lieutenant, in a regiment of Foot, head of White's party from Nottinghamshire. At first, he was located with Lieutenant Griffith on the Endless River, which did not answer his expectations. He was subsequently removed to Albany, and the location assigned to him was near Capt. Butler's and Mr. Joseph Latham's, on the Assegai River. The outbreak of the Xhosa in 1834-5 drove him to Graham's Town, where he became Major of the local Volunteers, and Acting Deputy Quarter-master of the burgher forces. During the whole of the campaign he was actively employed in making an accurate topographical survey of the Xhosa territory, and in prosecution of this, his favourite object, he had ascended an eminence near the encampment, for the purpose of sketching the surrounding country.

Four men of the Cape corps had been ordered to accompany him, and they were posted at different points of the hill to guard against surprise. In spite, however, of this precaution, the wily Xhosa, crouching stealthily in the long grass, succeeded in approaching the spot unobserved, and; suddenly springing upon him and the Corporal, despatched them with their assegais before the other men could afford them the slightest assistance or even apprise them of danger. On the first alarm a party proceeded from the camp to the spot where his body was lying with many wounds on the head, loins and back. His remains received a soldier's grave, dug under the shade of a bush with no other implements than the bayonets of his companions.

He was of high literary and scientific attainments, considerable property, and a large and successful flock-master. A memorial tablet in St. George's Cathedral, Graham's Town, erected by public subscription, records the melancholy event of his untoward death in the following terms:—

> Sacred to the Memory of
> Thomas Charles White,
> a native of Nottinghamshire, England, Major of the Albany local Volunteers, and Acting Deputy Quartermaster-General to the Burgher forces, formerly Lieutenant in Her Majesty's 25th Regiment of Foot, who, after many years of persevering and successful effort as an agriculturist to promote the welfare of his fellow-settlers and improve the country of his adoption, to which he emigrated in the year 1820, was slain by Xhosa on the 14th May 1835, on the banks of the Bashee River, whither he had marched with a detachment of the British forces, under the command of Colonel Smith, C.B., to

punish the calamitous and unprovoked irruption of the Xhosa tribes into this Colony in December 1834. He thus died as he had lived, in the active service of his country, cetatis XLIII. This tablet is erected by the public as a tribute to those talents and that worth by which he was distinguished alike in social as in public life.

Major White left two sons, who occupy the farms adjoining Graham's Town, viz., Thomas Charles White, Esq., J. P., Table Farm, and George White, Esq., Braak Kloof, married Miss Bliss Atherstone, and are known for their independence and enterprise as sheep-farmers.

Wood, George

A colleague of Mr. Godlonton's throughout his parliamentary career, and a co-operator with him in every undertaking for the good of the Settlement, was. George Wood, who came with the Sephton or Salem party in the Aurora, as an apprentice to Mr. Richard Smith, being then fourteen years of age, and subsequently to Mr. William Thackwray.

He was early thrown on his own resources, and his industry, energy, and aptitude for business soon obtained for him a good position. As his large family of sons and daughters grew up around him, assisting him in the shop and store, he prospered as no other settler did, and died reputed a millionaire. As a business man he was shrewd and far seeing, cautious to a degree, but never above hard work.[153] He was no counter-jumper of the modern style, and never feared soiling his fingers. He donned the shop-man's apron and swept his own shop long after the prosperity of his business would have justified the employment of others to do manual work, and withal was as courteous to his customers and as good a hand at driving a bargain as the best of modern salesmen. He recognised the nobility of work, he practised it himself, and brought up his sons in the practice of it.

As prosperity rewarded his efforts he increased the sphere of his business operations, built "larger barns" and storehouses, and speculated so judiciously that wealth flowed in upon him almost without a check. His business instincts were

---

153. A story told of Mr. Wood by several sources is that he was on a trip into the native areas to trade with the Xhosa. He brought a batch of three-legged iron pots. These were very popular, and he did not have enough stock. He was worried about his safety as his customers were becoming insistent on also receiving pots. He climbed into his wagon to give him an opportunity to think. There he found a packet of iron shot (for a shotgun). He proceeded to sell these "pot seeds" to his inexperienced customers. He told them they would grow to be a pot. But if they did not he would return shortly with more pots. One would think grudgingly, they accepted his word. He then hared back to Grahamstown, bought more pots and returned to his customers to provide them with the replacement for the "seeds".

early taken advantage of by the promoters of trading, insurance, and trust companies, and none of these prospered so well as when he was the practical managing director.

The Eastern Province recognised in him a man of wide experience and sound judgement, and for many years returned him in at the head of the poll, or among the first five at each general election. He was most punctual and diligent in attendance on his duties in the Legislative Council, even when advancing age and infirmity deprived him of the use of his legs, and when he had to be carried and wheeled from place to place, hauled on board ships and lifted to upper rooms in hoists.[154] His spirit was an indomitable one. Such pain and paralysis of the limbs as he suffered would have curbed the spirit and deprived many more robust than he of all energy and interest in public affairs.

He was most punctual in attendance at his office, at the Divisional Council meetings, at Board Meetings, and, when in session, at Parliament, retaining up to the last, even when sight and hearing had failed him, a memory of the most retentive and tenacious description. His public benefactions were considerable. His assistance was never asked in vain for any worthy object, whether in the promotion of institutions connected with religious or secular bodies. He gave liberally whether for the erection of the Cathedral Tower, for the erection or founding of the Wesleyan High School, or for the Baptist Sunday School.

The one exception to the local institutions with which his name might have been naturally associated was the Jubilee Memorial Tower. He was deemed too young to be ranked among the Settlers, only those of eighteen years of age and upwards being so regarded. This slight he resented very much, and in consequence the tower was built without any money assistance from himself or any of his sons. He died at his residence, Woodville, Beaufort Street, Graham's Town, 1st November 1884, aged seventy-nine years and six months.

George, came out as an apprentice to Mr. William Smith Owen[155], with the Sephton party in the *Aurora*, being then fourteen years of age. After completing his term of engagement with Mr. Owen, and after with Mr. W. Thackwray, he struck out for himself and set up on his own account in a modest way in Bathurst Street, Graham's Town, where he kept a shop and supplied all sorts of necessaries and useful articles.

---

154. On a trip to Britain he had fallen down an elevator shaft that left him paralyzed.

155. This contradicts the information in the first paragraph. These paragraphs came from different parts of the original.

He married Susannah Garbett, stepdaughter of Mr. Joseph Donovan, one of Mr. Willson's party of settlers, by whom he had a numerous family—eight sons and five daughters. He died at his residence, Woodville, Beaufort Street, Graham's Town, 1st November 1884, aged eighty years, his wife following him in 1890, aged eighty-one years.

- His eldest son, George Samuel, was admitted as a partner in his father's business in 1851. He was the first Mayor of Graham's Town, and was elected to the same office twice afterwards. He represented the City of Graham's Town in the House of Assembly from 1864 to 1868. He married Fanny, daughter of the Hon. J. C. Hoole, and died in Graham's Town in 1884, aged fifty-six years.
- John Edwin, also became a partner in his father's business in 1851. He, like his brothers, took an active part in all the institutions established for the advancement of the town, was second Mayor of Graham's Town, and represented the constituency of Albany in the House of Assembly from 1864 to 1866, and was returned to represent the City of Graham's Town in 1887, and continues to hold that seat. He married Charlotte, daughter of Mr. William Wright.
- William died in Cradock, 8th January 1856, aged twenty-four years and six months.
- Joseph Garbett, engaged in farming pursuits at Summer Hill, near Bathurst. He represented the Albany constituency in the House of Assembly from 1884 to 1887. He died at Graham's Town, 25th September 1892, aged fifty-nine years.
- Henry Richard joined his brothers in business about 1863, from which time it has been continued under the style of Wood Brothers. He is a director of several joint-stock companies, and also Deputy Sheriff for Albany.
- Ben Horace, also joined his brothers in business in 1863, but retired from the firm in 1870, going to Natal, where he is engaged with his large estate known as Clairmont.
- Alfred Jesse is now in London, where he is practising his profession of an artist, having for several years been under the tuition of Sir — Firth, Royal Academy.
- Garbett, the youngest son, died at the age of seventeen years.

The daughters
- Susannah, married Mr. Jonathan Ayliff;
- Eleanor, married Mr. George McKiell;
- Harriet, married Mr. G. N. H. Curzen;
- Elizabeth, married Commissary-General Sir W. H. Drake;
- Lydia, married Mr. George W. Impey.

Wright, William

William Wright, one of Mr. Mills's party from London, by the *Sir George Osborne*. He was married, and brought his wife, one daughter three years of age, and one son a twelve-month-old. He was chiefly engaged in mercantile pursuits, taking his share in the various political, municipal, and general efforts at improvement of the town and district. In 1855, he was elected member of the

House of Assembly for the constituency of Cradock; and at the same election was returned for the electoral district of Victoria East. He resigned his seat, and represented neither constituency. He died at Graham's Town in 1857, aged sixty-three years and ten months, leaving his wife a widow, who survived him till 1867, when she died, aged seventy-four years, and several daughters, and the son who had come to the country as an infant.

The widow, Mrs. Rosa Wright, built and endowed the beautiful church, called Christ's Church, at Oatlands, part of Graham's Town, of which the Rev. M. Norton is the present rector.

- Martha, married Mr. Charles Henry Caldecott, M.L.C., and died 1892;
- Julia, married James Henry Greathead, Esq., a merchant of Graham's Town, surviving her husband and living at Fairlawn, Graham's Town;
- Charlotte, married John Edwin Wood, Esq., M.L.A.;
- Emily, married first William Wood and second Joseph Gadd, Esq., who represented Victoria East in the House of Assembly in 1867, and was, with her husband, cruelly murdered by their own servants, October 1894;
- Eliza, married Dr. Spackman;
- Rosa Isabel, who married Frederick Charles Bate, Esq., also a merchant at Graham's Town, who are now living at Queen's Town.
- William, married Sophia Rowan, and died 5th March 1891, aged seventy-one years.

Bibliography

Batts, HJ (Unknown). The story of 100 years: 1820-1920. Maskew Millar.

Cambell, Colin Turning (1897). British South Africa. John Haddon & Co.

Cowan, Robert Ernest (1923). Norton I, Emperor of the United States and Protector of Mexico Quarterly of the California Historical Society.

Dugmore, H.H. (1871). Reminiscences of an Albany Settler. Richards,

Dyason, Isaac (1866). *Rough Outlines*. Anglo-African.

    Part I   23.6.1866.

    Part II   30.06.1866

Maxwell W.A & McGeogh, RT (1978). The Reminiscences of Thomas Stubbs. AA Balkema, Cape Town.

McCleland Dean (2018). "Port Elizabeth of Yore:The Macay Bridge over the Sunday's River". http//thecasualobserver.co.za.

Pringle, Thomas (1835). Narrative of a Residence in South Africa. Edward Moxon.

Rainer, M. (Ed) (1974). The Journals of Sophia Pigot (1819-1821). A.A. Balkema, Cape Town

Redgrave JJ MA; "Port Elizabeth in Bygone days."; The Rustica Press Ltd.; Wynberg Cape; 1947

Rivett-Carnac, Dorothy E.; "Thus came the English in1820"; Howard Timmins; 1961; Cape Town

Schoeman, Karel; "Baillie's Party, The new Land, 1820 – 1834"; Protea Book House; 2019; Pretoria.

Silva, PM (1982). The diaries of Thomas Shone. MA Thesis, Rhodes University. Available at: http://hdl.handle.net/10962/d1005799

Thompson, George (1827). Travels and Adventures in Southern Africa. Volume 1. Henry Colburn, London.

Wilmot, A & Chase, JC (1869). History of the Colony of the Cape of Good Hope. Juta, Cape Town.

Alphabetical Index

Ainswick, Rose..................................180
Ainswick, Thomas..............................180
Aldum..49
Alfred, Prince of Wales.....................116
Allison, Frank....................................44
Armstrong, James.............................136
Atherstone, Ann................................170
Atherstone, Bliss.......................169, 233
Atherstone, Caroline.........................169
Atherstone, Catherine....................169p.
Atherstone, Charles..........................170
Atherstone, Dr John............44, 138, **169,** 185
Atherstone, Edwin.............................170
Atherstone, Emily..............................169
Atherstone, Fanny.............................170
Atherstone, John...............................169
Atherstone, Walter Herschel............170
Atherstone, William Guybon.......169, **170**
Attwell, Benjamin Booth...................171
Attwell, Brooke..................................171
Attwell, Richard.................................170
Attwell, Richard L.............................170
Attwell, Sarah....................................171
Attwell, William.................................170
Aylesbury, Thomas............................230
Ayliff..............................49, 148, 172p., 193
Ayliff, Elizabeth.................................174
Ayliff, James.....................................**173**
Ayliff, John.......................................**172**
Ayliff, Jonathan..........................173, 235
Ayliff, Reuben...................................**172**
Ayliff, Reverend John......................**171**
Ayliff, William...................................**173**
Bacher, Mary.....................................191
Bager, George...................................135
Bailia, Archibald Hope......................156
Bailie, Alexander Cumming.............158
Bailie, Archibald Hope......................158
Bailie, Charles Campbell..................159
Bailie, Charles Theodore............156, 158
Bailie, Isabella Bennett....................159
Bailie, John................................**155,** 157
Bailie, John Amelius..................156, 159
Bailie, John Crause....................159, 184
Bailie, Miss.......................................207
Bailie, Thomas...........................157p., 184
Bailie, Thomas Cockburn..........156, 159

Barker, Reverend George................100
Barker, Reverend William................146
Bate, Frederick Charles...................236
Batts, HJ..144
Bean, Leonard.................................220
Bell, Charles Hurland......................208
Bennet, Philosopher........................104
Bennett, Samuel................................91
Biddulph..43
Biggar, Alexander............................**174**
Biggar, Ann......................................**174**
Biggar, George................................**174**
Biggar, Helen..................................**174**
Biggar, Jane....................................**174**
Biggar, Margaret Graham...............**174**
Biggar, Mary....................................**174**
Biggar, Robert.................................**174**
Biggs, Mr...140
Bingham, Reverand.........................139
Bisset, Alexander Charles...............175
Bisset, John Jarvis..........................175
Bisset, Lieutenant.............................95
Bisset, Lieutenant Alexander....162, **174**
Bisset, Sarah Maria.........................175
Bissit, Commander..........................210
Bissit, General Sir John..................185
Blaine, Henry...................................224
Blakeway, John................................185
Blakeway, Richard Harris................185
Blakeway, William John..................185
Boardman, Rev William..................**175**
Boardman, Reverend........................51
Boland, Thomas Parsons................163
Bonin, Susan...................................204
Booth..49
Booth, B..176
Booth, Benjamin..............................**176**
Booth, Elizabeth..............................180
Booth, Miss.....................................171
Bowker....................................26, 43, 92
Bowker, Anna..................................169
Bowker, Bertram Egerton...............**177**
Bowker, Holden.................................57
Bowker, J.M.....................................224
Bowker, James Henry....................**178**
Bowker, John Mitford.....................**177**
Bowker, Miles...........................**176,** 181

Bowker, Miles Brabbin...................**176**
Bowker, Octavius............................**177**
Bowker, Robert Mitford..................**177**
Bowker, Septimus Bourchier...........**177**
Bowker, Thomas Holden.................**177**
Bowker, W.......................................192
Bowker, William Monkhouse..........**176**
Bradfield, Edward...........................**178**
Bradfield, John................................**178**
Bradfield, John Jnr..........................**178**
Bradfield, John Linden....................**178**
Brown, George................................139
Brown, Mr.............................73, 112, 141
Bubb, E..200
Buller, Joe.......................................133
Burnet, E..200
Butler, Captain Thomas............99, 163, 168, **178**
Butler, Joseph..................................220
Caldecott, Alfred Edward...............**180**
Caldecott, Alice Annie Martha.......**180**
Caldecott, Charles Henry.............**179p.**, 236
Caldecott, Charlotte Isabella..........**180**
Caldecott, Dr Charles...............91, **179**
Caldecott, Emily..............................**180**
Caldecott, Frederick Horatio..........**180**
Caldecott, Frederick Reginald........**180**
Caldecott, Harry Stratford...............**180**
Caldecott, Jessie Lucretia Baldwyn...............**180**
Caldecott, Maud Isabella................**180**
Caldecott, Robert Torkington.........**180**
Caldecott, Rosa Wright...................**180**
Caldecott, William Shaw................**180**
Camm, John Philip..........................210
Campbell...26
Campbell, Alexander Gumming.....**184**
Campbell, Ambrosina Georgina van der Dupen
....181
Campbell, Captain Duncan..........176, **181**, 196
Campbell, Dr Ambrose George......**180**
Campbell, Dr. Peter.........................**184**
Campbell, Edward Andrews...........**183**
Campbell, Frederick.......................**183**
Campbell, Janet Isabella Suffield...181
Campbell, John................................**183**
Campbell, Lionel Donald Williams...............181
Campbell, Major-General Charles..100, 180, **183**
Campbell, Margaret Ann.................**184**
Campbell, Mary...............................100
Campbell, Peter...............................216
Campbell, Rosina Jane....................**185**
Campbell, Sarah Lucy Cecilia........**184**
Campbell, William..........................**183**
Carlisle, Edmond.............................**185**

Carlisle, Fanny................................206
Carlisle, Frederick...................**185**, 216
Carlisle, John............................**185**, 216
Carlisle, Robert...............................**185**
Carlisle, Sydney..............................**185**
Carlisle, William Montagu.............186
Carney, Mr......................................142
Cary, Dennis...................................133
Cawood.....................................59, 92
Cawood, David..............................**186**
Cawood, James..............................186
Cawood, John.................................186
Cawood, Joseph.............................186
Cawood, Joshua.............................186
Cawood, Samuel.....................186, **187**
Cawood, William............................186
Chaband, John Anthony.................220
Chalmers, Reverend.......................156
Chase...156
Chase, Frederick............................188
Chase, Frederick Korston..............189
Chase, Harry..................................189
Chase, Henry..................................188
Chase, JC..94
Chase, John Centlivres...................**188**
Chase, LC.......................................189
Clark, Mr..72p.
Clark, William................................227
Clayton, Bill...................................132
Clayton, George.............................44
Cloete, DJ.......................................96
Cock, Cornelius..............................**191**
Cock, Nathaniel..............................**191**
Cock, Thomas.................................162
Cock, William..........................27, **189**
Cock, William Frederick................**191**
Cockcroft, William.........................137
Collett, James.................................189
Collis, James..................................162p.
Comfield, Mrs.................................74
Cooper..44
Corydon, Selby..............................180
Coryndon, Blanche........................200
Cowderoy, Lieutenant....................95
Cowie, Dr.......................................169
Coyle, Miss E.................................164
Crause..156
Crause, Amelia..............................156
Crause, Captain Henry...........103, 132
Crause, Lieutenant Charles...........92
Crause, Major John........................175
Cumming, George..........................169
Currie, Helen Maria.......................206

Currie, Joseph..206
Currie, Lieutenant Walter..............................191
Currie, Mary Ann..216
Currie, Sir Walter..................................59, **191**
Currie, Walter..162
Curzen, GNH...235
Dale..113
Dalgairns, Eliza..73p.
Dalgairns, Magdalene.....................................73
Dalgairns, Miss..72p.
Dalgairns, Mr..............................72, 74pp., 217
Damant, Edward...**185**
Damant, Elizabeth...169
Damant, Hugh...185
Damant, John..185
Daniell, Lieutenant Richard....................98, 184
Daniell, Priscilla..184
Daniell, William Henry.................................181
Davies, Joshua...139
Davies, Mr...139
Davies, Reverend William....................147, 150
Dewes, Mr...220
Dick- Lauder, John EA..................................180
Dickson, Charles A.......................................184
Dickson, Emily...170
Dixie..148
Dixie, Mrs...136
Dold, Mrs..44
Donovan, Joseph...235
Drake, Ella..180
Drake, Sir William..180
Drake, WH..235
Driver, Edward..37
Du Plooy...157
Dugmore, Mr...215
Dukesbury...49
Dunbar, Sir Drummond M............................228
Dunell, Owen..208
Duxbury, Reverend SM................................**147**
Duxbury, William..148
Dyason, Durban..194
Dyason, George............................91p., 96, **193**
Dyason, Isaac..89, 91, 193
Dyason, Joseph.......................................91, 193
Dyason, Robert......................................91, 193
Dyason, William...194
Eddie, Dr...185
Ella..58
Elley..73
Elliott, Cecilia...112
Elliott, Elizabeth...112
Elliott, Joseph...112
Evatt, Captain...111

Fairbairn, James..219
Fitchat, Lt. James..200
Fleming, W...213
Forbes..44
Forbes, Alexander...**194**
Ford...148
Ford, Miss...209
Forse, Tom..142
Foss, Thomas..137
Foxcroft...44
Frames, WB..113
Franklin, John George..................................169
Fraser, Colonel George Sackville...................99
Freemantle..46
Gadd, Joseph...236
Garbett, Susannah...235
Garcia, Arthur...195
Garcia, Egbert...195
Garcia, Maurice..**194**
Gilfillan, Dorothea Mounsey........................201
Gilfillan, Lieutenant William........101p., 201, 223
Gilfillan, William..201
Gillfilian, Dora..207
Gilliebrand, Arthur.......................................208
Girdlestone, Armeni.....................................170
Glass, Benjamin..195
Glass, Daniel...195
Glass, James...195
Glass, John..195
Glass, Thomas..**195**
Glass, William..195
Godlonton, Robert.......42, 54, 94, 156, 171, 173, 187, 190, **195,** 196pp., 233
Goldswain, Jerry...48
Gradwell, William...37
Grant, Miss..217
Gray, George...199
Gray, James Wakelyn...................................199
Gray, William..198
Gray, William Marsden.................................199
Greathead, DCR..200
Greathead, George Alfred.............................200
Greathead, Herbert Harding..........................200
Greathead, James....................................**199,** 228
Greathead, James Henry....................199p., 236
Greathead, John Baldwin..............................200
Greathead, Julia Emily..................................200
Greathead, Octavius Ernest...........................200
Greathead, Rosa..200
Greathead, Walter Horatio............................200
Greathead, William Wright...........................199
Green, Rev. E. P..201
Griffith, Anna Elizabeth...............................201

Griffith, Charles	200
Griffith, Charles Duncan	201
Griffith, John	200
Griffith, John Valentine	201
Griffith, Mary	201
Griffith, Valentine	200
Grocott, Thomas	149
Gumming, Mary Anne	184
Gumming, Thomas	184
Gurney, Charles	113
Gush	49
Halse, Emilie	199
Halse, EV	200
Harding, George	228
Hart	83
Hart, Robbert	44
Hart, Robert	171
Hartley, Benjamin	**201**
Hartley, CH	202
Hartley, Henry	203
Hartley, Jeremiah	202
Hartley, John	201, 203
Hartley, Mary	203
Hartley, Mr	136
Hartley, Thomas	202
Hartley, William	37, **201**
Haw, Charles	204
Haw, Edward	204
Haw, Simon	**204**
Haw, William	204, 227
Hay, Reverend Alexander	145
Heley, Mrs	136
Higgins, Mr	213
Hillier, JB	180
Hiscock, Mrs	141
Hoar, Benjamin	158
Hobson	145
Hobson, Carey	37, 58, 204
Hobson, David	**204**
Hobson, DE	204
Hobson, Jonathan	204
Hobson, Samuel Bonin	204
Hodgkinson	135
Hodgkinson, George	141
Holditch, Dr	163
Holditch, Dr. Robert	**205**
Holland, Benjamin Herbert	208
Holland, Frederick	208
Holland, JA	111
Hoole, Abel	205
Hoole, Benjamin	205
Hoole, Fanny	235
Hoole, James	**205**
Hoole, JC	235
Hoole, TT	205
Hoolke, James Cotterell	205
Hope, Major	156
Hudson, Andries	206
Hudson, Charles	206
Hudson, Dr	206
Hudson, George	207
Hudson, Hougham	91, **205**, 224
Hudson, Hougham Jnr	206
Hudson, John	207
Hudson, Mary	207
Hulley Family	141
Huntley, Agnes	208
Huntley, Amy D'Esterre	208
Huntley, CH	159
Huntley, Charles	207
Huntley, Charles Hugh	**207**
Huntley, Douglas	207
Huntley, Gordon Merriman	207
Huntley, Henry	207
Huntley, Hougham Charles	207
Huntley, Hugh Campbell	207
Huntley, Jessie	208
Huntley, May	208
Hutton, Henry	169
Impey, George W	235
Impey, Rev William	224
Ingram, John	163, 167
Ingram, T	137
Innes, Doctor	170
Jaffray, Edith	191
James, Mr and Mrs	148
James, Mrs	43
Jarvis, Frederick	208
Jarvis, George	173, 208
Jerman, Thomas	137, 139
Judge, Canon	170
Keeton, Benjamin	**209**
Keeton, Bucher	209
Keeton, W. Parry	209
Kestel	44
Kidwell	145, 148
Kirkwood, JS	116
Korston, Mr	188
Krohn, NP	174
Kuhr, Mr	174
Lamont, Miss	210
Lawson, Thomas	95
Ledger, Fanny	117
Lee, William	32
Lindsey, Mr	137
Longlander, Herbert Penderell	181

Lord	145
Lucas	54
Lucas, Frederick	210
Lucas, Jessie Malet	183
Lucas, Philip	**209**
Lucas, Philip William	209
Lucas, PW	175
Lucas, William Tyndal	210
Lyons, Colonel	228
Mahoney, Jessie	210
Mahoney, Mr	72
Mahoney, Thomas	**210**
Mandy, Francis	211
Mandy, John	63, 134, **211**
Mandy, John Wilkinson	211
Mandy, Joseph	65, 211
Mandy, Mary Ann	65
Mandy, Stephen Day	211
Mandy, William	211
Maritz, Miss	219
Marsden, Elizabeth	198
Matthews, William Henry	51
Maynard, Charles	174
Maynard, James Mortimer	212
Maynard, Joshua	212
Maynard, William	212
McArther, Corporal	139
McCarty, Corporal	137
McCarty, Mr & Mrs	136
McCarty, Mrs	138
McCleland, Adelaide	213
McCleland, Anna	213
McCleland, Elizabeth	213
McCleland, Georgina	213
McCleland, Margaret	213
McCleland, Rev Francis	**212**
McCleland, Reverand Francis	163
McClelland, Frank	213
McDonald	54
McDonald, Donald	132
McKiell, George	235
McLeland, George	213
Merriman, Esther Louisa	200
Metelerkamp, William	220
Metlerkamp, WR	116
Meurant, LH	197
Middleton, Mr	210
Milbank, John	110
Miller	49
Miller, Ann	149
Miller, John	144, 146, 148
Miller, Mrs	149
Miller, William	144, 146p., 149
Mills, Catherine	213
Mills, Daniel	**213**
Mills, Harriet	213
Mills, James	213
Mills, Maria	213
Mills, Martha	213
Moodie, Benjamin	**214**
Moodie, Donald	72, 217
Moodie, Lieutenant Donald	**214**
Moodie, Lieutenant JWD	**214**
Moorcroft, James	**214**
Moorcroft, Sidney	214
Moscrop, Mr	142
Neat	145
Nel, Martha	184
Nelson	145
Nelson, Matthew	164
Nelson, Mrs	148
Nelson, Thomas	133
Netherton, Lucy	191
Newson, Edward	163
Newson, John George	163
Nicolson, Captain	228
Norden, Mark	113
Norden, Sarah	119
Norman	44
Norton, John	119
Norton, Joshua Davis	**119**
Norton, Louis	119
Nourse, Temple	216
O' Flinn, Dr Daniel	110
O'Connor, Miss	74
Oates	49
Oates, John	**214**
Oates, Mary Ann	215
Opperman, Field-Cornet	84
Overs	148
Overton, Rev CF	174
Overy	44
Owen, William Smith	234
Paine, Mr	146
Painter, Richard Joseph	215
Painter, Samuel	**215**
Palmer, George	**215**
Palmer, James	215
Parker, William	163p.
Parties	
Bailie's party	25, **155**
Bailie's party	188, 196, 205, 220, 229
Barker's Party	91
Bradshaw's party	25
Butler's party	26
Carlisle's party	26

Clarke's party 26	Patrick, Martha 231
Clarke's party 229	Philipps, Thomas 105
Cock's party 25	Philips 26
Cock's party 189	Philips, Miss 200
Dalgairns' party 26, 204	Phillipps, Frederick 186
Damant's party 169	Phillipps, Thomas 185, **216**
Dyason's party 25	Phillips, Catherine 185, 216
Dyason's party 193, 205	Phillips, Charlotte 216
Erith's party 229	Phillips, Edward 216
Gardner's party 26	Phillips, Frederick 216
George Smith's party 147, 227, 230	Phillips, John 142
Gush party 144	Phillips, Sophie 216
Hayhurst's party 25	Piggott 26
Hazelhurst's party 186, 201	Pigot, Elizabeth (Nee Tomkinson) 72
Holder's party 25	Pigot, George 72, 217
Holder's party 224	Pigot, Sophia 72, 217
Howard's party 26	Pike 49
Hyman's party 25	Pike, Mrs 138
Hyman's party 189, 230	Pinnock, Mr. 136
Irish party **163**	Plackett, Widow 219
James's party 25	Pote 133
Knowles's party 220	Pote, Charles 218
Liversage's party 26	Pote, Peter 218
Mahoney's party 25	Pote, Robert 217
Menzies party 26	Pote, Robert 218
Mills' party 26, 235	Price 54
Morgan's party 26	Pringle, Dodds 210
Mouncey's party 25	Pringle, Thomas 78, **219**
Norman's party 26	Prinsloo, Willem 86
Nottingham party 178, 201, 209, 215	Prior 145
Osler's party 25	Pullen, Adelaide 220
Owen's party 219	Pullen, Augusta 220
Parker's party **163**, 194	Pullen, Charles 219
Richardson's party 25	Pullen, Dorothy 220
Scanlan's party 205, 217	Pullen, Edward 219
Scotch party 26, 91	Pullen, Ellen 220
Scott's party 25	Pullen, Emily 220
Scott's party 214	Pullen, Harriet 220
Sephton's party 223, 233	Pullen, John Arthur 220
Sephton's party 25, 176, 212, 214p., 227	Pullen, Julia 220
Smith's party 25	Pullen, Lavinia 220
Smith's party 204	Pullen, Mr. 179
Southey's party 195	Pullen, Octavia 220
Thornhill's party 25, 91	Pullen, Tendall 219
Turvey's party 26	Pullen, Thomas **219**
Wainwright's party 201	Pullen, William Turner 219
Weight's Party 91	Purdon 44
White's party 232	Rafferty 54
William Smith's party 26	Rafferty, Mr. 132
William Smith's party 227	Rafferty, Mrs. 132
Willson's party 25, **159**	Rainer, Mrs. 146
Willson's party 171, 174p., 191, 208, 228, 235	Ralph 145
	Randal, Nathaniel 113

Randall, Thomas..162
Raymond, Miss..220
Reed, Amy Flora..117
Reed, Anne Elliot...117
Reed, Arthur Clarence..117
Reed, Cecily Emily Mabel....................................117
Reed, Eliza Anne..115, 117
Reed, Emily Jane...117
Reed, George...115p.
Reed, George Thomas...................107, 113, 117
Reed, Henry John..117
Reed, James Joseph...117
Reed, James Samuel...**107**
Reed, Louisa..110, 117
Reed, Sara..107
Reed, Sarah Eliza..110
Reed, William........................107, 111, 116p.
Reed, William James..................................115, 117
Rennie, George...36
Rivers, Harry...92, 96, 105
Roberts..49
Roberts, Dr Edward...**220**
Roberts, Samuel...223
Roberts, Samuel Henry......................................223
Roberts. Dr Edward..196
Robinson, Mary Anne..204
Rowan, Sophia..236
Rowles...145
Sanderson, Sarah..184
Sargeant..49
Sauer, JJ..180
Sauer, Johanna...180
Scanlan, John...222
Scanlan, Sir Thomas C..223
Scanlan, Thomas Ross.......................................223
Scanlan, William..222
Scanlen, Charles...222
Scanlen, Hannah...223
Scanlen, William...163, 221
Scrivener, HM..213
Sephton, Hezekiah..184
Seton, Thomas..164
Shaw, John..191, 225
Shaw, Matthew Ben..223
Shaw, Rev W Jnr..223
Shaw, Rev William...**223**
Shaw, William.......25, 48, 63, 93, 181p., 211, 223
Shepperd...145
Shepperd, William...145
Shepstone...49
Shepstone, John...**224**
Shepstone, Theophilus..224
Ship

Albury.............................91, 178, 201, 209, 215
Aurora............176, 184, 212, 214p., 223, 234
Belle Alliance................171, 174p., 191, 228
Brilliant................68pp., 91, 144p., 179, 230
Chapman 64p., 109, 118, 156, 185, 188, 196, 198, 205, 207, 220, 229
Dowson....................................180, 194, 209
East Indian.............163, 194, 205, 217, 221
Fanny..163, 178
John...201
Kennersley Castle..........195, 199, 216, 224p.
La Belle Alliance.......................................208
Nautilus.....63, 110, 135, 144, 170, 211, 214, 219p.
Northampton...........................204, 210, 229
Ocean..169, 185
Salisbury..183
Sir George Osborne...................21, 213, 235
Stentor.....................................147, 200, 230
Weymouth................174, 176, 181, 189, 230
Zoroaster....................................91, 193, 205
Shone, Elizabeth...141
Shone, George.........................136pp., 141p.
Shone, Henry..138
Shone, Mary...138
Shone, Sara..138, 142
Shone, Sarah...138p., 143
Shone, Thomas..**135**
Sievwright, Mr..220
Slater, Charles..**227**
Slater, George..204, 227
Slater, John..227
Slater, Thomas...**227**
Smith, CT...200
Smith, John..220
Smith, John Hancorn...228
Smith, Joseph..210
Smith, Letitia..191
Smith, Mary..228
Smith, Mr..73
Smith, Richard...233
Smith, Stephen..145
Smith, Thomas W..228
Smith, WE..216
Smith, William.................199, 207, **227,** 228
Smith, William Benstead...................................228
South..145
Southey, George...**225**
Southey, R..192
Southey, Richard.......................................131, 225
Southey, Sir Richard.......................................**226**
Southey, William..225
Southey's party..25

Spackman, Dr.	236
Stanley, John	26
Stanton, Catherine	228
Stanton, Robert	228p.
Stanton, Sarah	228
Stanton, William	132, 228
Staples, John	31
Sterley	145
Stirraker, Harry	37
Stockenstrom, Andries	169, 177, 181, 206, 224
Stokes, GF	216
Stretch, Lieutenant	83
Stringfellow	132, 156
Stringfellow, Miss	228
Stringfellow, Thomas	196, 229
Strut, Thomas C	227
Stubbs, John	131
Stubbs, Thomas	**131,** 229
Stubbs, William	229
Surmon, Edward	221
Surmon, George Thomas	221
Surmon, Henry	221
Surmon, James	221
Surmon, James Edward	221
Surmon, John	221
Surmon, Thomas	221
Surmon, Walter	221
Surmon, William Henry	220p.
Synnot, Walter	163
Taberer, Rev. C. F.	228
Taylor, John	164
Temlett, James	144, **229**
Temlett, John	230
Templett, James Brilliant	230
Thackwray, John	37
Thackwray, William	233
Tharratt, John	142
Thompson	54
Thompson, George	98
Thornhill, Christopher	25, 91, 100pp., 115
Thornhill, John	102
Trollip, John	230
Trollip, Joseph	59, 189, **230**
Trollip, Stephen	230
Trollip, William	230
Trotter	145
Tucker, Kidger	58
Turpin, Rev. William Henry	199
van der Reit, F.	181
van der Reit, Johanna Sophia	181
Wainwright	43
Walker	49
Walker, Joseph	44
Walker, Richard	176
Walton, Captain	220
Warner	44
Warren, Fanny	180
Wathall, Miss	218
Webb, Christopher	**68**
Webb, Dr.	44
Webb, Mary (Nee Evans)	68
Webber	145
Wedderburn, Christopher	230p.
Wedderburn, Esther	231
Wedderburn, John	231
Wedderburn, William	230
Wentworth, Lieutenant	163
Wheeldon	145
Whiley, Miss	170
White, George	170, 233
White, Thomas Charles	232p.
Whitnal, R. M.	216
Williams, James	113
Williams, PM	114
Wills, Mr.	96
Willson, Thomas	159
Wilmot	145
Wilmot, Benjamin	162
Wilmott, James	162
Wilson's party	33, 51
Wimble, Skeleton	228
Wood	54
Wood, Alfred Jesse	235
Wood, Ben Horace	235
Wood, Eleanor	235
Wood, Elizabeth	235
Wood, Garbett	235
Wood, George	173, **233**
Wood, George Samuel	235
Wood, Harriet	235
Wood, Henry Richard	235
Wood, John Edwin	235p.
Wood, Joseph Garbett	235
Wood, Lydia	235
Wood, Susannah	235
Wood, William	235p.
Woodcock, Robert	163
Woodfield, Matthew	207
Wright	54
Wright, Charlotte	235p.
Wright, Eliza	236
Wright, Emily	236
Wright, GG	158
Wright, Julia	199, 236
Wright, Martha	179, 236
Wright, Rosa	236

Wright, Rosa Isabel..236
Wright, William..............................179, **235,** 236

Yelling, Miss..219

www.ingramcontent.com/pod-product-compliance
Lightning Source LLC
Chambersburg PA
CBHW070302010526
44108CB00039B/1511